You *are* a Medium

About the Author

Psychic since childhood, Sherrie Dillard has been a professional intuitive, medium, medical intuitive, and teacher for over thirty years. Among her international clientele are spiritual leaders, celebrities, and business executives. Sherrie's love of service combined with her intuitive ability have catapulted her intuitive practice around the globe. She has given over 50,000 readings worldwide.

Sherrie has taught intuition and medium development classes at such diverse places at Duke University and Miraval Resort and across the United States, Europe, Costa Rica, and Mexico. Her passion for the fusion of intuition, spirituality, and conscious self-growth has made her a popular speaker and teacher at retreats and conferences. She has been featured on radio and television for her innovative books and her work as a psychic detective, medical intuitive, and medium. Sherrie is the award-winning host of the weekly radio program *Intuit YOUniversity* on transformationtalkradio.com.

With a lifelong devotion and dedication to be of service, Sherrie has worked with diverse populations in unique settings. Along with her work as a professional intuitive, she has helped to house and feed people who are poor and homeless in New York City, and in San Jose and San Francisco. She has built simple water systems in Indian villages in the mountains of southern Mexico and Guatemala and created art therapy programs in treatment centers for troubled youth in North Carolina and Georgia.

Sherrie holds a B.S. in Psychology and a M.Div. in New Thought pastoral counseling. Originally from Massachusetts, Sherrie has made Durham, North Carolina, her home for the past eighteen years and can often be found walking along the river with her dogs.

You *are* a Medium

Discover Your Natural Abilities
to Communicate with the Other Side

SHERRIE DILLARD

Llewellyn Publications
Woodbury, Minnesota

FIRST EDITION
Third Printing, 2014

Cover art: iStockphoto.com/17781941/Лилия Файзуллина, 75183/Björn Kindler,
    12880651/Fuat Kose, 15625077/temmuz can arsiray, 6201476/sbayram
Cover design by Kevin R. Brown
Editing by Andrea Neff

Llewellyn is a registered trademark of Llewellyn Worldwide Ltd.

Library of Congress Cataloging-in-Publication Data:
Dillard, Sherrie, 1958–
  You are a medium : discover your natural abilities to communicate with the
other side / by Sherrie Dillard—First edition.   pages cm
  Includes bibliographical references and index.
  ISBN 978-0-7387-3792-8
1. Channeling (Spiritualism) I. Title.
  BF1286.D55 2013
  133.9'1—dc23

Llewellyn Worldwide Ltd. does not participate in, endorse, or have any authority or responsibility concerning private business transactions between our authors and the public.
  All mail addressed to the author is forwarded but the publisher cannot, unless specifically instructed by the author, give out an address or phone number.
  Any Internet references contained in this work are current at publication time, but the publisher cannot guarantee that a specific location will continue to be maintained. Please refer to the publisher's website for links to authors' websites and other sources.

Llewellyn Publications
A Division of Llewellyn Worldwide Ltd.
2143 Wooddale Drive
Woodbury, MN 55125-2989
www.llewellyn.com

Printed in the United States of America

Other Books by Sherrie Dillard

Discover Your Psychic Type
(Llewellyn, 2008)

Love and Intuition
(Llewellyn, 2010)

Dedication

This book is dedicated to my spirit family, helpers, allies, and angels who patiently and devotedly guide and watch over me.

Acknowledgments

Special thanks to Angela Wix, the best acquiring editor an intuitive writer could have, Andrea Neff for her insight and editing advice, and the expert marketing and publicity team at Llewellyn. I send love and gratitude to the many clients who have joined me on this journey of spiritual exploration and allowed me to share their stories.

Thank you, Austin Morris, for your skilled legal advice.

Contents

Author's Note

The examples, anecdotes, and characters in this book are drawn from my work as a psychic, medium, and spiritual counselor, as well as my life experience, real people, and events. Names and some identifying features and details have been changed, and in some instances people or situations are composites.

Philosopher Thomas Carlyle spoke a truth I have long felt. He said, "Blessed is he who has found his work; let him ask no other blessedness." I am a psychic and a medium and I love what I do. A psychic is able to tune in to and put words and meaning to energy information, while a medium has the ability to connect to and communicate with beings in the spirit realm. As a medium, I have communicated with those on the other side almost daily for the past twenty-five years. Even though I am frequently able to provide peace and closure to people who are grieving the passing over of their loved ones, I often feel as if it is I who benefits. I am constantly amazed, inspired, and deeply touched by the poignant coming together of my clients with their loved ones on the other side.

Our Evolving Connection with the Other Side

Years ago when I first started giving readings, people were often surprised that I had enough clients to do this work full-time. They felt like brave pioneers coming to my office and initiating contact with their loved ones on the other side. Most of the time they did not want their friends and family to know they were consulting with me. While their desire to communicate with their loved ones was compelling enough to overcome their apprehension, I was still a hush-hush secret. Over time I have seen my clientele become more open and deepen their respect for and knowledge of the spirit world. In some ways, the unseen realm has become almost as commonplace as prime time television. On a daily basis we can watch ghost hunters, paranormal experts, psychics, and mediums all living as normal people. Thanks to the magic of television and film, even vampires, werewolves, and otherworldly beings touch our hearts.

With global technology, the world may be shrinking, but at the same time it is expanding. We are more and more comfortable with what was once thought of as spooky and mysterious. There is an increasing acceptance of life beyond the physical, and we desire and seek more knowledge, wisdom, and personal experiences with it. This is leading us into new territory, as we are more aware than ever that the spirit realm is a part of who we are. The line that seems to separate the physical from the spiritual, the seen from the unseen, is becoming blurred. As our connection with the other side evolves, the veil that separates us in thinning. Those on the other side are drawing closer, and our desire to connect with them is stronger than ever. Our ability to influence one another is also growing and expanding.

As you go about your daily activities, your thoughts, emotions, and actions are intersecting with those on the other side. You may have noticed this yourself. Have you ever had an instantaneous thought or idea that gave you valuable insight into a problem or concern? Have feelings of love and comfort spontaneously soothed you during a time of crisis? Maybe the lights in your home have blinked or prematurely burned out? Have you ever felt a warm but invisible hand on your shoulder or smelled the scent of your deceased grandmother's perfume? Has a bird ever seemed to linger on your window sill and you had the odd feeling that it was sent to you as a message of love from someone on the other side? Maybe you have had a dream of a loved one that feels more like a real encounter or seen the fleeting image of a loved one in the corner of your eye? These are common ways that our loved ones make contact with us. Our worlds are not as separate as they may appear to be, and just as you long to communicate with them, they desire to make contact with you.

Why People Visit Mediums

People go to mediums for a variety of reasons. Many clients have come to me by way of their loved ones in spirit who are anxious to communicate with them. With an invisible push and silent prodding from the spirit realm, new clients will often tell me that they just felt like they needed to make an appointment with me and are not sure why. Sometimes people seek out a medium because they miss their loved ones and need to know that they are alive and well. A family member or friend may have passed unexpectedly, and they are in shock and wonder where they are. Sometimes the last contact we had with a loved one was difficult. The person may have been very ill and in pain, and we want to know that they are happy and close to other family members in spirit.

A loved one's passing over to the other side can be distressing and life-altering. Feelings of loss and grief can be overwhelming. I often get referrals from grief counselors and suicide support groups. People who have lost loved ones in traumatic circumstances often seek closure from the other side in order to move forward in their lives. It is also not unusual for people to tell me that they do not know why they want a session. I am often contacted by individuals who heard about a friend's experience with me and are curious.

Your Loved Ones Are with You

Although I have been giving people messages from their loved ones in spirit for a long time, I am still surprised by what those on the other side have to say. I begin sessions by tuning in to the spirits that are present. They will often tell me their name, but if they do not, there are other ways to identify them. Because I am able to visually see those on the other side, I can tell my clients the color of their loved one's hair, their height, body type, and the expression on their face. If I have a client who is more skeptical, they will sometimes desire more specific information that only their loved one would know.

I recently had a session with a client who asked me for more "proof." My description of her father's body type, hair color, and health issues were not enough. Fortunately, those in spirit will oblige. In answer to my client's skepticism, her father showed me an image of antique chairs, tables, and other home furnishings.

When I shared this with my client, she remarked, "Well, he did love to buy and sell antique furniture."

I then saw an image of her having dental work done as a young girl. When I asked her if she had struggled with significant dental problems when young, she seemed convinced.

"I had congenital problems with my teeth and had extensive dental work done as a child. This is my father," she told me.

Sharing personal information with my clients that only someone close would know helps to open their heart and mind and receive more from the session.

After I identify who is present, I simply listen and relate to my client what I have heard, seen, and felt and the impressions that I receive. Sometimes those on the other side will talk about their passing, their activities on the other side, and what they are learning. They will offer advice and guidance on many of my clients' concerns and express love and gratitude. Loved ones will also often share memories, favorite places they may have visited with my clients, and special events and anniversaries. Whatever the reasons for coming in for a session, my clients are often surprised at the amount of detail their loved ones know about their lives and the scope of information they are able to share.

Those on the other side likely know much more about you and your daily activities than you might suspect. They will often comment on my clients' redecorated homes or describe the hallway where a picture of them hangs. They may give career and health advice, and they may know when a client's car needs repair and where the client is going on vacation. I have had those in spirit tell me what my client had for dinner the night before and offer advice to improve their health. Those on the other side know your worries and stresses, and they celebrate in your achievements and victories.

People come in expecting to simply say to their loved ones in spirit, "Hello, are you happy?" Instead, they are often startled at how close and connected their loved ones really are. You are seen, known, and loved by them.

How This Book Came About

Several years ago, my communication with the other side began to deepen. One morning I had a session with Claudia, a woman who had come to connect with a dear friend of hers who had passed over several months prior. The session began like most others. Her friend quickly came in to let her know that she was with family and in peace, and she shared a few happy memories. She thanked Claudia for all of her help during a prolonged illness. Toward the end of our time together, Claudia's father came forward. He had died several years earlier after a brief illness. Claudia was startled by his presence, as her parents had divorced when she was young and she had rarely seen him after that.

However, his message to Claudia was clear and direct. "I want to apologize for not being in your life," her father said. "Your devotion to your friends and family has taught me so much. I didn't give your needs much thought. I am sorry. I have a lot to learn from you about how to open my heart and give. Watching you love and care for others inspires me."

After Claudia left, a little shaken and surprised by both her friend's and her father's presence and messages, I realized that this kind of session was becoming more common. The depth of sharing from those on the other side was expanding in its scope and substance. Although those on the other side had always shared their love and offered support and guidance to those still in the physical realm, more and more often they were expressing how their loved ones were helping them. I was beginning to understand that the role we play in helping our loved ones after their death might be more significant than what I once thought.

Inspired by this session with Claudia, I began to review records of my past sessions. What I discovered surprised me. In reading after reading, there were accounts of friends and family in spirit who had communicated similar types of experiences. Fathers discussed how their son's or daughter's ability to express love helped them to open their heart. Side by side with their physical loved ones, those on the other side read self-help and inspirational books. Those in spirit who were dismissive of intuitive and psychic abilities while on earth were developing their intuitive skills along with their physical family and friends who had similar interests. Loved ones in spirit who had passed over due to drug and alcohol problems went to addiction counseling with loved ones who were experiencing similar challenges. People who had worked hard all their lives and then died without ever enjoying leisure time were traveling, climbing mountains, and visiting exotic locations along with their adventurous loved ones in the physical realm.

As I reviewed these past sessions, I had an experience similar to what happens when we suddenly decipher the words of a song that we have listened to over and over but could never quite make out, or the flash of understanding that sometimes comes when we learn a new language or solve a math problem. All of a sudden, the brain connects the dots and confusion lifts. I understood in a new way what I had been hearing for years.

Although I had always been aware of how those in spirit help us in countless ways, I had not fully grasped how much we also help them. Through our personal choices, struggles, and actions, those who have passed over are inspired, encouraged, helped, and healed. In session after session, it became clear to me that we often serve as living examples of how to succeed at the sometimes difficult life lessons that we all are confronted with in the physical world.

Why the Other Side Needs Us

We come to the earth to learn how to love ourselves and others, activate the power of our spirit, and accomplish the lessons and tasks that our soul most needs in order to evolve. Although the realm of spirit is one of love, forgiveness, wisdom, and joy, we do not go to heaven as much as we grow into heaven.

After we pass out of the physical body, we experience the healing and love of the other side. Family and friends who have passed over welcome us, and we are nourished and renewed in the light of the heavens. With angelic support, we review our lives here on earth. We become aware of what we have learned, where we have grown, and what still needs our attention, forgiveness, and healing. This process of understanding where our soul has made advances and where we have allowed fear, negativity, and other human challenges to thwart our progress is done in the spirit of love and compassion. The choices we made that were motivated by fear, pain, and self-centeredness and those that we made through love become obvious. We forgive and are forgiven, and we heal and come into wholeness. But this is just the beginning. We must then learn how to integrate this new awareness into every aspect of our being.

One of the ways that our loved ones who have passed over continue to heal and evolve is by drawing close to those of us in the physical world who are experiencing similar life lessons. When our loved ones in spirit go through their life review, they become aware of the decisions and actions they took while in the physical world that sabotaged their soul growth and evolution. Inspired by the all-knowing awareness of the heavens, they begin to understand how they have limited their ability to manifest and experience their highest good. This is where we come in. By watching and observing our positive efforts in confronting our day-to-day challenges, healing our emotional wounds, developing our talents and skills, and showing kindness to others, they have the opportunity to vicariously experience a new way through us.

The Importance of Your Choices, Intent, and Actions

Life on earth, as most of us know, is not always a picnic in the park. While it is beautiful, loving, fulfilling, and a source of great happiness, it can also be tough and demanding. But life on earth is a precious opportunity. Our loved ones in spirit are immersed in the soft cushions of divine love. Angels watch over them like doting parents, applauding their growth and lighting their path with love. It is we, the physical living, who often wander in the dark, making our way through challenges like fear, financial and relationship stress, aging, and illness, usually unaware that celestial help is available. We try to do the right thing. We want happiness and all the good that life has to offer, but we frequently feel lost in the fog. Yet when we love, forgive, and evolve here on earth, the heavens cheer and heave streams of translucent confetti our way.

Transforming anger, eliminating negative thoughts, and forgiving those who have hurt us are powerful acts that elevate us to the heavenly realms. Our struggles have meaning. Every decision and action that we take that is derived from love, including the small and seemingly insignificant daily acts that happen in secret, have tremendous power. Not only do we evolve and forever move beyond the clutches of negativity and darkness, but our actions reach out beyond time and space and touch the lives of family and friends and past generations. Even those you barely knew or didn't know at all in the physical world can richly benefit by what you do and who you are. Our actions are like stones thrown into a still pond; the effect ripples, expands, and reaches out far and wide and into the realm of spirit.

How This Book Will Help You

My hope is that as you read through the pages of this book, you will more fully recognize and tune in to the eternal and vital connection you share with those in the spirit realm. Not only do your loved ones on the other side assist, guide, and help you to heal, you do the same for them. When a loved one passes over, the grief process can be arduous and difficult. Knowing that you connect to and affect your loved ones on the other side in positive ways can ease the ache of separation. Those on the other side desire to communicate and share with you. They benefit from this interaction and are closer and more involved in your day-to-day life than you may think.

Even though you may not know it, you are already communicating with the other side. It is so common and natural, most people are not aware that they are doing so. Once you become aware of your innate medium ability, further development comes faster and easier. The last section of this book will empower you to ignite and harness the medium within you. At any time you can skip forward to this section and get started.

In the first section of the book, I discuss how the conditions and circumstances of my early life encouraged me to connect and communicate with those on the other side. My decision to become a professional medium was in part inspired by my interactions with guides, angels, and loved ones in spirit. I will explain the differences and similarities between these three types of spirit allies and help you to understand how they guide and help you.

After poring over my notes and journals from past sessions, I discovered many tender, funny, surprising, and inspiring stories. In the second section, I share these with you in the hope that you will see a bit of yourself in them. We all share common earth school lessons. Whether it is through confronting fear, addictions, or financial or relationship concerns or through pursuing joy and fulfillment, we are evolving through our everyday struggles and successes. Your choices and actions create a better life for you here and in the here-after and influence your friends and family in their celestial home.

In the third section of the book, I help you to become aware of how you unknowingly interact with your loved ones on the other side. You have within you the qualities of a medium and a particular way of communicating with the other side.

In my book *Discover Your Psychic Type*, I revealed how we all have a particular way that we absorb and receive intuitive energy information. We do this through our thoughts and emotions, our physical body, and our energy field. I have heard from many people who, after reading this book, are now better able to understand the spontaneous and often perplexing thoughts, feelings, bodily sensations, and inexplicable knowing of information that they sometimes experience.

In this same way, you are often unknowingly connecting and communicating with those on the other side. A flash of light or color or an image that quickly passes in and out of your vision is easy to ignore, yet it may be a loved one on the other side trying to let you know that they are with you. The waves of emotion that sometimes seem to come out of nowhere, the conversations that go on in your head, or the spontaneous awareness of ideas and solutions to problems may also be real encounters with those on the other side. That sudden feeling that you are not alone and that there is a guiding presence with you may be someone in the spirit realm offering you a helping hand. Once you become aware of how you interact with those on the other side, you can better develop and enhance your natural medium abilities.

The third section includes a quiz to help you become aware of your innate medium tendencies, as well as meditations and step-by-step development exercises for each medium type. In the last chapter of the book, there are exercises to help you further assist those in the spirit realm. This includes practical ways to help your loved ones who are making their transition into the spirit realm and exercises to assist lost souls and ghosts into the safety and light of the heavens.

Whatever your interest may be in connecting and communicating with the other side, it promises to be an exciting and enlightening adventure. As you make your way through this book, you may identify with some of the events and influences that led to my becoming a professional medium. You may also recognize some of your own challenges and experiences in the stories of my client sessions. As you read about how those in spirit have been helped by their loved ones' positive efforts here on earth, you may be more motivated to fully embrace your life lessons. Yet this book is not meant to simply be a testament to my abilities or the experiences of others. My hope is that you will more fully understand and embrace your own innate medium abilities and further develop them. In the last section, I empower you to further dig in and embrace your inner medium.

Now, relax, sit back, and enjoy your visit with the spirit realm. Don't be surprised if you intuit and sense a loved one (or two) on the other side reading along with you.

Section 1

My Path to Becoming a Medium

1

THE GOOD DEAD: MY EARLY YEARS

~~~~~~~~~~~~~~~~~~~~~~~~~~~

Many of my clients want to know how long I have been communicating with the other side. The answer, I tell them, is simple: as far back as I can remember. My connection and ease with interacting with the other side has never felt like an extraordinary feat or a leap into the mysterious. From a young age I felt and saw the presence of those in spirit, and it was a source of love and comfort. It has never been odd, unusual, or strange for me. I believe that this is in part due to the circumstances in my family before I was even conceived. You could say that the road to my becoming a medium was in many ways paved before I was born.

Angel Sister

I don't remember how old I was when I first heard the story of my sister's birth. It was a tragic family story that was told many times. It happened years ago during the time when fathers drank coffee and smoked cigarettes in the waiting room of the nursery section of the hospital. Not invited to participate in the birth process, they instead occupied themselves with magazines and small talk while waiting for a nurse to signal to them that their baby had been born.

Unlike with my mother's first pregnancy, this labor was long, too long, and difficult. My father paced back and forth in the waiting room for hours. Finally the doctor arrived. My father said that when he saw the doctor enter, he wanted to feel relief. Instead, an uneasy sense of dread pounded in his head. He knew something was not right.

"It is your decision," the doctor said while tensely looking at the clock on the wall.

Tired and drained after hours of pacing the floor and watching the clock, the answer was obvious but painful. Looking down at the floor, my father said the words he never thought he would have to say.

"You must save my wife."

Moments later, tears of love for his baby daughter who would never breathe her first breath silently fell down his cheeks.

My older sister, Dawn Marie, died at birth. Twelve hours into a painful delivery, the doctor discovered that she had hydrocephalus, a condition of fluid in the brain. She did not survive the birth. Less than a year later, I was born.

When I was growing up, my mother often spoke of Dawn Marie. I was conceived within weeks of her passing and was born on my father's birthday, a minor miracle that did not go unnoticed by my grieving parents. My mother said that she was pregnant for eighteen straight months. People she knew from the grocery store, bank, and her other everyday errands would stop her and ask, "Isn't that baby born yet?"

From a young age, I knew that I had a sister in heaven. She was a part of my life, and it felt as if she were a part of me. I confided in her when I said my prayers at night. She was my playmate, my friend, and as I got older I shared my teenage secrets with her. I could see her as an outline of sparkly light and curly blond hair. I recognized her presence as warmth and comfort. My connection with Dawn Marie was natural, and I felt lucky to have an angel sister.

The Beloved Dead

In my home, the dead were the good ones. My mother's favorite brother died before I was born. He was a New York City firefighter who died as a result of an injury he sustained while fighting a fire. We had his fireman's hat in our hall closet. Like him, it was honored and revered. When I was a toddler, my father's brother, a New Hampshire state police officer, also died in the line of duty. He was taking blood to the hospital to save a man who had been injured in a car accident. Winding down a mountain road, he was hit head-on by a speeding car and died at the scene. We loved him, too.

The beloved dead also included my mother's best friend, Aunt Marianne. She was the kindest person I had ever met. She tirelessly played games with us and was the first adult I knew who seemed to actually like being with me and my siblings. She never married and had no children of her own, and I often wished that she was my mother. She died of cancer when I was about ten.

Yet, perhaps the strongest presence of the dead in my home was my grandmother, my mother's mother. I often saw my grandmother as a translucent outline sitting next to my mother at the kitchen table. She would also follow my mother in and out of the car, into her bedroom, and into the basement when she did the laundry. I didn't know if she could see me.

My mother spoke of her mother often. She died while getting ready for church when my mother was seventeen. According to my mother, she died of a broken heart.

"My father killed her," she told us. "He left her for another woman."

My mother was bitter and angry much of the time, and when I was young, I believed this to be my grandfather's fault.

In time, my father also proved to be what my mother referred to as a "good for nothing, deadbeat alcoholic." He, along with many other living folk who crossed my mother's path, could not be trusted. The dead, I learned, were good, but the living, not so much.

I don't know if our dead's honored place in my home had any-thing to do with my ability to see, hear, and communicate with the other side, but it motivated me and made it comfortable enough for me to trust and allow my natural medium ability to develop.

All Life Is Energy

My first memory is an intuitive one. One early morning, standing in the garden of a house we lived in when I was two, I saw purple, gold, and green light surrounding the flowers and plants. The sun was rising and I remember staring transfixed as colors and light shimmered and glowed. The garden was sparse. It had just a few flowers and bushes and flat stones that led through its center, but for me it was a magical place where I felt surrounded by comforting and warm company. Everything that is alive emits energy. Animals, plants, people, the sky, water, and even the wind have life force en-ergy. When we physically die, it is our energy body that lives on. Sometimes the energy body is observed as a vague outline, some-times as streaks of light and color, and other times as a three-dimen-sional physical person.

I never heard the words *intuitive, psychic,* and *medium* until I was much older. I did not need to define the tingly presence of energy and color that I regularly experienced. A rush of warm air that came out of nowhere, an inner surge of love, dreaming of future events, and the instantaneous knowing of information were commonplace. Seeing the distinct outline or image of a person and hearing them whisper to me or share a smile was not unusual. I didn't need any words to describe this. It was normal and natural.

One of my first experiences of seeing a spirit in a solid-looking human form happened when I was about eight. Up until that time the dead people I saw were more wispy and transparent-looking. I was riding my bike up and down the hilly streets of my neighbor-hood. One side of my street bordered the woods. This is where I spent most of my days with my friends, building forts and picking blackberries. On this particular day, I was riding past a field of grass and wildflowers and in the distance I saw a dark-haired woman in a white dress waving to me. She had a kind face and a big smile. My heart leapt with joyful recognition when I saw her. Without a second thought, I jumped off my bike and ran as fast as I could to her. But when I got to where she stood, she was gone. She had vanished. Running to the edge of the field and into the woods, I looked all around for her. For several minutes I was on the verge of tears. I felt unexplainable feelings of love for her. I had no idea who she was, but I wanted to be with her. For years I looked for her in this field. I have never seen her again.

Religion and the Supernatural

The more I experienced of the supernatural, the more I wanted to know. I was surprised that my friends did not always seem to share my enthusiasm. I grew up in a predominantly Catholic neighborhood. My friends all went to Catholic school, confession on Saturdays, and mass on Sundays. We were Baptists and attended church just as regularly. For me, going to church was as boring as going to school. It was something that I had to do. It seemed to have no connection to the "real" world as I knew it. My mother was reverently involved with the church, and she wanted her children to share her devotion. But I never took to it the way I was expected to.

In my church, children went to Sunday school in the basement. We sang songs and the teachers moved felt Bible characters around on a sticky mat. Baptists are not known for being especially open to communication with those on the other side, psychics, and the supernatural. From a young age I heard warnings about the activities of the devil and the importance of following Jesus, yet I wasn't completely sure what that meant. The devil I imagined made people do bad things, like steal, smoke cigarettes, and hurt others. My naivety and stubbornness protected me. I knew in my heart that what I was experiencing was not bad or of the devil. I did, after all, have an angel sister who was always close by. The sparkly light around flowers and plants was beautiful. Knowing what others were thinking had helped me more than once, and the spirit visitors were harmless and often warm and kind. This was not evil, scary stuff.

From the Bible stories that I regularly heard, I knew that Jesus had performed miracles and communicated with angels and saw the future. It seemed to me that he had had one exciting adventure after another. That is, until he was crucified. Yet, rising from the dead, he told his disciples that we did not really die. He was still alive, and after we died we would also be spirits. At least this is how I interpreted it.

While my friends were trying to be good and say their prayers, I preferred to embrace a different message from my religious upbringing. I wanted to explore the mysteries and miracles that Jesus spoke of. I wondered if others could walk on water and bring the dead back to life. I thought it unlikely, but I wanted to know for certain.

Searching for Walt Disney

I did my best to encourage my friends to join me in exploring the unknown. I don't remember how I knew what a séance was or how to conduct one, but it seemed like an exciting activity. As far back as I could remember, I had been aware of the presence of people who had passed over, but I had never summoned someone at will. I wanted to see if I could.

One hot summer afternoon, I persuaded my younger brothers and a few friends to hold a séance with me. We went into the basement, which was always dark and cool, even on the hottest of days. Sitting on the cement floor, my friends looked to me as the leader of this supernatural adventure. We didn't have a candle and matches, so I made do with a small flashlight. With all of us sitting in a circle around the flashlight with our knees touching, I pretended to know what I was doing. Contacting the dead was the kind of nervous fun that I enjoyed. Because not all of my friends shared this passion,

I acted with confidence. I announced that everyone had a vote in whom we chose to contact, but no one seemed to have an opinion. The room went silent. None of my friends volunteered a name, and most seemed reluctant to try to conjure up the spirit of a relative or anyone they knew.

I knew that I had to pick someone whom we would all be enthusiastic to visit with. Every Sunday night we would all gather in our living rooms to watch the *Walt Disney Show*. I knew that this was everyone's favorite show. Walt Disney, I quickly remembered, was no longer alive. He seemed like the perfect spirit to call forward. Fortunately, my friends agreed.

I began the séance. "Mr. Walt Disney," I repeated over and over, "please come close and let us know that you are here. Give us a sign."

After a couple minutes of quiet interrupted by restless giggles, a crashing noise came from the shelves not far from where we were seated. Our giggles turned into shrieks. The light was turned on, and we found that a board game and a couple of G.I. Joe action figures had fallen off the shelf.

Was this a sign from Walt Disney? we all wondered. *It had to be,* we concluded. *It would be just like him to play with our toys.* And so we were convinced. *Walt Disney had paid us a visit.*

I do not know if this was truly the spirit of Walt Disney. After many years of connecting with spirits, I now know that another spirit may have taken the opportunity to rattle our nerves and give us a thrill. Manifesting physical phenomena is a common way for the other side to let us know that they are present. They can cause lights to blink and flash, create humming sounds on phones, manipulate electric currents, and cause television reception to get fuzzy or spontaneously change the channel or volume. They can also move and hide things (like our games tumbling from the shelf), drop pennies in our path, and stop, speed up, or slow down watches and clocks.

My Grandfather

For the next several years, my connection with the other side continued in a satisfying and often fun kind of way. I still felt and saw the presence of my sister and other family members, and my intuitive and psychic sensitivity continued to increase.

One afternoon while eating lunch, my mother announced that her father had died. For years the wall of silence separating my mother and her father had been thick and impenetrable. They did not speak or communicate in any way. It wasn't until my mother received a card from a relative several months after her father's death that she heard the news. She did not seem particularly sad or upset when she told us of his passing. Her attitude was more matter-of-fact, and there was no further discussion about him.

My grandfather was a poor Italian immigrant when he came to this country as a young man. He settled in New York City at the time when Italians were thought of as dirty and subservient. He was from Northern Italy and had light hair and blue eyes. After changing his last name to a more American-sounding name and learning English, he "passed" as non-Italian. Many years later as a successful businessman, he wore a suit wherever he went and drove a shiny black car. This is how I remembered him from the few times we had met.

My grandfather's death proved to be the beginning of our relationship. It is not uncommon during readings for a family member whom my client did not know well to come through. My client usually reacts to this by explaining to me that they did not know the parent, grandparent, aunt, or uncle who is present very well. They are often surprised and uncomfortable when someone they are not familiar with comes through from spirit with a message for them. We assume that if we did not have a relationship with a family member in the physical world, then we do not have one in the spiritual realms, but this is far from the truth. Once our family members are on the other side, they soon realize that healing the family connections they did not honor while in the physical world is vital to their growth and evolution. It was only after my grandfather's passing that I got to know him. My connection with him began a new chapter in my connection with the other side.

Family Healing

About a year or so after his death, my grandfather paid me a visit. One morning while sitting in my room reading, I started to feel drowsy and closed my eyes. Instantly in my mind's eye I saw an image of him. He was dressed in a black suit and had a serious look on his face. I knew it was him.

"I am your grandfather," I heard him say. As he came closer, I began to feel a little nervous. I was confused and didn't know what to do. I was used to seeing spirits, but they were not as forceful and determined as he seemed to be.

With equal determination I sent him a telepathic message back. "Go away," I said.

Telepathy is the ability to send, receive, and become aware of others' thoughts. By that time, I was becoming accustomed to exchanging messages with the spirit world in this way. I then got up, left my room, and tried to forget about the encounter.

A few days later, he returned. Again, I was alone in my room and I suddenly felt him close. I closed my eyes and saw an image of him similar to the one at our first meeting. I was curious and wanted to see if I could observe him without interacting, like I did with most of the spirits I encountered. But he had a purpose for this visit.

"I have a message for your mother," he abruptly announced. In my mind, all of the stories that my mother had told me of the sorrow and pain he had caused her came rushing in.

"Go away!" I inwardly yelled. "And don't come back."

This was the first time that I was uncomfortable with my connection to the spirit world. Although I had gotten a bit flustered by my earlier séance and had watched a few scary movies and heard stories of ghosts who haunted places and people, I felt confident in my special world. Now I did not know what to do.

My grandfather, however, would not be turned away so easily. He persisted. I was becoming accustomed to his visits, and it wasn't long before he once again returned.

The next time I felt him, I paused before running away. I was by then accustomed to his intense presence. So this time I tried to relax, focus, and tune in to him. As usual, he was dressed in a dark suit, and he seemed to have a look of concern on his face.

"What do you want?" I tried my best to summon some confidence.

"Tell your mother that I am sorry and that I love her," he telepathically broadcast my way. Then he was gone.

Fat chance of that, I thought. *After all he put her through, I don't think she would even believe me.*

Now I was truly perplexed. I knew that if I gave this message to my mother, it was highly likely that she would get angry. She had a fierce temper. There was a silent but strict policy in my home: Do not talk about her family. There was also the issue of her believing me. We did not share the same awareness of those in spirit. This was my private world, and I did not want to open myself to her scrutiny. I hoped this would all just go away, but it did not.

Within a few days, my grandfather again made his presence felt.

"Please tell your mother that I am sorry," I heard one morning while I was waking up. In a half-asleep state, I saw my grandfather standing near my bed. "I did not know," he pleaded. "I was too proud. She needs to know that I love her."

In my drowsy state, I could feel his emotions more acutely, and they were real and deep. I knew that this was important to him. Covering my head with my pillow, I waited a minute or so, then got up and tried to shake off the overwhelming feelings that I had received from him.

I knew that I had to do something. My grandfather would not give up until I talked to my mother. By then, I knew that with his strong will and determination, he would persist.

I soon got my opportunity. Walking into the kitchen one Saturday morning, I saw my mother sitting alone at the table drinking coffee. I was anxious as to how to approach her, but I knew this was my chance.

With no introduction and in the most nonchalant voice I could muster, I said, "Maybe your father loved you."

I was ready for the wrath of hell to break open, but to my surprise she simply said, "Why do you say that?"

"Well," I continued, "maybe he loved you, but he was confused and didn't know what to do and how to tell you."

My mother looked out the window. "It's funny you should bring this up," she said. "A few nights ago I had a dream about him. Then yesterday while I was folding the laundry, I remembered something that I had forgotten. Soon after my mother died," she continued, "he asked me to move back into his house. I was living with a friend at the time. My father told me he wanted me to come home. I told him that he had hurt my mother and that she had cried every day. It was his fault that she had died. I hated him for this and told him I would never speak to him again. He looked at me with tears in his eyes, and I knew that he loved me. But I had to be loyal to my mother, even after her death. I couldn't let him into my life. I thought I owed this to my mother. Maybe I did want him to be a part of my life. Maybe it could have been different."

I had never heard my mother speak of her father without resentment in her voice. With a distant gaze, she continued to stare out the window. A look of peace came over her.

"He loves you and he is sorry for all of the pain" shot out of my mouth. I was ready for her onslaught of anger. But, still looking out the window, she just nodded her head. Before she could collect her thoughts and come back to being the mother that I knew, I left the room. We never spoke of this again.

❧ ⚜ ☙

Several days later, I received another visit from my grandfather. I was in my backyard when I felt his now familiar spirit.

"Thank you," I heard him say. "You and your mother have both helped me."

For the first time since our visits had begun, I felt the warmth of his love reaching out to me. I assumed that I had helped him by giving my mother his message. I was not sure how my mother had helped him, but I suppose he needed her forgiveness and she had come closer to this than I had thought possible. This was the first time since our encounters had begun that I felt peace with him. A shiver of energy moved up my spine and into my heart. The hair on my arms stood up as I felt a rush of love flow over me. Then he was gone.

Love Transcends Time and Space

At the time, I did not fully understand the impact and significance of this encounter, but I knew that my connection to the other side had changed. The spirit realm was no longer simply fun and games. My mother had changed in a way that I had not thought possible. If only for a magical moment while staring out the window in the kitchen, she had remembered that her father loved her. Maybe more importantly, through some kind of miracle that I could not fully grasp, she had felt his love.

My mother and grandfather had come together in a way that they were not able to while my grandfather was alive on earth. They needed each another's love and forgiveness. I had witnessed a transformation in my mother that no friend, therapist, self-help protocol, or positive affirmation could equal. I had never known my mother to express anything but bitterness and anger toward her father. I saw the light of hope and forgiveness peek out of her, and it was wonderful.

Since my early days as a medium, I have come to realize that being able to communicate with the other side is just part of the story. In the thousands of readings I have given since my encounter with my grandfather, I have witnessed a similar kind of power that changes lives. It heals, forgives, and fills in the gaps where our human frailties keep us stuck. It resides within each one of us and is greater than any one of us. With this power, those on the other side help, comfort, and heal us, and with it, we heal, comfort, and help them.

2

SPIRITUAL HELPERS, ANGELS, AND GUIDES

᷈᷈᷈᷈᷈᷈᷈᷈᷈᷈᷈᷈᷈᷈᷈᷈᷈

Even though from an early age I was able to communicate with those on the other side, I had no desire to become a professional medium. Although I love what I do and cannot imagine doing anything else, I have not always felt this way.

For most of my childhood, I knew I was different and that some considered my natural ability to communicate with the other side to be odd. I did not know of anyone else who was able to see hear, feel, and sense the spirit realm in the way that I did. As I got older, my encounters and interactions with those on the other side intensified. There seemed to be nothing that I could do to turn off my sixth sense. As interesting and comforting as communicating with the other side could be, there was a part of me that wanted to fit in and be like everyone else.

As I got older, the idea of broadcasting my intuitive talents went against my natural reserved tendencies, and I did all I could to go in the opposite direction. You may be a bit like me. You, too, may have experienced some form of contact with the other side. Everyone has innate medium capabilities. Yet many of us also hesitate, deny, and do not readily claim our abilities.

My path to becoming a professional medium has involved much more than refining my intuitive abilities. I have had to confront my inner fears and resistance and heal and grow in many areas of my life. Along the way, I have had the wise and loving support of many, including those in the physical and spiritual realms. Yet it has been the determined and persistent prodding from my spirit guides and angels that has led the way.

A Variety of Spirits

When I was young, my awareness and ability to communicate with those on the other side was not limited to my family members who had passed over. Through clairvoyance, which is the ability to visually see spiritual energy, I became aware of a variety of spirits in my environment. There were some whom I did not recognize and felt no connection to. Others were more intuitively familiar. My perception of the spirits in my environment, however, was not always clear and understandable. Sometimes their visual form would fade or drift. At times I would see a partial image that looked more dreamlike. Less often they would be three-dimensional in appearance. I also became aware of spirits through clairsentience, which is the ability to sense energy. You may also feel the presence of spirits in this way. Have ever been driving in your car or awakened at night with the feeling that there was someone beside you? You might not know who it is, but you sense that you are not alone.

When I was young, I did not know who many of the spirits were that I encountered and why I was able to see and sense them. Yet as perplexing as this was, I was never frightened or upset when I saw a face staring back at me from the mirror or observed solitary, transparent figures walking in the woods or down the street. Most did not interact or make contact with me. There were, however, a few spirits who did seem to be aware of me. They felt oddly familiar, and I looked forward to their visits. I now know that these were encounters with my spirit guides.

Spirit guides do not incarnate in the physical world during our life span. They have completed their time in the here and now. From the spirit realm they continue to evolve and grow by helping those in the physical realm who have the same challenges and interests that they experienced when here. You, too, have a spirit guide, and during the course of your life, several will come and go. Even though you may not be aware of their presence, they assist and help you in a variety of ways. Because of their diverse knowledge and expertise, they can guide you in all areas of your life, no matter how practical or mundane. You may not, however, always recognize their positive influence and presence. My first encounters with the spirit whom I later realized was my guide were just simple fun. There seemed to be no agenda and no significant purpose behind our meetings.

My Guide by the River

Growing up, I spent a lot of time in nature. My mother was a great lover of hiking and camping, and on most weekends throughout the spring, summer, and fall, we would pack up our tents and other gear and head for the beach or mountains. One of our favorite places to go was in the Berkshire Mountains in Massachusetts. After a short drive of just over an hour, we could have our tents set up on the banks of the river along the Mohawk Trail before sunset on a Friday afternoon. In a grove of trees on the other side of the bridge that led to our favorite camping spot stood a statue of a Mohawk Indian with his arms raised to the sky. Known for the Native Americans who lived in the area, the mountains and rivers were alive with their spirits. It was here that I became friends with my first spirit guide.

When we are young, we connect with our guides in a natural way. Most children still feel and interact with the spiritual realm without giving it much thought. My connection with my guide crossed over into that fuzzy zone of imagination, make-believe, and pure spiritual presence. At the time, I would not have called him a spirit guide. He was integrated within the essence of the environment. I first felt him as part of the trees, the sky, and the river. Later I caught a few glimpses of him, standing tall with a broad smile and kind eyes. As his presence became more familiar, I experienced feelings that I could not put into words. Sitting on big stones in the river listening to the hypnotic rush of water and wind, I could feel him sitting next to me. He was unlike the other spirits I had encountered. Feelings of warmth and connectedness and surges of love beyond my comprehension would flood my heart when he was near. Although in the past I had felt emotions and feelings while in the company of spirit beings, this was different. I felt as if I were under the influence of a magical and secretive spell. There was a tingle in the air, and the water sang and laughed. A moment in space opened, and I could feel the rivers and mountains, as he did, alive and vibrant.

My family went on camping trips to this same spot year after year, so my connection with him continued in this way into my teenage years. As soon as we crossed the bridge onto the Mohawk Trail, I felt his presence. In my twenties, my peaceful bond with him abruptly intensified. Up until this time, my contact with him had been limited to our camping trips. Once back home, I did not encounter or even think much about him. However, one day he startled me by paying me a visit.

My Cosmic Rodeo Clown

At the time, I was working as an artist and art therapist. Although I also gave medium readings to friends and friends of friends, I had no desire to work professionally in this way. I loved being an artist, and I spent most of my time working in the small art studio in my backyard. It was here that my guide from the mountains appeared in an unexpected way. One day while painting, I felt a tangible presence behind my shoulder. At first I did not give it too much attention. I tried to ignore whatever or whoever was with me, but it would not go away. Wondering who or what this was finally got the better of me. Focusing on the presence, I heard a voice ask me to meditate and better tune in to his presence. In my studio I had a small area padded with cushions, for daily meditation. I went and sat down in this spot, closed my eyes, and began to breathe and relax. Within a few minutes I began to see colorful and vibrant images of a Native American riding a horse. As I focused on the images, I realized that this was my spirit friend from the mountains, and he was clearly trying to get my attention.

I telepathically sent him a message. "What do you want?"

Instead of answering me, he started to do tricks on his horse. He was hilarious. Like a funny rodeo clown, he would tumble through the air making faces and leaping in crazy jumps. Besides making me laugh, there initially seemed to be no other message. Eventually he faded away. I continued meditating for several more minutes, then went back to work.

Several times a week, for a few months, this continued. While meditating, spontaneous visions of him twirling and jumping through space on his horse would appear. It was funny and enjoyable, and I looked forward to his visits. Then one day he startled me and told me his name.

"I am Techyouwatchyu," I heard him say in a deep voice. "I am here to help you."

However, Techyouwatchyu was not big on talk. After he told me his name (which took me years to finally realize was "Teach You Watch You"), he said little else. Even so, I suspected that he had come to help motivate me to work full-time as a psychic and medium. For months prior to his arrival, I had been receiving the intuitive message that it was time for me to work with others. Although I was giving a few medium readings a week, I felt a consistent inner nudge to work with others on a larger scale. Yet I resisted. Techyouwatchyu, I intuited, was here to help hasten the process. Still, he seemed in no rush to do anything but make me smile. He continued to entertain me during my meditations and seemed content to make me laugh at his crazy antics. One afternoon after a particularly funny bout of spiritual acrobatics, I asked him the obvious question.

"Why are you leaping and jumping through space? Am I supposed to be learning something from this?"

His answer came in a wave of energy. Like the river and wind from my young days on the Mohawk Trail, I felt a soothing ripple of energy move through me. He then sent me wave after wave of gentle yet stimulating energy. I felt lulled into a hypnotic, peaceful mood.

"This is what the spirit realm feels like," I heard him say. "I want to teach you how to move in these currents of vibration."

I then felt my spirit lifted along an invisible current. It felt a bit like lying in a raft on the ocean. In this flow of energy vibration, I was able to easily access and connect with nonphysical streams of energy information. For a few months I practiced releasing my spirit into these vibrant cosmic streams. As I did this, I became adept at learning how to find, retrieve, and—with Techyouwatchyu's guidance—interpret and understand the energy information that I received.

Just as I was feeling more competent and enjoying this newly acquired skill, it abruptly changed. Another spirit guide made his presence known and took me to my next level of development.

The Elder

The next spirit guide that came forward to assist me in my emergence as a medium was the Elder. I first met him when I was a teenager. I was in my basement sorting clothes and doing laundry when I became overwhelmingly tired. I sat down on an old couch, closed my eyes, and felt as if I were being pulled inward. I couldn't resist the inner force of energy. Somewhat like a dream that I had no control over, a rush of energy swiftly moved me through an inner space. Suddenly in my mind's eye, the image of an older man appeared. He was dressed in white, and there was a golden glow surrounding him. With authority and kindness, he spoke to me for several minutes. Then abruptly, I was wide awake again. Even though I could not remember what he had said, I knew that it was significant. This happened two other times. Each experience was similar. Pulled inward by an incredible force, I heard him speak and then, just as abruptly, I was again in a normal state of consciousness. Once I was out of this trance-like state, I could not remember what had been said.

As I was meditating in my art studio several years after our last encounter, his unmistakable presence suddenly reappeared in a soft inner vision. Instead of me being pulled inward, he gently spoke to me. He told me his name was the Elder and that he was going to be working with me. Even though I was a bit confused by his sudden reentry into my life, I wanted to know him better. After my enjoyable sessions with Techyouwatchyu, I was ready for an entertaining interaction. However, what happened could not have been further from what I expected.

Channeling

In preparation to communicate with the Elder, I went to my meditation spot. I began to breathe, calm my mind, and get into a receptive state. However, I was jolted out of my relaxed state by an influx of energy entering my body. I was suddenly uncomfortable with my posture. I realized that I was not sitting up straight. I lifted my head, sat taller, and stretched out a bit. My body felt tight, and I was aware of myself in a new way. I felt confident and self-assured, feelings that at that time I was not used to. I was detached but at the same time accurately aware and sensitive. New perceptions began to emerge. In a surprising insight, I realized that being an artist might not be my purpose. I felt a fear of working with others lurking in my mind and heart that I had not been aware of. Yet my apprehensions now felt silly. Ready to more fully engage with others, I felt a renewed sense of devotion to developing spiritually and as a medium.

The Elder communicated in a no-nonsense manner and insisted on my full attention, but he did not speak to me telepathically, through images, or through my intuiting energy information. Instead, in a deep and calming voice, he literally spoke through me. At the time, I did not know what was happening. Although I was a bit unnerved, it was also an exhilarating experience. My curiosity compelled me to allow this interaction to continue to unfold. I now know that this is called channeling. Channeling differs from psychic and medium communication. Instead of conversing with a spirit being or receiving energy information, it felt as if the Elder was within me.

For several months, a few times a week during my meditations the Elder's energy would enter my consciousness energy field and my body. He would then speak to me about various aspects of spirituality, the spirit realm, and communication with the other side. He asked me to tape-record our conversations. I complied, and in session after session he communicated to me in this manner.

Noble in his approach to psychic awareness and medium abilities, he expected me to respect myself and honor my abilities. I was told to eat a healthy diet, get plenty of sleep, and live a disciplined life. Given boundaries and guidelines as to how to approach the spirit realm, I was shown how to share information and guidance with my clients and help them to heal and spiritually evolve.

"It is an honor to work as an intermediary between realms. If you do it correctly, you will advance. If you do not, you will only create confusion," he told me.

The Elder was patient, and his teachings were wise and helpful. Yet the biggest gift he gave me was his generosity in sharing his energy with me. I felt purposeful and confident in his presence. At that time in my life, those kinds of feelings were not always commonplace, and I soaked in his kindness.

Giving Readings with the Elder

Once the Elder came into my life, events started to evolve and unfold rapidly. Although I was not advertising my services, I began to have more requests for medium readings. When I sat down with my first client since the Elder's arrival, I did not know what to expect. I closed my eyes and said a prayer to begin the session. Before I finished the prayer, I felt his energy enter my body and consciousness. He announced himself to my client and, to my surprise, proceeded to give her guidance and information. Surprisingly, she did not seem unnerved or shaken by his presence and the obvious change in my voice. Before long, I was popular and busy. Just as with my first client, the Elder continued to work with people through me. His guidance was accurate, his sense of humor charming, and his confidence magnanimous. No one seemed alarmed or concerned that this was a spirit they were interacting with. Instead, this seemed to have the opposite effect. While I was talking to a client before a session one morning, she reminded me that she had come to hear from the Elder and not me.

Within a few months, however, I felt his presence begin to fade. I no longer experienced his unmistakable robust energy guiding me and prodding me to sit up straight and be confident. Then one day, as I was starting a session, he was not present. He may have gone deeper within me or into a higher dimension altogether. I am not sure. There was no goodbye. We did not review our work together, and he did not pat me on the back and say, "Good job." I continued to give readings, and a few times I called out to him for assistance. He would immediately be present and helpful, but I knew that his work with me for the time being was complete.

My "Accident"

I would like to tell you that with this boost of supernatural help, I confidently went forward and pursued my psychic and medium practice. But this is not what happened. Instead, I stubbornly resisted. I did a few sessions a week. However, most of my effort and energy remained devoted to being an artist. I still went to work most days in my studio and lined up several art exhibits. While being a medium was interesting, I did not feel ready to fully commit to it as a profession. I continued to feel a cosmic push in this direction, but I did my best to deny it and tune it out.

However, despite my resistance, there was a different plan than mine at work. One sunny morning while driving to a store to pick up some supplies, my art career ended. I did not see the car to my left run the red light. Instead, I heard a large boom and felt the side door of my car crash against my arm. As I watched my metal fender sail brilliantly through the sunlit sky, I realized that my car was airborne right alongside it. Yet, instead of feeling fear, I experienced a surreal moment of awakening.

I heard myself say, "Okay, I get it. I will be a medium."

I knew that this was no accident. It was a clear message. Although my car was totaled beyond repair, I sustained only minor injuries. My shoulders, neck, and upper back bore the worst of it. Weaving and silk painting, my art of choice, required the continuous use of my upper body, shoulders, back, and arms. While I may have eventually been able to do art for an hour or so, I could not physically manage the long hours that were required to make a living.

Earth School Lessons

As I lay on the couch recuperating and thumbing through a magazine the first week after the accident, I came across an ad for a program that trained and certified spiritual counselors. It was starting in a couple of weeks in a town not far from me. I called the number and set up an interview. Within a week, I was enrolled. If I was going to be a professional medium, I wanted to be prepared.

As I continued to recuperate and heal from my injuries, I had a lot of time to think. It occurred to me that there was an important lesson in what had just happened, one that I recognized was in my best interest to fully grasp. As I mulled over the recent events, I considered my work with the Elder. The instructions and advice that he had me tape-record now seemed more significant. As I went through the tapes and notes from my earlier work with him, I came across what I was looking for.

Several months prior to my accident, the Elder told me that before our birth into this life, our angels and spirit guides help us to design a life plan. We agree to experience specific earth school lessons that will promote our soul's growth and evolution.

"Once you are in the physical life," he said, "your angels and spirit guides watch over your progress and steer you into those situations that will benefit your life plan. You will know when you are in sync with your life plan when events and opportunities flow smoothly and things seem to fall into place. Even though not everything always goes your way, you feel an inner assurance that you are on track. Despite the ups and downs of life, you know that you are where you are meant to be."

The Elder encouraged me to listen to these internal nudges and persistent feelings. He told me that guides communicate through the still, small voice within, through gut feelings, and through synchronicity. These intuitive messages let us know when everything is going to work out and when we may need to reexamine and change the path we are on. Our spirit guides and angels fill us with courage and determination when we need to go forward and try to steer us in another direction when we are detouring from our life plan.

"Angels and guides communicate to you through either opening or closing doors to opportunities and plans. If you are not on track with the lessons that you agreed to participate in previous to your birth, expect conditions to right themselves. Sometimes this happens in what appears to be random circumstance, loss, or disruption," he said.

As I reviewed his guidance, it sunk in better. At the time that he had shared this with me, I thought it was interesting, but I did not fully grasp its significance. I now realized the importance of listening within and following my inner guidance. Of course, had he told me that my car would go sailing through the air, I might have paid more attention. I have since come to realize that when we fail to listen to the signs and our inner voice, the message intensifies and hits us harder.

The Elder told me that our spirit guides and angels also communicate to us through our everyday experiences. Often these messages are subtle and appear to be luck and chance happenings. You may have experienced this yourself. Have you ever had a day where everything seems to fall into place? You readily drive through the green lights, you impress your coworkers with a unique solution to a problem, and your family notices and thanks you for the little things you do to make their lives easier. Events and circumstances flow effortlessly. You are at the right place at the right time. Then there are other days when you get stuck behind a bus and miss the beginning of an important meeting, plans that you had been looking forward to fall through, and your friends are too busy to keep a much-needed lunch date. When you are going in the right direction, life flows along smoothly. When you are not, obstacles, interruptions, and disruptions impede your progress. Your spirit guides work behind the scenes to help you attract the right opportunities and avoid the people and situations that will cause you stress and grief. If you are pushing too hard in a direction that conflicts with the experiences and lessons that you have come here to learn, your guides will let you know by creating difficulties and frustrating delays.

Emotional Stress

As I studied the Elder's teachings more closely, I became more motivated to pursue work as a medium and counselor. I devoted myself to school and began to give medium readings in earnest. Although I continued to work part-time as an art therapist, I rented space in a healing center and put effort into building more of a spiritual practice. I was fortunate to quickly become busy with clients.

However, I soon discovered another inner obstacle. I had initially thought that my resistance to intuitive work was due to my desire to be an artist. It wasn't long, however, before I realized another inner hindrance. I was very emotionally sensitive, and not just to energy and the unseen world. Feeling the pain, grief, confusion, and distress of others was at times overwhelming. Many of the people I worked with were experiencing hardship and great loss. Mothers grieving the passing of a child and others who had lost their jobs and were in physical pain or emotionally distressed and lonely came to see me for guidance and advice. Their pain and confusion began to emotionally affect me. Waking up at night thinking of my clients and feeling their stress and pain at all hours was becoming the norm. To add to my stress, I began to wonder if I was actually helping anyone.

Feelings of inadequacy and oversensitivity to others' suffering became more and more consuming. I knew that these thoughts and feelings were not healthy. I needed to get a grip on my emotions and reactions, so I sought advice and help through a number of different sources. I read books written by psychics and mediums, but no one seemed to address what I was experiencing. I meditated and turned to my guides for support, and I sought the counsel of other healing practitioners. Yet again, help came in an unexpected way.

Angelic Healing

The angelic realm came to my rescue. Growing up in a religious home, I was familiar with the concept of angels. In my young Sunday school days, I learned that angels lived in heaven in peace and harmony. I knew that they were pure emanations of the divine or God force and were quite different from us humans. Yet even though I had been told that they comfort, love, heal, protect, and guide us, I did not feel very close to them. From what I had learned in church, angels seemed so good and holy. I had difficulty believing that they would pay me much attention. Yet, like many of my previous held beliefs about who I was and what was possible, this perception was also about to fall by the wayside. I soon experienced and better understood the practical and down-to-earth ways of the angels.

Unlike the dramatic arrival of my spirit guides, my introduction to the angelic realm was softer and gentler. Their presence quietly emerged one morning while I was giving a reading to a woman whose young son had died of a heart defect. The grief and sadness that my client felt was oppressive. It surrounded her like a heavy, damp blanket that could barely be lifted. Although I was able to communicate with her son and her father, who was also in spirit, the emotional and psychological heaviness that she felt continued to hold her tight in its vise. I felt it. Yet I knew that despite my compassion and desire to help her, there was little I could do to alleviate her suffering.

As I sat with her, I suddenly saw a translucent light above my client's head. I psychically tuned in to it, and to my surprise, it was an angel. She was encircled by an orb of turquoise, gold, pink, and white light. Speaking softly, she told me to tell my client that she could let go and release her sadness to her. Although it was a simple message, the effect was tremendous. As I told the grieving mother the angel's message, waves of love and compassion filled the room. I could feel it, and I knew that my client could too. Almost in a trancelike state, we sat quietly for a few minutes in the aura of angelic love.

Healing came to both of us. My client was able to release some of her crippling grief. She accepted the angelic compassion being offered to her and felt the close presence of her son. I was able to let go of the critic within me that told me I was not doing enough to help my clients. My heart opened, and I let go of my stress and anxiety. In its place I felt peace and the assurance that I was not alone. Although my desire to free my clients from their pain was heartfelt and sincere, the angels sent me the message that this was not my place. Being loving and compassionate and assisting others in their healing had its limits. The angels knew, much better than I did, what was in another person's highest good. I further realized that we all come into this world with predetermined challenges that are important for our soul's evolution. It is in our life plan to confront, heal, and learn from them.

This session, although subtle and tender, had an enormous effect on me. I was freed from my belief that I could and had to do it all. The angels were much better and more effective at healing others than I could ever be. From that day on, I started to invoke and invite the presence of angels at the beginning of every session, and I have never been disappointed.

In the many years since this first angelic encounter, I have discovered that angels are a diverse group of celestial beings who do much more than play harps and float aloof in heavenly harmony. Their influence can be quite practical and down-to-earth. Like spirit guides, they can inspire, guide, comfort, motivate, and assist us in all of our earthly concerns. Although they are pure light and love, there is little that happens here on earth that intimidates them.

In a reading a few days ago, I saw an image of an angel that expressed their diverse nature. In this clairvoyant vision, I saw a beautiful female angel dressed in white. She had translucent wings, and a golden halo-like energy surrounded her. On her feet, however, were large heavy-duty rain boots. She was up to her knees in mud, yet she trudged through it with a force that I could tangibly feel. This was no faint-of-heart angel. Instead of a flute or harp, she carried what looked like a shovel in her hands. I knew she was helping to clear the path for my client who felt stuck in her career.

Understanding Celestial Help

As the weeks and months of giving readings turned into years and now decades, I have continued to encounter many celestial helpers. Always curious as to who might draw close from the spirit realm to assist me during readings, I have never been bored or disappointed. They are as unique as we are. Spirit guides, angels, and loved ones on the other side interact and help us in ways that we cannot always logically comprehend. This love and support is given freely and abundantly. It is the way of the spirit realm.

Everyone has a guardian angel. Since your birth into this life, a bit of the love of the heavens has tenderly watched over you. Guiding, protecting, and comforting, angels soothe your suffering, heal your pain, and encourage you to love and help others. You may feel your angels as warmth in your heart or a hand on your shoulder in times of need. When frightened or nervous, you may feel their reassuring presence whispering in your ear that everything will be all right.

Many of your loved ones on the other side love and support you in similar ways. They are aware of what is coming your way, and they help you to avoid pitfalls and problems that may arise. They may try to signal you to take a different route to work to avoid a potential accident, direct the right buyer to your home that is for sale, or influence a prospective employer to hire you. I have an uncle in spirit who was an aerospace engineer. When I was in college, I floundered in a calculus class that I needed to pass in order to graduate. One day while trying to study for a test, I felt his presence guiding me. In the aura of his calm confidence, I began to see and understand the complicated numbers in a way that finally made sense. Within a few hours, I grasped the problems that had previously eluded me.

Like your angels and loved ones on the other side who help you with day-to-day decisions, your spirit guides are adept in both celestial and practical matters. Is there a special skill, ability, or hobby that you would like to learn? There is a spirit guide that can assist you. Many spirit guides, while alive on the earth, achieved high levels of expertise in areas that may also be important to you. It may be part of your life plan to participate in athletics, technology, medicine, entertainment, and other fields. It may also be important for you to acquire knowledge and advance in specific areas of study. Your spirit guides may be supporting you as you assist others as a teacher, healer, author, speaker, or therapist. They work through your heart center, igniting feelings of passion and drive to pursue certain activities. Gently and silently, they guide you to comprehend and master knowledge and develop specific expertise by influencing your thoughts and ideas.

Your spirit guides lead you to be in the right place at the right time and to encounter others who help further your development. Along the way, they inspire you to acquire patience, be kind to others, and develop a more spiritual consciousness. Yet they will not simply do what you want them to do. If you are not able to participate and affect others in loving and positive ways, they will not support your involvement in certain activities or undertakings. Spirit guides tend to be most active with people who are interested in helping and healing others. Highly evolved spirit guides and angels are drawn to those who wish to develop healing, intuitive, and medium abilities and are interested in spiritual growth. Their help can be invaluable in opening energy pathways to access nonphysical energy information. They can also prepare your physical body to accept and integrate higher vibrations of spiritual energy that make connecting with the other side easier.

In the physical world, we often ignore the presence of our spirit guides and angels. Because we usually cannot see or speak to them, hear their voices, or touch and feel them with our physical senses, it is easy to deny their existence. Despite my ability to see and communicate with the spirit realm, I have stubbornly tried more than once to ignore celestial guidance. On the other side, spirit guides and angels cannot be denied. Once we pass over, we immediately enter their reality and encounter the guides and angels who have been close to us during our physical lives. They guide us through our life review, helping us to understand and become aware of the choices, decisions, and actions we took that furthered our soul growth and evolution and those that set us back. We are accountable for both what we do during our physical lives and the intent that motivated our actions.

Just as we have a life plan in our physical lives, we also devise a plan for activities in the spirit realm that will further our soul growth. It is during this process that some souls are assigned the task of visiting and interacting with certain individuals on earth. If there is an earth lesson that a soul has not yet been able to fully master and embody, they may need to draw close to the physical realm and observe and learn from a loved one who is engaged in a similar lesson. If, during the life review, a soul realizes that their responsibilities to others in the physical realm have not been completed, they will also be encouraged to draw close and assist them and act as a positive influence.

Through my many years of psychic and medium work, I have been surprised, shocked, excited, calmed, healed, comforted, and enlightened by the spirit guides, loved ones, and angels that share our space. Perhaps you, too, have felt and experienced the opening of new life and new energy through your connection with the spirit realm. In the last section of this book, I include development exercises and meditations to empower you to further communicate with your loved ones, angels, and guides.

In the next section, I share stories from client sessions that demonstrate the surprising extent to which you unknowingly help and interact with your loved ones on the other side. The positive daily choices, decisions, and actions that you take influence your family and friends on the other side and your soul's evolution.

Section 2

How You Help the Other Side —The Sessions

3

OVERCOME FEAR: ACTIVATE YOUR COURAGEOUS SPIRIT

Transforming fear is one of the earth school's most familiar lessons. At some time or another, we all have to contend with the stress, concern, and worry that accompany fear. Our fear has many disguises and can show up in any and every aspect of our lives. Fear can feel like anxiety, anger, nervousness, stress, and an impending sense of doom. Not only do we fear what we do not want to come into our lives, we can also feel fear about the good things that come our way.

There is a biological component to fear. It can keep us alert and aware of danger and signal us to pay attention and devote more time and effort to certain parts of our lives. But for the most part, fear runs out of control and is crippling. It can freeze us into inaction or motivate us to act in ways that create more stress and heartache for ourselves and those we love. Only on the earth do we feel fear. It is, in a way, the disease of the planet. Throughout time, fear has generated more suffering, devastation, and pain than almost any other human emotion.

Can You Imagine Having No Fear?

There is no fear in the spiritual realms. I have never encountered a spirit who had even a hint of the dread and stress that so many people live with on a day-to-day basis. On the other side, we understand that there has never been anything to be afraid of. We are safe and always have been. Love is everywhere.

Life is very different on the other side. Instead of dealing with daily economic, health, and relationship concerns, you rest in safety and love, knowing that all of your needs are taken care of. You do not have to struggle for what you want and need, as the climate is one of abundance and support. Imagine fear, anxiety, and stress falling away, just slipping away, and in their departure, love, possibilities, and inspiration taking their place. The skies are soft, multicolored orbs of translucent light. Flowers are always in bloom, and their fragrance whispers love into the atmosphere. There is never any pollution, trash, or smog. All living beings thrive. There is no death.

Once you pass over, you are graced with an enlightened view of your earth life. Through this transformed perspective, you wonder why you took your fears so seriously and allowed them to control and limit your ability to express your full potential. Like a dream that seemed so real, you now know that you are always safe and love is never far. You become aware that fears kept you from taking advantage of opportunities to create and participate in positive ways and to develop abilities and talents. The choices, decisions, and actions you took that were motivated by fear kept you in the dark and separate from the truth of your most beautiful and authentic self. You want the opportunity to reclaim your spirit and heal that part of you that embraced fear and dismissed love.

On the other side, you also remember all of the people you love and care for who are still in the physical realm. You send waves of love and support to them. You want to reach out and let them know that you are alive and finally at peace. Some of your loved ones on earth still live in fear and make decisions and choices that cause them pain and stress. You understand all too well why they do this.

But there are others who are in touch with the power of their spirit. They dive deep into their soul and, with courage, make choices from the heart of love. They accept their lessons and do their best to live their truth. How brave they are! You admire their courage and want to learn from them. You draw close ...

Courage in Action

The following session involves a fear that is common to many, especially women. Fear drives many of us to lose our power in relationships. Fear of not being loved and being alone causes many of us to repress our true self and live according to someone else's expectations. Some people feel dependent on others and stay in negative situations and relationships because they fear that they are not worthy or that they cannot financially take care of themselves.

When I first met Teresa, she was a few minutes late for our session. She was rushing from a long workday and was a little flustered when she sat down on my couch. She wanted me to begin the reading right away, as she was concerned that we would not have enough time to get to all of her concerns.

I began the session and immediately saw a woman dressed in a tailored jacket and skirt with her hands folded in her lap.

"Is your mother on the other side?" I asked Teresa, who nervously sat across from me.

"Do you mean is she dead? Yes, she died five years ago."

"A woman came in as I started the session who I believe is your mother. I hear the name 'Gloria.' She is nicely dressed, but is not saying very much. She seems to be waiting for me—"

"That would be like her. She was a quiet woman, and yes, her name is Gloria," Teresa said, interrupting me. She started to fidget.

"She is showing me an image of a small dog. I feel like it is a dog that is in spirit with her. She seems happy to be close to him."

"That is probably Sami. I think he was the love of her life," Teresa sighed.

At this, Gloria became more active. "Please tell my daughter that I love her and that I am sorry," I heard Gloria repeat over and over. I relayed this message to Teresa, and she bowed her head.

"Your mother says, 'I am learning so much. I was not there for her in the way that she needed me to be. Tell her that I am not afraid anymore. I want her to know this. All of the fear goes away when you are here, just falls off,'" I told Teresa.

Teresa nodded in agreement. "My mother was full of fear. She avoided conflict and could not handle disagreement of any kind. She would just shut down. When she became ill and was dying, she was very distant. She was afraid to die and lingered for days and weeks. We all knew that it was fear keeping her here. Ask her about her passing. Did her mother or father come for her? I was so hoping that they would help her."

Gloria was quick with a reply. "Your mother is saying that it took her a little while to realize that she had died. She says that she woke up and the stiffness in her body was gone. The constant ache in her joints had subsided, no more pain." I started to get some intense images from her. "Your mother is showing me an image of the sun, a glowing sun coming through what look like lace curtains. She tells me she felt its warmth, and I feel her relax—"

Teresa interrupted me. "My mother died at night."

"I believe that the sun your mom is showing me was the light of the other side. She thought it was the sun. Now I see her mother and father coming out of the sun toward her. She shows me an angel that took her hand. She had a peaceful passing. She wants you to know it took her a while to realize that she had died. It was so different than what she expected. She says that there was nothing to be afraid of. She wishes she would have known."

As I gave her this message, Teresa seemed to relax and told me, "She was so closed down and unable to let go. I am relieved to know that she is at peace."

I was not too surprised at Gloria's desire to apologize to her daughter. Many sessions with loved ones in spirit involve healing and forgiveness. Gloria was surprisingly good at communicating with me. For a spirit who was initially shy, her presence and message were clear and strong.

"Your mother says that she is with you more than you know. It is necessary. She says that the angels tell her she needs to learn from you. Even when you are afraid, you find the courage to move forward. You didn't get this from her. Your mom tells me that she was full of fear."

Spirits communicate with me in a variety of ways. Gloria sent me both thought and visual messages. I again began to see more images. I told Teresa, "I see what feels to me to be your father. He is yelling and being a bully. I see your mom cowering and feeling small and powerless. I get the feeling that she did not know what else to do. She shows me a young girl. I think it is you. You are looking at her for help. But she does nothing."

As I gave this message to Teresa, I heard her begin to cry. I handed her a tissue, and through her tears, she explained.

"My mother was always quiet. My father would storm around the house screaming and getting his way. We were all afraid of him. He could be mean, and we never did anything right in his eyes. My mother would cower and never stand up to him. I felt unprotected, and for a long time I was mad at her. I understand now that she did the best she could do. Her father was an authoritarian parent, and she was raised to believe that a woman's place was to cook and clean and give her husband what he wanted. She never challenged this. My father was a brute, and my brothers were just like him. It took me a long time to find my power and to learn how to take care of myself."

"Your mom is very sorry," I told Teresa. "She understands how she was not there for you. She is also telling me that she is learning from you. She says that you have courage. She shows me an image of you. I believe that this is your home. You are in the kitchen with two children. Your mom is there in spirit. I see her watching you. She is very proud of you. I get the impression from your mother that you are a single parent and that you are raising your children on your own. Is this true?"

Teresa responded, "I am divorced with two sons. It has not been easy. I have had to go back to court several times to get child support. My ex just won't pay. Says he will. Then there is always an excuse. I married someone just like my father. He was charming and said the right things, but the anger was there. I didn't want to see it at first. I did my best to make him happy, skirt the issues, and try to calm him. It didn't work. He just got angrier and more demanding. I knew I had a choice. I could pretend it wasn't happening, and I did for a while. But I couldn't bring up my boys to be like this. I had to give them a chance. I didn't want them to grow up with the same fear that I felt. Soon after my mother died, I started the divorce proceedings. I have had no regrets. I did the right thing. I can feel it in my heart."

"Your mom is proud of you. She tells me that she never taught you how to take care of yourself, and now you are helping to teach her. She is learning from you," I told Teresa. "When you make positive choices and act on what you know in your heart to be the right thing, you are helping her. She knows the difficulties that you have had to endure. Now she can understand her part in it. Through your healing and self-empowerment, your mother has the opportunity to experience a different way of responding."

"Is that really possible? How do I help her?" With a perplexed look on her face, Teresa tried to take this all in.

"Love creates a bond that spans time and space," I tried to explain. "Even though your mother is in spirit, she is still learning. Sometimes our lives on earth are so full of stress and anxiety, we do not know how to change. We lack the courage and allow ourselves to be powerless victims. When we transition to the other side, we become aware of the power of our spirit. We begin to realize that the power to create a better life is within us. In our physical life, we may not have known this, and if we did, we may not have acted on it. Your mom knows that she could have done things differently. Now, through you, she has the opportunity to feel and experience what it is like to have courage and strength."

"Wow." A smile spread across Teresa's face. The lines in her forehead were gone, and she looked more relaxed. "I had no idea that my struggles were helpful to anyone but me and my boys. For a long time I was mad at my mother. I felt that she did not love me enough to take care of me or herself. That anger turned inward, and I felt I didn't deserve to be loved and cared for. When I became a mother, I began to see things differently. I understood better what my mother experienced. She did not work and had no marketable skills or education. Feeling stuck, she tried to make the best of it. It feels good to know that my struggles are helping her. Don't get me wrong, I know what it is like to have my knees shake with fear. But I somehow move forward anyway. Maybe my mom is helping me with this. This makes me feel good, very good. Please tell my mom I love her and I forgive her. I know that she did the best she could."

I explained to Teresa that she did not need me to give her this message. "She sees you, hears you, and feels your love," I assured her. "You don't need me to let her know. Just hold the love in your heart and imagine sending it her way. She will receive it."

Activate the Courage Within

Fear is a disconnection from your most powerful self, your spirit. When you are cut off from your inner power, life becomes a series of external events that you have no control over. You are tossed here and there in the winds of change and you become a victim to outside influences and forces that seem to come and go at whim. We do not know what is coming our way and when. This provokes fear in every area of our lives. We might lose our job, a relationship may end, or we may become ill or be involved in an accident.

Fear motivates many people to seek out the service of a psychic. There is a widespread belief that tapping into the unseen will yield information and guidance on what is to come and how it will affect one's life. We look to the wise counsel of the heavens to better negotiate the ups and downs and practicalities of life on earth. I have found the spirit realm to be surprisingly helpful in providing guidance to those who confront earthly issues of financial stress, career decisions, relationship concerns, and illness. Despite the sublime and transcendent nature of the heavens, our concerns on earth are heard and addressed.

Although knowing and predicting the future is what most people expect from a psychic, another truth also becomes apparent. Psychic awareness is not just about predicting outcomes and knowing the future. It is also the awareness that we have the innate power to influence outer conditions. Most people want me to tell them the conditions and opportunities that I see coming their way. I give them my most accurate predictions, but I also remind them that they have free will. Once we are aware of what we are creating in our future, we can also choose differently and affect future outcomes.

Fear Creates an Energy Wall

Not too long ago on the recommendation of another psychic, a woman came to me for a reading. As I tapped into her energy, I felt as if I had literally hit a brick wall. Despite her desire to consult a psychic, her fear and defensiveness made it almost impossible for me to give her an accurate reading. Luckily, her very helpful and psychic cat suddenly appeared in my mind's eye. Had it not been for this cat psychically providing me with accurate insight and information, I might not have been able to do the reading. After the session, I asked her why the other psychic had recommended me to her.

"She couldn't read me," my client told me. "She told me that I was harder to read than anyone she had ever worked with."

"I completely understand," I told her. "I had a difficult time also. I felt a fair amount of fear when I began the reading. Are you sure you wanted one?"

With an innocent look on her face, she told me, "Well, yes, I guess I did. But, to be honest, I was afraid of what you might tell me. I didn't want to know if I was going to get ill or be told that something bad is going to happen."

Fear acts in this way in our lives. Like a dense wall surrounding us, it is a visceral inner resistance that we erect to try to guard and protect ourselves from what may or may not come our way. Yet this never works. Instead of protecting us, fear keeps us from accessing the inner power of our spirit.

Where there is fear, the awareness of the power of your spirit is repressed and hidden. The cure for fear is to activate your inner power. Instead of looking for outside solutions or becoming numb with stress, go within and listen. Summon and awaken the quiet power of your spirit. Breathe into your body, open your heart, and feel the power in your solar plexus. If you feel led to take action, activate the courage buried within and go forward with integrity and positivity. You only truly know the power of your spirit when you allow it to lead you. Take a risk and confront your fears. When you do, they fall away. The earth school lesson of fear is a call to activate and employ the power of your spirit.

Financial Fear

It is no surprise that most people harbor some degree of financial fear. The world broadcasts daily the looming threat of financial collapse and the devastating personal and collective disasters that may befall us in the process. The fear of poverty, lack, and unexpected financial expenses constantly nips at our heels.

The contrasts between physical and spiritual perceptions of money are impressive. In the spiritual realms, there is no money. Can you imagine never having to worry about paying bills or an empty bank account? In spiritual reality, money represents energy, abundant and infinite energy that is everywhere. Can you imagine what life would be like if you were able to live every day with the realization that, like energy, there is an infinite supply of money available to you?

Despite your daily earthly financial concerns, you can tap into the infinite abundance that is everywhere. Just as in the spiritual realms, money is energy. Learning the earth school lesson of activating your inner spirit to confront fear enables you to take back your power. When you know that the source of your supply is not dependent on outer forces, you become aware of the never-ceasing flow of abundance that is within you.

Overcoming the Fear of Lack

The following session addresses the common fear of lack and financial security. Even those who have money in the bank and a steady income can experience anxiety, stress, and worry about money. When our ability to connect to the power of our spirit is repressed and denied, we experience some form of fear in our external life.

This session speaks to the fears associated with not having enough. It illustrates how we can help those on the other side who may have allowed financial fear to control their earth lives. It also includes the story of how certain pets come into our lives and act as helpers and guides, even when it comes to our finances. Although they cannot communicate to us through words, they are able to transmit feelings and messages. Even though it may look like your dog or cat is simply relaxing in the sun or staring into open space, they may also be conversing with the angels.

The Giving Veterinarian

Kevin came to see me to communicate with his beloved dog that had died in a tragic accident. Prince was a mixed-breed, long-haired, spunky dog that Kevin had adopted from a shelter when he was about three months old. One of the several jobs that Kevin had held during his college days was in a dog shelter. Although Kevin had plans to go to veterinary school and was busy with his studies, when he saw Prince curled up in his pen he knew that this was his dog.

Prince seemed to understand Kevin's busy schedule and was remarkably calm for a puppy. Through college and then veterinary school, they ran together in the mornings and, when time allowed, explored the mountains not far from their home. Kevin eventually became a veterinarian and opened a low-cost spaying and neutering clinic. In addition, he bought a mobile vet unit that could go into low-income neighborhoods and offer services at a reduced rate. His income was far less than that of the average veterinarian, but he did not seem to care. He loved his work.

Prince was Kevin's constant companion. The dog's quiet and wise demeanor was a source of strength. Accustomed to going to the clinic with Kevin, Prince was hit in the parking lot one morning by a car that was attempting to quickly turn around. Kevin rushed Prince into surgery and did everything he could do to save his life. Even though the dog was badly injured, Kevin felt confident that Prince would make it. He came through surgery successfully but never recovered. An infection set in, and Prince died.

On the day of our session, Kevin drove his mobile vet van to my office. He had just finished a morning of onsite vet visits in the inner city. Never having been to a medium before, he was a little apprehensive. As I began the session, I was surprised at the number of dogs, cats, and other animals that were close to him in spirit. Although they were all loving and seemed to want to connect with Kevin, I knew that it would not be possible to talk to all of them.

"There are quite a few dogs, cats, and other animals close to you," I told him. "Is there any particular pet or animal that you would like for me to connect with?"

Quite often when I ask a client this question, spirit answers. Immediately this happened and I told Kevin, "A brown, long-haired, medium-size dog just came forward."

Dogs, cats, and other animals tend to communicate with me through visual images. This is what Kevin's dog began to do.

"He is showing me a bedroom. It has several large windows that look out over a yard. There is a large red dog bed in the room. I take it this is his bed. I see him lying in it."

I look at Kevin and I see that he is staring straight ahead. "This is why I am here," he said. "That is my dog Prince. The bedroom you described is mine. His bed is near my bed."

"Prince is also showing me an office. He shows me it from a dog's point of view. He is looking up at the table. I get the impression from him that he is trying to help you."

"Is he really with me?" Kevin asked. "Or is he showing you images from the past?"

"I am not sure," I told him.

I tuned in to Prince, and he seemed very happy. He was wagging his tail. "I am getting the message that he is with you now, in spirit, sleeping near your bed and in your office with you."

"That is interesting. I have had the feeling that he is still with me. This is why I decided to come in for a session." Kevin looked more serious and continued. "I woke up from a deep sleep soon after he died, hearing him moan. I thought it was my imagination. But it happened a few more times. Then one day in my office I was working on a dog that was lethargic and weak. I was not sure what was causing this. Then in my mind's eye I saw my dog Prince. I felt like he was trying to help me. It was almost like he was directing me to certain areas in the dog's body. I felt like I was crazy."

I explained to Kevin that animals do not view death like we do. Prince was with him. There was no doubt of that. He was a wise soul who wanted to be helpful to Kevin in any way that he could.

"He was a wise soul when he was in body, too," Kevin enthusiastically told me. "I could always depend on him. He gave me strength. I know it sounds strange, but I felt like he gave me the courage to start the mobile unit. I always wanted to do this, but I was not sure I could make a living. It was expensive to get going. I knew I would have to take out a big loan. Mobile units are a great way to reach animals and their owners, but they do not make much money. My financial fears almost kept me from following through. But Prince just seemed to calm my nerves. I miss him so much."

Prince had a few other things to share with Kevin. It meant a lot to Kevin to know that he was alive in spirit and still with him. As I was finishing up my communication with Prince, Kevin's grandfather also came through for a visit. He was proud of Kevin and his accomplishments.

"You did it all on your own," he said. "I wish that I could have helped you. But I guess you didn't really need it."

I was about to end the session when another man came in that I could not immediately place.

I told Kevin, "There is a thin, medium-height man with gray hair who just came in. He holds himself tightly. I feel like he was a family member on your mother's side. His name begins with a *B*, maybe Bill or Bob. I get the impression that he was successful in business."

"I am not sure who that is." Kevin looked confused.

"Let me tell you the message," I said. "He is telling me that he had plenty of money, but it didn't make him happy. He was stressed and fearful when he was here. He held on tight to what he had. Didn't share and give, even when others needed help. Now he doesn't know why he lived like this."

"That sounds like my Uncle Bo," Kevin said. "My mother's brother. He had his own insurance company. Made a lot of money, but he was really stingy. We didn't know why. When my grandmother needed help with her mortgage after my grandfather died, we all thought he would help her. But he didn't, and he told my mother to stop whining and asking for a handout. He always thought that people were trying to get his money. There was a rumor that he kept a loaded gun under his bed. He was so sure that someone would try to rob him. He always lived in fear. I am really surprised that he is here. We were not very close."

Uncle Bo was listening intently and was ready to continue. "Your uncle says that he has to learn from you," I shared with Kevin. "He says that he does not know how you do it. You give so much away. You could be saving your money or buying a bigger home, retiring early. But you give it away. To animals, no less, stray dogs and cats. The angels like you. Your uncle says that you can help him to learn how to give."

"I am glad I can help," Kevin continued. "We never understood why Uncle Bo was so unhappy. Tell him that I wish him well and that I give because it makes me happy."

Uncle Bo still had more to say. I told Kevin, "Your uncle is beginning to feel the joy of giving through you. I get the impression from him that after he passed out of the physical body, it took him a while to leave the earth realm. He shows me his home and things. He did not want to leave them. I see an older gentleman, maybe your grandfather, encouraging him to join him in the light of the heavens. I feel that when he finally went into the light, he was surprised at how much love and forgiveness he felt. I get the impression that his life review was quite an eye-opener. He experienced his selfishness and fear in a very different way. The angels guided him to you to help him understand how good it feels to give."

As we ended our session, Kevin thanked me, looked at his watch, and told me that he had his afternoon rounds to make in the mobile unit. The look in his eyes as he said goodbye was one of strength and renewed motivation. It was a wonderful session for me, too.

4

HEAL ADDICTIONS: EXPERIENCE YOUR SPIRITUAL POWER

~~~~~~~~~~~~~~~~~~~~~~~~~~~~~~

At some point in the course of your life, you will cross paths with an addict. Whatever the person is addicted to is not necessarily important. Whether it be alcohol, drugs, sex, shopping, food, gambling, or playing video games, it is their all-consuming passion and the focus of their life. For the addict, there is little else as important as feeding the need and desire for their drug of choice. A higher high, a release from the pain, a dulling of the external senses, and a false sense of connectedness are what the addict seeks. Addicts are relentless in their desire for sensory pleasure and willingly give their mind, body, and soul over to an external fixation.

The earth school lesson of addiction is a harsh wake-up call from one's spirit. When we persistently ignore and place no value on our spirit, it eventually recedes into the murky recesses of our consciousness. In the all-consuming grip of addiction, the spirit is deadened, vague, and out of reach. The addict is surrounded by darkness and immersed in material and sensual desire that can never be fulfilled. This lesson is a difficult one. Yet a soul elects to pursue an addiction in order to experience a profound awakening.

I know it seems like a paradox. Why would our soul intentionally put us through such misery, loss, and the possibility of death when what it really desires is that we become aware of its light, warmth, and love within us? Sometimes we have to go fully down a path in order to see where it takes us. Those on the other side often tell their loved ones during sessions that there was little anyone could have done to stop their addiction. Although it may make no sense, the addict relentlessly pursues a false material god in order to ultimately discover the divine power within.

Until we are completely cut off from our spirit, we do not fully understand the magnitude of its importance and irreplaceable worth. In this same way, we do not know happiness if we have never felt sadness. We value and embrace the warm days of spring after the harsh, cold winter. Illness makes us honor our health. When the spirit is denied, repressed, and hidden, we are shaken out of our ambivalence. Our suffering eventually wakes us into reluctant but illuminating awareness. We understand our spirit's value, its light, wisdom, love, and magic. We become motivated to embrace, appreciate, and cherish our spirit.

Death Through Addiction

When someone passes over as a result of an overdose or if alcohol or drugs were a contributing factor in a person's death, their entry into the light may be delayed. Especially in the case of an overdose, it may take some time for them to realize that they have died. An addict's spirit may hover over their body, lost in a fog as to what is happening. In some cases, they follow their body long after they have physically died. In extreme cases, they stay stuck in the astral realm.

When we pass over, the astral realm is the energy vibration in between the heavenly realms of all love and the physical world. When an addict passes over, they are often confused. They are at risk of becoming wandering and lost spirits who do not always recognize that they are no longer in the physical body. Their spirit may roam in the astral realm attempting to inhabit places where alcohol or the drug of their choice is available or congregate around other addicts or drug and alcohol users.

There are angels and loved ones in spirit who try to assist these lost souls. They reach out and attempt to guide them into the love of the heavens. An individual may resist this help and choose instead to continue to drift close to the earth in a desire to satisfy their addiction. Eventually, though, most willingly accept that they must advance into the light of love, where they can heal.

Addiction Lingers after Passing

One of the biggest surprises for people with active addictions who pass over is that they still crave their drug of choice. The physical body is released from the addiction, but the emotional, spiritual, and mental addiction does not evaporate upon death. Addicts must still go through the process of freeing themselves from their reliance and dependence on their drug of choice. In the light and love of the heavens, there are energy "treatment centers" where these souls can heal. Here they are given angelic care and attention. This detox period is in some ways similar to detoxing from the physical addiction.

Addicts on the other side must, however, go through an intense review period where they see, feel, and understand how their addiction affected their soul plan and the people in their lives. This is not an easy process, as the soul must feel at deep levels what others felt as a result of their actions. In the spiritual realm after this review, addicts often return to the emotional state they were in previous to becoming addicted. Loved ones in spirit who struggled with dependency issues often tell me that they have returned to the emotional age they were before their addiction began. This is essentially when they stopped growing and developing. By returning to this time, they are able to work through whatever issues they were avoiding and denying by turning to an outer substance. All of this is done under the guardianship of loving and healing angels and spirit guides.

A soul's progression through this detox period varies in length. I have communicated with some on the other side who have been reluctant to grow and remain "in treatment" for many (earth) years. Others embrace their growth and evolution and move through this process more quickly. Once a soul has completed their healing, they join their family and friends and move into other areas of interest and continue their growth and evolution.

Like Mother, Like Son

Some of the most difficult medium sessions that I conduct are with mothers and fathers who have a son or daughter who has passed over as a result of drugs, alcohol, or other addictions. Because addictions often repeat generation to generation, it is common to have clients and their loved ones on the other side working through the process of recovery simultaneously. One family member's recovery can have a far-reaching energetic effect on others. We often view our challenges as our own. We suffer in silence and can feel isolated and separate from others who appear less burdened and troubled. Yet our struggles are not as personal as they may appear to be. We are all one. This includes our challenges as well as our victories. Your healing helps others to heal.

Sarah came to see me one Saturday morning. She was so quiet when she came in and sat in my waiting area, I did not know she was there. I opened the door to my office to check for her, and I saw an attractive woman sitting with her hands folded looking out the window.

I invited her into my office, and in a faint voice she told me her name and waited for me to begin. Because I work as both a psychic and medium, I am never sure what kind of session people want when they schedule with me. I have learned that it is best not to ask, but to simply begin the session and see where my angels and guides lead me. I always invite loved ones in spirit into the session. Sometimes their presence is so strong that I have no choice but to begin the session with whoever has come in from the other side.

Before I finished saying a short prayer with Sarah, her father, grandmother, and another male came in. I began by talking to her father. He quickly introduced me to another male who was by his side.

"There is a young male close to your father that he wants me to communicate with," I told Sarah. "I hear the name 'Brian.'"

I heard a gasp from Sarah. "My son's name is Brian. This is why I am here. I wanted to see if you could communicate with him."

"He is here," I told her. "I see an image of him when he was young dressed in what looks like a sports team outfit. He seems happy. He wants you to know this. I get the impression from him that you two were very close. In his early life, you had a lot of fun together."

Sarah interjected. "It was just the two of us, and yes, we were very close."

Despite the happy memory, Sarah looked sad and distant.

"Brian is telling me that his death was not your fault. He wants you to know that he made his own choices. I get the impression that alcohol was involved. But I am confused. I feel that he is talking about you, too. That somehow you have had some issues with alcohol. Is this correct?" I asked Sarah.

"I was an alcoholic from the time Brian was little. When my husband left, I felt overwhelmed and I began to drink. I started with just a few drinks after work once in a while, then every night, then every day. By the time Brian was in middle school, I would be drunk by the time he came home." Sarah was quiet for a few moments, then added, "It was my fault. This is all Brian knew."

"Brian is showing me an image of a truck, a red truck. He is rounding a turn. I get the impression that he is driving the truck and there is an accident. Then I feel a lot of confusion. He doesn't know where to go. I feel like he tries to go back to what looks like a party. I know that doesn't make sense. Is this how he passed over, in a car accident after a party?"

"Yes," Sarah confirmed. "Brian died alone in his truck. He had been drinking and was way over the legal limit of alcohol. He drove off the side of an embankment and into a deep ditch. It should have been me," she continued. "I drove drunk many times and nothing ever happened to me."

As I continued the reading, I became aware of Brian's confusion after he died in the accident. I did not want to make this harder on Sarah, but Brian's ability to communicate with me was excellent and he seemed to want me to explain some things to his mother.

I went on. "I am not sure that Brian was aware that he had died. This sometimes happens when a person is under the influence. He shows me that he wanted to go home. I feel that he was close to you for a while. I am not sure how long. He shows me an image of you in what I believe is his bedroom. You are crying and going through his things. He is with you trying to talk to you, telling you that he is alive. He shows me what looks like a colorful poster or picture over his bed. It seems important to him. It reminded him of something from the past, a good memory."

Sarah looked surprised. "Oh yes, that was a poster that we got from a trip we took to Boston to see the Red Sox play when he was young. That was his favorite team, and we went to see them play on his tenth birthday."

I felt the presence of Sarah's father. He wanted her to know that he helped Brian after he passed. "Eventually I feel that your father helped him to go with him," I told her. "I see a fishing pole in his hand. Your father coaxed him over by asking him to join him on a fishing trip."

"Please thank my dad for me. He died when Brian was young. I know that he always wanted to go fishing and do other activities with him. I guess he is getting his chance now."

There was more that Brian wanted to share with his mother. I continued. "Brian is showing me the image of a group of people. It feels as if they helped him. He wants you to know that he is not confused anymore. He is learning about himself and life. There is a sense of peace with him. You are part of this. He shows me another image of you. You are in this group of people. Hmm ... I thought this was an image from the other side, but maybe not. Do you belong to any kind of support group? I believe that this is what he is trying to show me."

Sarah looked puzzled. "After Brian's death, I was a basket case. I wanted to die. I drank myself unconscious every night. I was on the verge of losing my job. My supervisor called me into her office and told me that she was going to have to let me go. She did not want to. She knew that Brian's death had had a devastating effect on me. In our conversation she disclosed to me that she was a recovering alcoholic. Alcohol, she told me, almost ruined her life. After a failed marriage and bankruptcy, she realized that she needed help. In desperation she went to an AA meeting. She was ten years sober, and she told me about a meeting not far from our office. I went to it that day after work. I couldn't afford to lose my job. I thought if she knew that I took her advice and went to a meeting that she would not fire me. That was seven years ago. I have not had a drop of alcohol since. Maybe this is the group that Brian is showing you. Is it possible that he was there with me?"

"I believe that this is the message. He was close to you, in spirit, in the meetings. I get so much warmth and love from him to you. He is proud of you and wants you to know that this helped him. You have in some way been recovering together. Brian wants me to tell you that he loves you. His drinking was not your fault. He likes being in spirit. Brian is funny. He says it's more fun than video games. He is playing some other kind of game, with light, color, and sound. It feels very creative. By the way, do you have a dog? He keeps showing me a medium-size, light-colored dog. I feel like when he is with you in your home, your dog is aware of his presence."

"Yes, that's Molly. She has been a constant companion. I call her my angel dog. She helped me to get through this. Tell Brian I am so proud of him and I love him."

Follow-up

We ended the session soon after this last exchange. Sarah contacted me a few months after her session. She wanted me to know of the peace that she now felt.

She explained, "I didn't know what to say after our session. I was at a loss for words. For so long I have lived with the overwhelming weight of guilt. I felt that if I had not been an alcoholic, then Brian would not have been one either. I didn't know what to think during our session. The message from Brian that my meetings were helping him was almost too good to believe. It has taken me a while to let go of my self-hatred. I feel like Brian is helping me to do this. Just knowing that he is alive in the spirit realm and happy makes every day better."

The Spiritual Cure of Addiction

Addiction is a disease of denial. In its clutches you no longer participate in your life. Addictions subdue the voice of the spirit, and the individual's emotional and mental development ceases. Fully consumed, addicts give themselves over to the energy of a force outside of themselves. They become its puppet and enter the realm of shadows and darkness. The ultimate distraction—being high, strung-out, loaded, and under the influence—keeps them from feeling, thinking, and being in the flow of conscious awareness.

No one sets out to become an addict. What they are searching for is not so much the drug or activity that they eventually become addicted to. Instead, their motivation is escape from the dulling pain that often comes with the ups and downs of everyday life. We can, for the most part, deal with pain, loss, and disappointment. What we cannot live with for long is pain, loss, or disappointment that has no meaning. When all of life seems futile and pointless, when what we experience feels random and empty, we suffer.

Every day, in a multitude of ways, this world broadcasts illusionary and soul-deafening ways to find bliss. We are told that external things like money, clothes, physical attractiveness, trips to exotic places, expensive objects, and fast cars open the happy gates where we all revel in life's luxuries. This is simply not true. We are at peace when we are whole. When you are consciously in the flow of your soul purpose, mind, body, and spirit, life has meaning. Whatever comes into your life is transmuted and used for your highest good. In this way, your spirit takes back its power from the world.

It is not surprising that Alcoholics Anonymous, Narcotics Anonymous, and other twelve-step programs based on giving one's will over to a higher power are the most successful recovery programs for addiction. Every addict began their addiction from a deep desire to experience oneness with a source of power and energy much greater than the self. The lesson for the addict is to embrace their ability to fully surrender to what is within.

Many of the deceased people who come in during medium sessions were alcoholics and drug users here on earth. They tend to have left a fair amount of unfinished business. If you have or had a mother, father, sister, brother, friend, lover, wife, husband, or other loved one who suffered from an addiction, you are most likely painfully aware that despite their physical presence in your life, they were essentially absent. You cannot have a true relationship with an addict. For this reason, as a medium I communicate with many souls who left this earth with an active addiction and are healing in the spirit realm. If you had a loved one who had an addiction pass over, know that in the spirit realm they are working hard to grow, evolve, and heal and that they are likely also learning from you.

It's All in the Name

I had an interesting session a few years ago that involved a mother who had given her daughter up for adoption at birth. An active drug user, the birth mother of my client came through during our session to connect with the daughter she never knew. What I found interesting in this session was the bond that these two shared despite never having had a relationship in the physical realm.

"It's nice to meet you, Maria," I greeted my next client as she walked into my office.

"Nice to meet you, too, but my name is Linda." With a look of puzzlement, she took a seat on my couch. "Not a good way to start the session," I told her. "I apologize."

I began the session by explaining that before a reading, I say a short prayer. During the prayer, I again embarrassingly referred to Linda as Maria.

I apologized once more. "I don't know why I want to call you Maria," I told her.

As readings go, this one started off fairly typically. I received messages for her from her angels and loved ones on the other side. As I got ready to ask her if she had any questions, I began to hear, "Mother, mother, mother …," repeated over and over. The image of a tall, dark-haired woman crowded my inner vision.

"Your mother is coming in from spirit, and she would like to talk to you," I told Linda.

"But my mother is very much alive," she told me with a look of surprise on her face.

Hmm, I thought to myself, *who is this woman?* I continued to hear, "Mother, mother …." I described the woman spirit's appearance to Linda. A look of surprise came over her face.

"I was adopted. I never met my birth mother," she explained. "That might be her?"

As Linda talked, her mother in spirit began to show me images, one after another. I began to try to describe all of the images and thoughts that I was receiving.

"Your birth mother wants you to know that she loves you. Her life was difficult. I feel like she had a problem with drugs. She shows me images of an older home; it feels empty. I feel a lot of confusion inside of it. I see bottles of pills and hypodermic needles. She is sitting in this house. I feel like she was lonely and scared during her pregnancy with you. Now she shows me an image of herself in the hospital. She is holding a baby. I am sure it is you. I get the feeling from her that she wanted you to have a good life, a different life than she could offer you. She wants you to know she always loved you." I looked over at Linda and she was expressionless.

"I have had a good life," she told me. "I love my parents and my family. My life is not at all like her life. She is a stranger to me."

I listened to Linda and kept part of my awareness focused on her mother. I felt her pull on my energy. Despite Linda's reluctance to communicate with her birth mother, she went on. There seemed to be a lot her birth mother wanted to say.

"Do you want me to continue?" I asked Linda. "Or I can move on if you prefer."

I gave her a moment to think. Cautiously she replied, "No, please, I want to hear what she has to say. I am just surprised that she is here. I did not expect this."

"Your mother is showing me the image of what looks like a clinic. I am not sure why. But I think this has more to do with you than with her. It feels more present time. I see people needing help. Does this make any sense to you? She keeps showing me an image of you in the clinic."

Linda looked startled and told me, "I work in a treatment center. Maybe this is what she is showing you. I am an addictions counselor for teenagers. It has its challenges, but I love my work."

"I get the impression from your birth mother that at times she is present with you in the clinic. You are not aware of her presence, but you are helping her. She tells me that her drug use started when she was young. She shows me herself in spirit, learning about herself and why she chose drugs. She tells me that your work with the teenagers helps her. Even though she is no longer in a physical body, she still has to work through the choices she made when she was here and their consequences."

"I didn't know that something like this was possible." Linda looked like she was trying to take all of this in. "Do you know when she died? Did she ever get off of drugs?"

"I get the feeling from her that she died of a drug overdose not long after you were born. She tells me that she gave up on life. You are the best thing that came from her life. She is very proud of you."

"Do you have any other questions for your birth mom?" I asked Linda. She looked at me with a blank face. I knew that this was a lot for her to take in and that it might take some time for her to fully understand and process all that she had heard.

"I did not expect my birth mother to come into this session today. I do not think much about her, and I don't know what I would ask her. It's funny, but because of my work in the treatment center, I guess in a way I do know her or I know what her life must have been like. It's strange. I always wanted to help people with these kinds of problems."

The session ended soon after this encounter. As Linda was getting ready to leave, she put her hand on the doorknob and turned to look back at me. "I didn't tell you this earlier, but on my original birth certificate my birth mother named me Maria."

There Is a Move Coming

I included the following session because it involves an addict, his father, and an enlightening glimpse into the spirit realm. I gave this reading many years ago, early in my practice. It was before I fully understood the beauty of the heavens and what I call the "light."

I had given several readings to Greg before he came to see me one afternoon. From previous sessions I knew that his adult daughter Jamie was living with him. In her thirties, she had lived on her own for only a couple of years. Addicted to drugs and alcohol, she was unable to keep a job and had little money. After several years of her living in his basement, Greg began to understand that he had enabled Jamie. A single parent, he struggled to do the right thing. He eventually went to therapy and began to take positive steps to better help himself and Jamie.

This is a short excerpt from a longer session that I had with Greg. We talked about many things, but foremost on his mind was his daughter. When I sat down and started the reading, he looked both hopeful and nervous. I began the session with a prayer. Before I had a chance to listen and receive messages from the spirit realm, he began to ask me questions.

"How is Jamie?" he anxiously asked me. "I am so nervous. She is at a residential addiction treatment center right now."

"I feel that Jamie is both confronting her issues and looking forward to being released," I told him. "She is learning a lot about herself and her choices and decisions. It isn't always easy, but she has a lot of help."

"I am not worried about Jamie right now," Greg explained. "But she is coming home next weekend and I don't know what to expect. What do you see? Will she go back to using drugs?"

"I am seeing an image of her working. It looks like a store of some kind. I feel that she makes friends there," I told him.

"She has a job lined up at a department store. What else do you see?" he asked me.

"I get an image of her working on a computer. She seems to be intense and focused. I am not sure why this is coming in, but it seems significant. I am not getting a good feeling about this. Someone is coming in from spirit, a beautiful angel, magnificent really. She is saying that you have done all that you can do. She wants you to feel her peace. She says that she is here for you."

"This worries me. Jamie bought drugs on the computer, pharmaceuticals from illegal online drug stores all over the world." Greg looked nervous as he told me this.

I suddenly saw a woman near Greg and I told him, "I see an attractive woman close to you. I am feeling a lot of love from her to you. Feels like you are in love. I see pink and gold light around the two of you."

"This is the other thing I wanted to talk to you about. I met a woman. We have been dating and we are talking about moving in together. I have been single for so long. I didn't think that this would happen for me. I am in love. But I don't know what to do about Jamie. Rhonda, my girlfriend, isn't comfortable with her living with us. Jamie is going to be thirty-five next month. It is time she lived on her own, but I don't know if she can make it. I am so worried about this. What do you see coming for me? I don't want to lose this wonderful woman." Greg was visibly distraught.

"The angel is coming in again, so close to you. She is beautiful. I rarely get such clear and profound visceral connections with angels as I am getting now. There is so much love that she is sending your way. I get the impression that Rhonda is a blessing. The angel tells me that Jamie is going to be moving. You and Rhonda will be together," I assured him.

"Jamie is moving?" Greg said. "Where? That cannot be possible."

"I am not sure," I told him. "I will ask your angel. She shows me someplace warm. There is so much sunlight. It is relaxing. She seems very happy here. I do not feel her using drugs, either. She is getting help."

"I cannot afford another treatment program for her. I cannot imagine where she would move to. Is it Florida?" he asked.

I tuned in again to the location, but I was not able to locate it. I told Greg, "I am not sure where it is. But I can assure you that she is happy here. There is so much light. I feel that somehow this is all going to work out."

Greg and I continued with other concerns for several more minutes. Even though I had given him several other readings, I could tell that he did not fully believe that Jamie would move and everything would work out.

A few months after this session, Greg left a message on my phone.

"I want you to know," he told me. "Jamie died of an overdose last week. After treatment, she went to work and everything seemed to be getting better. But she continued to use drugs. I found her unresponsive in her bed one morning. She had a peaceful look on her face. Do you think that the 'move' you talked about to a warm and sunny place, where she is happy, is the other side? Do you think that she is there now?"

I assured him that she was in the light and at peace.

This session taught me a lot. It showed me that the energy of "death" is one of love and light. Although we view it as scary and often dark and mysterious, the light of the heavens is a safe place of love, even when we pass under difficult conditions. I also learned, and have witnessed many times since in readings, that when we cannot heal, learn, and evolve in the physical world, we may elect to do the work on the other side.

5

EMBRACE YOUR FREEDOM: BREAK FREE FROM CONFORMITY

~~~~~~~~~~~~~~~~~~~~~~~~~~~~~~~~~~~

The pressure to conform and fit in is widespread and unrelenting. Yet despite this, we have come into this life to experience freedom. From an early age, schools and religious groups, our families, and cultural influences push us to follow and obey certain behaviors, norms, and rules. For some, a feeling of belonging is comforting and provides a sense of identity, friendship, and connection. But the expectations of others can also create inner tension and conflict. Your soul has its own plan for its unique self-expression—one that may not always be what the outer world expects from you.

Trying to be who others want you to be instead of being true to yourself can cause all kinds of problems. When you become disconnected from your authentic self, you lose your most valuable asset. You can become confused, distrust your natural impulses, be indecisive, and feel empty. Repressing your true self can also cause depression, apathy, and physical fatigue. Some people believe that they are flawed or defective in some way if what they desire for themselves differs from what others expect from them.

Certain souls come to the earth with the specific challenge of expressing their individuality. Often they are born into families where they do not feel as if they fit in. Some may also live in a repressive cultural environment where they are forced to confront inner feelings of being different and at odds with what others accept as normal. Many of my clients have told me that as far back as they can remember, their political, spiritual, and innate heartfelt perspective on life has differed from those in their environment.

From a soul perspective, there are many benefits to the earth lesson of expressing our individuality. Although it can be challenging, it is an opportunity for rapid soul growth and development. Feeling different than others can motivate us to listen to our inner voice and strengthen our self-awareness and self-trust. We have come to the earth to discover and listen to our personal truth. Even though the worldly current of influence often seems to want to direct us in the opposite direction, we are here to listen within and discover what frees our heart and spirit and brings us joy. Although we all want to belong and feel close to others, when we accept who we are, we become free and harness our true power.

Real Freedom

In the spirit realm, it is our individuality that defines us. We are free. This is our natural state. We are able to create, experience, and participate in a reality that offers unlimited possibilities for self-expression. We have no money, cars, big homes, fame, or physical attractiveness. Material things are nonexistent and, unlike in the earth realm, we cannot be defined by what we own. Ultimately, all that we have and all that we are is our individuality. What we retain after physical death is the joy within our heart and soul.

Once we pass over, the many masks that kept our true self from shining through drop away. I sometimes see this with people who are dying. I have had a few clients who, in the last stage of life, seemed to be released from the false baggage that they had been carrying around for most of their lives. Problems, pressure, and stress fell away. They laughed easily, and love shined bright from their eyes.

Helping Conformists on the Other Side

Some people, who have come to this earth with the specific purpose of developing their individuality, may fail to fully express their true potential. For various reasons, they may be overly swayed by outer influences and fail to listen within and embrace their true self. When they pass over to the other side, they become aware of this missed opportunity. They feel the ease and joy of their individuality and realize the beauty and creativity that was theirs to share and give to others on earth.

Your ability to be yourself helps and inspires your family and friends on the other side who lived repressed and conformist earth lives. Those day-to-day choices, decisions, and actions that you take to be yourself that seem to go unnoticed and unappreciated are being watched and received by those in spirit. Often souls who have not been strong enough to take up the challenge of being true to themselves can learn this lesson from those still on earth. Encouraged by their angels and spirit guides, loved ones in spirit come close, observe your challenges, feel the power of your spirit, and learn through your individuality.

The following are just two of the many sessions that I have had where those in the spirit realm have been inspired and helped by those brave souls on earth who dare to be themselves.

A Father's Freedom

Ken contacted me from Alaska for a session. Originally from North Carolina, he called me at the suggestion of a friend of his who was a client of mine. On the morning of the session, I called Ken, and with the first hello, his dynamic and adventurous spirit came bounding through. He oozed joy and vitality. The angels, too, seemed to love being close to him.

We were midway into the session, talking about his work on a fishing boat, when I became aware of a man in spirit quietly listening and watching us. As I tuned in to him, I sensed that he wanted to communicate with Ken. But for some reason, he was a little timid.

"There is a man who just came forward. He is saying 'father.' He has a short gray beard and is about average height, and it looks like he has a little curl or wave to his hair. He is holding several books. I believe he is trying to tell me that he likes reading and learning."

"That sounds like my father. He loved his books."

As I further tuned in to Ken's father's energy, the differences between the two of them became obvious. Ken, with his lively and open attitude, thrived on excitement and new adventures. Currently living in Alaska, he was planning his next move, which would likely take him to China. He was an avid rock climber and wanted to go to Yangshuo, China, and climb the Moon Hill and White Mountain crags.

His father felt to me to be more of a thinker. He was a quiet soul. I encouraged him to communicate with me. It seemed to work, as he suddenly began to flood me with images and thoughts.

"Your father is telling me that you would be proud of him. He says that he is exploring and learning new things, things that cannot be found in books. He is showing me an image of a fishing boat. You are in it, and he is there with you in spirit. He loves the feeling that he gets when he is with you on the open sea. The wind and sea spray and ruggedness of working on the boat seem to appeal to him. Your father tells me that you would be surprised by this. He wants you to know that he better understands you now. I get the impression from him that he was focused on his work. He was serious and tells me that he took the safe route. His work was important to him. He didn't explore and travel like you do."

Ken took a deep breath and sighed. "It sounds like he is with me on the crab boat that I am working on. My father was an attorney and a partner at a law firm. My grandfather, his father, was also an attorney."

Ken's father continued to open up. "Your father is telling me that he now understands the pressure that he placed on you as a child. He wanted you to be who he thought you should be. Does this make sense to you?" I asked Ken.

"Yes, it makes a lot of sense," Ken explained. "From an early age, there was tension between me and my father. I liked to play outdoors. I liked nothing better than to get dirty and trample through the marsh down the street. I was diagnosed with ADD and a learning disability in the third grade. I know my father was embarrassed. Our relationship got worse as I got older. I wanted to please him. I wanted him to be proud of me."

Ken's father in spirit was intently listening. "I hear your father saying that he was unhappy and didn't know why. Not with you but with himself. He didn't understand you, and he realizes now how much his negativity affected you. Your father laughs and tells me that he was full of himself."

"Really, he understands what I felt as a child?" Ken said and clearly looked perplexed.

"Your father wants to apologize. When you were young, were you a Boy Scout or did you go to camp in the summer? He is showing me a scene in the forest. It looks like a camp. There are a lot of kids, and I think that this is you he is showing me. You are sitting alone. I feel a lot of regret from your father."

"I loved camp. I think I know what he is talking about," Ken told me. "When I was young, I went to a Boy Scout camp. On our last day there, our fathers were supposed to join us and spend the night. My father never showed up. I felt very lonely. The next morning he showed up right before we were supposed to go home. He said that he had been in court. That was the end of it, he never apologized. I was expected to understand. My friends seemed to have good relationships with their fathers. They shared hobbies and interests, even if it was simply watching sporting events together. I wanted my father's attention, but I never felt that I got it."

"Did your father not show up for your college graduation, either? He seems to be apologizing for this or something about a graduation. He shows me you in a college cap and gown. Again, you seem to be sitting alone. I get the feeling of anger from him. Not sure why."

Ken looked sad and explained. "I had no desire to go to college, but I attended a community college. I thought that this might make him happy. It wasn't easy. But I got through and then went on to a four-year local college to earn a bachelor's degree. Of course, my father didn't seem to notice. I did not get great grades, and I certainly did not excel at anything. After college, my desire to explore and travel intensified. I knew that I did not have the grades to go to law school like my father and grandfather. I know that this disappointed him. My mother made him go to my graduation, but he was silent and looked bored. Afterward, when I went home, he went into his study and shut the door. He didn't come out and he ignored me. I was humiliated. It felt as if no matter what I did, I was not good enough."

"Your father is telling me that he was not angry at you. He was angry at his own life. I get the impression from him that he wanted to do other things but did not know how to change. It feels like there was pressure on him from his family. He shows me images of tools, like carpentry tools. He says that he wanted to be a builder or maybe a craftsperson."

"That's interesting," Ken stated. "He had a workshop in the yard. It was full of old woodworking tools, big saws, and interesting things. My mother once told me that it was his dream to build his own house in the country and live closer to the land. I never saw my father work in his shop. Everything was old and full of cobwebs. We lived in an upscale suburban neighborhood. It's hard for me to imagine him working with his hands."

"Your father never lived the life he wanted to," I told Ken. "He admires you for pursuing your dreams."

"I thought that he was a sad man," Ken told me. "When I went to Thailand to teach English and then traveled throughout Asia, we had little contact. I would come home for the holidays, but we had little to talk about. My father seemed to be uninterested in my adventures, and I could not relate to the hours he spent behind the desk."

Opening old wounds and talking about his father seemed to be having a healing effect on Ken.

He continued. "On one of my visits, I opened the door and had an overwhelming feeling of dread. The next morning at breakfast, my mother, in a matter-of-fact tone, told me that my father had recently been diagnosed with advanced-stage stomach cancer. There was little that could be done, and he was given just a few months to live. I was in shock and very sad. I couldn't believe that he was still working and that they had not told me. Almost as if everything was fine, my father came home that evening and continued with his normal routine. This, however, did not last long. Within a few weeks he was unable to walk without assistance. I decided to stay home and help care for him. I wanted so much to hear him tell me that he loved me. I sat near his bed with him for a few weeks, but he said nothing. He refused food and slipped into a quiet, dark place. I didn't know what to do. He died in his sleep in the hospital about a month later. I stayed and helped my mother as best I could. But she, too, seemed distant and depressed. I didn't know what to do. I needed to work, so I went to Alaska to be a crew hand on a fishing boat. I can barely believe that this is my father." Ken looked at me with wide eyes. "Why now? After all of this time, what happened? What made him change?"

I focused my attention on his father, curious to hear his reply. "He doesn't seem to know why," I told Ken. "Your father tells me that he doesn't know what happened. I didn't expect any of this, he says. I thought that I would die and that was it. But that is not what happened. I feel things that I never felt, everything is new to me. A kind man has been helping me. He told me that I could not stay stuck forever. He coaxed me into this place of warmth and light. I have been learning so much. I know now that you were sent to me. You were my opportunity to experience life in another way. I needed to be encouraged to be myself. I guess I didn't do too well. I resisted. I reasoned that I loved you because all parents love their children. I realize now that I did not love you, not the way I could have. You were different, and I rejected you. I am sorry. I was afraid to be different. So now this man has encouraged me to spend time with you. It is never too late, he tells me. I am enjoying it. Being with you is fun. Stay free, just the way you are."

Ken became silent and stared at the floor. He wanted to change the subject and started to ask me about his upcoming plans to go rock climbing in China. But after this intense encounter with his father, he seemed a bit dazed and a little spacy. Before we finished the session, I asked him if he had any other questions.

"Just one," I heard him say almost in a whisper. "I would like to think that my father has changed, but it almost seems to be too good to be true. Can he affect my life in a negative way? I know that seems not very loving of me, but he has always criticized me and I am worried that he might still do this."

"I think that is a valid question," I told him. "If you do not want your father's influence, all you have to do is send him the mental thought that you are not ready to have his spirit close to you at this time. Tell him that you will send him the invitation to return at another time. We have power over who is close to us. Although it seems hard to believe, once we transition into the spirit realm, we are immersed in love. Our wounds and pain heal, and we experience compassion and forgiveness. Keep in mind that your father is learning from you. You are providing him with an opportunity to experience and evolve and grow. Like his male angel helper told him, it is never too late."

"Okay," Ken told me. Pausing for a moment, I heard his hopeful laugh. "I guess we may finally do some of the things I always wanted to do with him."

Ethereal Play

Once we shed the physical body, we experience a kind of freedom that often eludes us in the material world. On the other side, there is a vast variety of activities, pursuits, and opportunities available to us. We can learn new skills, acquire knowledge, and develop and express creativity. It is always interesting to hear what kind of things those in spirit are involved in. I have had people on the other side tell me that they go to parties, take cruises, paint, climb mountains, play cards, fish, sew, help others who have recently passed over, and learn about every subject imaginable. I have also been told that it is necessary on the other side to develop psychic abilities and learn how to create with energy, vibration, and color. Some on the other side are simply relaxing and healing in the vibrant streams of harmony, love, and peace. As they do this, they are balancing their mental, emotional, and spiritual energies, which enables them to heal and help those they left behind in the physical realm. It is also common to continue pursuing the same hobbies and talents and interests from the earth life.

If we did not take advantage of our time in the physical realm to practice and learn new things, we can make up for this in the spirit realm. Our spirit guides and teachers motivate us to become involved in specific areas of interest and encourage us to teach and help others in those matters where we have expertise. We might need to further develop specific talents and deepen our knowledge of certain subjects to enhance and refine our creative potential. The soul is nourished by experiences and possibilities. In its natural state, the soul evolves, grows, develops, and advances. In this way, we perfect our individuality. It is only on the earth that we become static and resist change.

The following story involves two relatives with distinctly different personalities. This was a fun and unexpected interaction that still makes me smile.

The Beauty Shop Mirror

It is unusual for me to communicate with loved ones on the other side when I am not working. Years ago, I learned how to turn my abilities on and off. I had to. It is not easy to continually be available to those on the other side. It can be distracting and emotionally confusing. Like everyone, I value my time off and I need it. For this reason, the following encounter with someone from the other side was a surprise.

One afternoon I went to get my hair cut at the salon that I usually visit. However, when I showed up for my appointment, they did not have me on the schedule. My usual stylist was not working that day, and the only person available was Kareem. I did not know him, but I received a good vibe from him, so I went ahead and sat in his chair. Kareem was quite talkative. Sometimes I zone out during these appointments and take some time to relax. But Kareem had so much charisma, I just listened.

Kareem began by telling me of his early life. Locally born and raised, he grew up on a farm not too far from the salon. He told me of how much fun he had exploring the then-undeveloped woods and streams, which are now a community of homes and a shopping center. At about eighteen, he moved to Los Angeles to pursue his dream of being in the film industry. For several years he went from audition to audition and took acting lessons. During this time he made his living as a makeup artist at a film studio. With his lifelong interest in and flair for design, makeup, and hair styling, the job came easy to him.

"Hair was important in my family," Kareem told me. "You couldn't go out looking anything but the best. Didn't matter where you went—the grocery store, the post office—people would look and talk. I did my grandmother's, my mother's, my aunt's, and even the neighbor's hair. I was good. The women loved it, but the men, not so much. I was teased and called all kinds of names. I was a gay boy. It was very obvious. I knew it and everyone else did too."

Kareem took a breath and went on. "From a young age, I was one of those flamboyant types. I liked to wear bright colors, take dance lessons, and be me. My dad didn't like this at all. He was embarrassed. The whole family had a hard time with who I was. I knew I had to leave. I didn't have too much of a choice. I am who I am."

In Los Angeles, Kareem became a popular makeup artist. He eventually went to England with an actress that he worked for. Even though he had grown up cutting and styling his family's hair, it was there that he took his first classes in hair styling. He loved it and continued his studies in Italy. Eventually he switched over to doing hair full-time. Kareem told me a few funny stories from his travels and then asked me what I did. He had been so self-disclosing that I felt it only fair of me to return his honesty. I told him that I was a psychic and a medium. We talked for a few minutes about my work, and he realized that a friend of his had had a reading with me not too long before.

"That's right," he said. "My friend told me how you talked to his mother, who passed a few years ago. He never thought that she approved of him. I am glad that he went to you. He was a lot like me. We just did not fit in. Not in our families, not in school, not in church. I used to think that God had made some awful kind of mistake plopping me in the middle of rural North Carolina."

"Well, you might be surprised how people change once they go over." I managed to slip this in as he talked.

"It's not just angels playing the harp, is it?" he said. "Not like the preacher made us think. You know my granddaddy was a preacher, used to be at the tabernacle just up the road in north Durham. I wonder what he must be thinking now. He thought I was over the top then. Lord, he should see me now!"

As I was listening to Kareem and enjoying his friendly conversation, I looked into the large mirror in front of the chair where I was sitting. I wanted to see the progress on my hair, but instead I saw an older African American woman with a big smile staring back at me.

"I think that someone from your family is here," I told Kareem. "I just saw an older, thin woman with white hair tied up in a bun in the mirror. I heard the name 'Elena,' 'Elaine,' or something similar."

"Oh, that's my Aunt Ellen. She was my mother's sister." Kareem looked surprised.

Instead of shutting down this psychic intrusion, I gently allowed Kareem's aunt's presence to get stronger. The image that I saw of her in the mirror was so vivid, I was intrigued.

"She has a big smile. I get the impression from her that she was depressed before she passed over. She says that she is happy now," I told him.

Kareem stopped cutting my hair and stared into the mirror. "She was always so quiet. We all knew she was depressed. Never married and never went out much. I always wanted to know her better, but she was quiet. She is the last person I would expect to pay me a visit."

"She wants you to know that she is with you quite a bit. I am getting images of different places. I see you laughing, having fun. She is with you, enjoying traveling and having new experiences. Your laughter is helping her."

Kareem, staring at the mirror, said, "You mean she has been following me around in spirit? Why?"

"Your aunt is telling me that she is learning from you. She says that she is making up for lost time. I get the image of a bedroom. I see her sitting there in a rocking chair just staring out the window. Not doing anything. I feel that her self-expression was stifled," I told Kareem. "My impression is that within her there was a very sensitive, artistic soul that she did not know how to let out."

"That would be her bedroom," he told me. "She would just sit there in her rocking chair staring out the window."

Kareem's aunt began to send me different images. "I see her dancing and painting in the spirit realm. She is learning new things. She says you are an inspiration."

Kareem looked at me in a more serious way. "Being different in my family was not easy. We all were expected to go to the same church, marry, and settle down close to home. When I came out as gay, my father stopped talking to me. I had to leave home. It was only recently, many years after his passing, that I felt like I could come home. I understand my aunt's depression. I wish her the best."

I looked at the wall on the clock. I had been sitting in Kareem's chair for an hour and a half, and my hair was much shorter than I had wanted. As I got ready to leave, Kareem stopped me.

"One more thing before you go. Tell my aunt to fly high and keep dancing. I will be watching for her."

Individuality Can Never Be Taken Away

True freedom and individuality is a gift. Many people believe that freedom means having enough money to do what they please when they please. Some of us feel that having no responsibility to others, to a job, or to societal norms keeps us free. Even though the idea of personal freedom is appealing to many, those we consider to be "free spirits" are often ridiculed. People who are individuals and follow the dictates of their inner conscience can surprise and baffle their friends and family. They may not always be appreciated for their individuality and may even be teased and bullied for being different.

The fear of being criticized and humiliated for one's personal choices keeps many people imprisoned. We want to be liked and accepted by others. We quiet our inner voice in favor of others' expectations. Yet our striving to fit in, be popular, and better than others is a false victory.

You are not meant to follow the dictates of others. A unique and individual expression of the divine, you fulfill your purpose by shining bright in your beauty. You have come into this material world to listen within and be true to who you are. When you do this, you discover a source of power that never goes away. No matter what the world throws your way, when you know who you are and unlock the joy in your heart and soul, it can never be taken away.

When you are an individual, you become a light to others. Your influence spreads far and wide, and you shake others out of complacency and the status quo. You act as a catalyst and motivate others to take chances, discover their authentic self, and risk being different. Not only does your individuality give your friends, family, and co-workers the courage to express their individuality, it helps those on the other side as well.

6

HEART DISEASE: A CALL TO LOVE

〜〜〜〜〜〜〜〜〜〜〜〜〜〜〜〜〜〜

The most common cause of death for both men and women worldwide is cardiovascular (heart) disease, according to the American Heart Society's website. More women die of heart disease than of the next four causes of death combined, including all forms of cancer. On average, 2,200 Americans die of heart disease each day. The main factors said to contribute to this disease are tobacco and alcohol use, poor diet, lack of physical exercise, diabetes, obesity, and heredity.

On the other side, there is no illness. There are no aches and pains, heart disease, obesity, poor diet, or alcohol or tobacco use, either. But the heart exists. It is as important in the spirit realm as it is in the physical world. Similar in some ways to the heart's function in the physical body, the spiritual heart is the center of the energy body. It is through the heart that we are connected to the pure, vital energy of the divine source. In the spirit realm, love feeds and nurtures the energy body, just as food and water are essential to the physical body.

Love is the spirit realm. When you pass over to the other side, you, along with your guides and angels, review your earth school lessons. The most important component of this is how well you loved. How much forgiveness, kindness, and compassion are you able to express to others and to yourself? Do you act on the positive and the good? Do you listen to your heart and make decisions that support your most loving self? These are the kind of questions that are of importance to your soul, both here and in the beyond.

Once on the other side, we continue to grow and heal with those whom we were in relationship with in the earth life. Many of my clients want to know if their loved ones in spirit are with other family members on the other side. They are often pleasantly surprised when those in spirit tell them that they are working things through with a sibling or parent whom they had a challenging relationship with while in the physical realm. Sometimes it is not until we pass over that we forgive and heal our earthly relationships.

Learning the Relationship Lessons

It is through our relationships that our soul can make great progress on its evolutionary path. Our earth lessons, for the most part, are centered on some form or expression of love. Before we come into physical life, we choose the people we will be in relationship with. Based on our shared lessons with them, we also choose the type of relationship that best supports our mutual growth.

Before birth, you know who your mother, father, siblings, and future partners and children will be. When I first became aware of this concept, I was taken aback. I wondered why I would have chosen such difficulties. Did I want to punish myself? Had something gone terribly wrong? It took me a while to realize that struggling through the significant relationships of my early life had forced me to discover my inner strength and individuality. Had circumstances been different, I might not have developed the intuitive path that I now cherish. The purpose of suffering is to become aware. The soul is willing to create whatever experiences we most need for our awakening, even if the human self would just as soon run away from the experience.

In the physical realm, we do not always understand the important role that others play in helping us to come into our most loving and powerful self. A distant or unloving father or mother may compel you to become independent and discover the love within yourself. A selfish sibling may help you to stand up for yourself. An abusive mate may force you to look within at hidden but deep feelings of unworthiness and shame and find your power. We regress when we become victims and do not take care of ourselves. Emotions like anger, guilt, shame, and resentment are like poisons. They are a toxic and dense vibration that robs your physical body of vital life force energy. The negative emotions that you may be holding on to cause your physical body stress and distress and eventually lead to illness.

Your Emotional Purpose

You have come into this world with an emotional purpose. If you suffer from cardiovascular disease, you may not be on track with your earth school lesson of loving yourself and others. Discover your emotional lessons. Examine your relationship challenges. Is there childhood hurt or pain that still needs to be resolved? Do you love yourself and allow others to love you? Have you forgiven yourself and others for any intentional or unintentional pain, slights, or unloving behavior? All of your lessons of love must be learned, either here or on the other side.

Becoming aware of the lessons inherent in even your most difficult relationships empowers you to learn and move on to more positive experiences. Loving yourself is essential for good health, mind, body, and spirit. Heart disease has many physical causes and contributing factors, all of which are important. When we truly love ourselves, it is easier to commit to eating nourishing foods, exercising, and adopting healthy habits. We feel good and become motivated from within to take of ourselves.

Healthy (Other-Side) Diet

People do not usually come in for a session to connect with a loved one who caused them pain. I do not blame them. Yet those on the other side often take the opportunity during medium readings to resolve pain and express forgiveness. This is what happened in the following session.

Andrea was a single woman in her late thirties. She started her career working in an insurance company but had been taking classes to become a personal trainer. Unsure if she would be able to financially support herself if she left her current job, she came in for a reading.

"Good morning!" I heard Andrea enthusiastically address me as I opened my office door. She quickly stood and shook my hand, and we went into my office.

"I have never had a reading before," she said. "You helped a friend of mine and I thought I would give it a try."

"Many of my clients have never had readings," I assured her. "Have a seat and relax. I do most of the work."

"How does this work? Do you need to know why I am here?" Andrea asked me.

"I begin with a short prayer and then tell you whatever information I receive. Then at some point, if you have any questions, you can ask them."

"Okay, that sounds good," Andrea responded.

I began the reading with a beautiful image. "There is a guardian angel coming in. She is encouraging you to go forward. She shows me your path. It is filled with light, and there are people from spirit on both sides of it cheering you on."

I continued communicating with her angel for several more minutes. I was discussing some upcoming changes in her life when I suddenly felt someone on the other side trying to get my attention.

"There is a woman coming in from the other side. I have to speak to her. She keeps drawing my focus to her. Is your mother over? I keep hearing, 'Mother, mother . . . .'"

"Yes, my mother passed over a few years ago," Andrea told me.

I focused my attention on her mother, who now seemed a little more distant. I waited and listened. "Your mother is apologizing. I get the impression from her that she is not sure that you want to hear from her. Is this correct?" I asked Andrea.

"I would like to hear what she has to say," she answered.

As Andrea said this, I began to feel her mother's energy grow stronger. I was now able to see her.

"Your mother has her hands on her chest. Did she have a heart problem? Is this how she passed? I believe that she is talking about her physical health and her emotional health as well."

"She had coronary artery disease. Why is she apologizing?" Andrea asked me with a curious look on her face.

"Your mother says that she missed out on a good life with you. She shows me a young girl. I believe that this is you. I get the impression from her that she did not love you the way that she now knows she could have. She tells me that she did not value you. I feel a lot of regret coming from her."

I heard a soft cry. Andrea was drying her eyes with a tissue.

"This means so much to me. You have no idea," she said with a sigh. "I tried so much to help my mother. But my love never seemed to be enough for her. I am glad to hear this. I just wish it could have been sooner."

"Your mother wants you to know that you were never the problem. You were a blessing. It was her. She felt your love and care all through her life, but she rejected it. She tells me that she was angry. I feel that this goes back to her childhood. I see a large family and I hear her say 'sisters.' I get the impression that she did not feel loved and cared for as a child. She built up a lot of resentment," I told Andrea.

"All of this is true," she confirmed. "My mother had three sisters. She was jealous of her oldest sister, June. I always tried to understand what happened that kept them from being close as adults. I know my mother felt June was her father's favorite. I think she may have spent a lot of her life trying to get the love that she never thought she received as a child."

Andrea's mother in spirit continued her honest and humble disclosure. "I get the impression from your mother that she had hoped you would be a boy. Do you have an older sister? She wants you to know that she now understands how much her disappointment at having another girl affected you. She is truly sorry," I told Andrea.

"I was supposed to be 'Andrew.' When she was pregnant, my mother was sure I was a boy. I have an older sister, and my mother wanted just two kids, a boy and a girl. She never understood how difficult it was for me when she told people that I was supposed to be her son."

"Your mother is aware of the pain that this caused you. She knows that you did not deserve this. She tells me that you were smart and beautiful and full of love. You were a blessing, she says. Your mother is also thanking you. I get the impression that you tried to help her with her health. I can smell food cooking. Did you try to get her to improve her diet?" I asked Andrea.

"I tried and tried. Her diet was horrible. She was overweight and she just wanted to sit in front of the television and eat junk food. Even when the doctors told her how ill she was, she wouldn't change. But I tried. When I could not get her to eat better, I cooked food for her and brought it to her home. I would come back a few days later and it would be sitting there untouched. It was very discouraging," she explained.

"Your mother wants you to know that it wasn't the food," I told Andrea. "It was the lack of love that she felt for herself. Your mother tried to fill her emptiness with food. Now she feels and knows all the love that was always there for her. No one could give it to her. She only had to let herself feel it. Your mother says that she carried resentment and jealousy in her heart, all of her life. Someone else always seemed to be getting more and better than she was. I know this might not make sense, but I get the impression from your mother that she is exercising and eating well in spirit. You would be proud of her, she says."

"Hmm, that is good to know. I just got a funny image of my mother in a sweatsuit working out and eating protein bars. I would like to think that there are gyms on the other side," Andrea laughingly told me.

"People on the other side are engaged in all kinds of activities. I wouldn't be surprised if there are spirit-realm gyms," I told her.

More images continued to come through from Andrea's mother. "I see an image of a woman with a slender build and dark hair next to her. I get the impression that this is your mother's sister. I feel as if they are together on the other side—"

Andrea interrupted me. "That is a surprise. June passed over a couple of years before my mother. Are they getting along?"

"Your mother says that it is not always easy, but she is learning how to forgive and let go. I get the impression from her that in this life she was meant to learn how to be part of a family. She needed to learn how to balance her personal wants and needs with what would benefit the whole. She knows that she resisted the lesson. Her stubbornness got in the way. I feel that she is still with her family and she is now learning this lesson. Your mother tells me that you are helping her. She is watching you and learning from you. Have you been in therapy? I get an image of you in a small group of people. Maybe this is group therapy? I feel that you have been able to work through some of the pain from your childhood. Your mother seems to be proud of you."

I knew that this was a lot of information for Andrea to digest. I looked over at her, and she was nodding her head in affirmation.

"I have been in both individual and group therapy," she told me. "I found myself making bad choices and decisions. I felt as if I were sabotaging my success, and I didn't know why. I learned a lot in therapy about myself. I had a lot of inner pain locked up inside. It felt very good to let it go. Do you think that maybe this helped my mother?"

"I feel that your courage in healing has been an inspiration to her. You are doing the difficult work that she could not do when she was here. Your mother wants you to know that she is healing and learning alongside you," I told her.

I began to feel love coming from Andrea's mother. For the first time since connecting with her, I felt her heart open as she sent her daughter waves of warmth and love. "Your mother loves you very much. Can you feel it?" I asked her. "Take a moment and just breathe, close your eyes, and imagine your mother's spirit."

Andrea sat back and closed her eyes. I was silent for a few minutes. I saw her face begin to soften, and I knew that she could feel her mother's love.

"Can you forgive her?" I quietly asked her. "Just send this energy to your mother."

A few tears rolled down Andrea's cheek. She opened her eyes.

"Thank you. I know that I need to forgive her to move on. It's funny, but I can feel her love more now than I was able to when she was alive in the physical world."

The Heart of Work

The earth school lesson of the heart involves love in its many forms and expressions. Quite often the love that we are asked to give and share is expressed through our career and work choices. To be passionate about what we do is a gift and a blessing. But this earth lesson goes beyond simply working at the coveted job or career of our dreams.

We tend to believe that we cannot be happy or satisfied until we do what we want to do. Many of my clients feel that they are stuck in jobs and careers that give them no joy. In order to pay the bills, take care of their families, and keep their homes, they believe that they must sacrifice what they most cherish: their day-to-day happiness.

The earth school lesson of the heart informs us differently. We are called to give of ourselves in a truly loving and authentic way despite the circumstances and conditions that we find ourselves in. Although it feels at times that our moods, feelings, and quality of life are controlled by outside influences, we have come here to recognize our true power. If you spend your days feeling stifled and victimized, your heart lacks energy and vitality. Eventually you can become depleted and ill. This lesson is less about your ego desires and more about loving where you are and what you do.

Give of Yourself

What makes you happy and where you most succeed is in those things that engage your spirit. The essential question is: What am I here to give, and how can I be of service?

The most difficult aspect of this lesson may be to accept that you are right where you are meant to be, doing exactly at this time what you are meant to do. When you discover something that you love in what you do, your heart pumps vital energy thoughout your entire body. It invigorates and makes your mind, body, and spirit smile. You become empowered from within.

Give of yourself wholeheartedly, wherever you are and whatever is asked of you. In this way, you complete your purpose. The doors then open and you are led to the experience that best suits your current soul needs. Find something to love about what you do. No matter where you are, discover the service that you are meant to be giving and sharing. The sooner you accept your purpose, the sooner you will move on to something better.

The lesson of expressing your authentic heart and living your passion centers on your willingness to give and love. As much as we would like to think that what we do defines us, it is really what we give to what we do that is important.

Some of the most spiritual and loving people I know work in corporations, organizations, and businesses that seem to be some of the least spiritual and loving of environments. Yet they fully give of themselves, day after day. You may be divinely and unknowingly guided to a certain job or situation for the purpose of being a catalyst for consciousness transformation and positivity to others. An open-hearted, loving person in an environment that is rigid and lacking in positive vital energy has a league of angels working with them. They are doing the difficult work of this planet. Planting seeds of love, kindness, and spirituality in places that lack life-giving essential energy is a masterful act of love. As with all service work, it also advances your soul evolution by leaps and bounds.

Other-Side Employment

On the other side, we do not have to work to make money to pay our bills, buy food, and pay for housing. But we are involved in some form of heart-centered activity. Many busy souls have come in during sessions to share their excitement in being of service. They may be involved in a variety of both earthly and celestial undertakings. Some help ill children, those in the military, and confused and lonely souls to feel comfort and peace. There are many who are a part of teams of souls who band together to bring constructive solutions to the planet. In such diverse areas as the environment, politics, poverty, hunger, and economic abundance and equality, they silently guide and send positive energy where they can have an influence. I have also talked to souls on the other side who share their specific knowledge and interests with other souls, helping them to evolve and grow. Whatever those on the other side are involved in, they share and give because it feels so good to do so. Like our oxygen, love is everywhere in the spirit realm, and the heart is the center of our being. When we selflessly give, we thrive.

The Mechanics

The following story is a common one. Most of us know of someone who suddenly and without warning died from a heart attack. The family and friends of those who pass in this way are usually shocked. Looking back on the events that led up to their loved one's passing, they try to discover clues or warnings that they may have missed. Along with their grief and mourning, many also feel a sense of insecurity and fear about the randomness of life. Although many heart attacks appear to be unpredictable and sudden, they often occur after a lifelong or prolonged period of repression of the heart and spirit. Although there are many significant dietary and lifestyle choices that contribute to the heart's sudden failure, the ability to express and share love is often a core factor.

Unlike many of my clients, Brian contacted me for a reading when he was most interested in connecting to his spirit guides. He did not elaborate on why this was important or what he was hoping to learn, yet just knowing that this was his interest told me that his spiritual life was important to him. The morning of our session, Brian came into my office with a broad smile and warmly shook my hand. Many of my clients are nervous before we begin the session, but not Brian. He seemed comfortable and excited.

I began the session with a prayer and immediately felt the presence of his father. I knew that Brian most wanted to communicate with his spirit guides. But sometimes loved ones can be so intent on being heard, I cannot continue with the reading until I allow them to communicate.

"Your father is here," I told Brian. "He very much wants to talk to you. Would you like to hear what he has to say?"

"Yes. My father died when I was in college. This is a surprise. For some reason, I did not expect to hear from him. Yes, please, what does he have to say?"

"I get the impression from your father that a blast or jolting shock went through his body. Did he pass over as the result of a heart attack? He is clutching his heart."

"He died at his job, on a Monday morning," Brian confirmed.

"I hear the name 'Jim' or 'Tim.' Is this your father or someone in your father's family? It feels like another man might also be coming in," I said.

"He has a brother Jim who is on the other side. My dad's name is Curtis. They were not particularly close. I am surprised that Jim is here. I didn't know him very well."

"I have to tell you, there is someone else. I see three men. This feels like your grandfather. I get the feeling that you did not know him. He passed over before you were born. Is this correct?"

"You're right. I never knew my grandfather. He died when my father was young. We do not have longevity on my father's side of the family. All three of these men died of some type of cardiovascular disease. Why are they all here?" Brian asked me with a perplexed look on his face.

"I get the impression that they are all here to thank you. I feel a lot of love and gratitude coming from them to you." Words could not fully convey their feelings. I only hoped that Brian could feel this, too.

"Thank me for what?" Brian asked me.

With this question, I immediately began to receive images and impressions from Brian's father. "I take it your father and his father worked with their hands. I see a shop or garage? It seems busy. I get the feeling of dread with this, though. I am not sure that he liked his work," I told Brian.

"That is an understatement," Brian said. "My father, his father, and his father before him were mechanics. My father worked for a while in the family business, a garage. It goes way back. They worked on engines almost from the time that they were invented. My father hated it, though."

"I get the impression from your father that he was a jack of all trades. Did he sell cars, too? I see him in what looks like a car lot."

Brian quickly answered. "Yes, he sold cars for a while. Then he went on to selling insurance. His last job was as a manager at an auto parts store. He was always searching for the job that would make him happy. I don't think he ever found it, though."

"Your father is telling me that he wanted to be free. He felt that work was a burden. He is apologizing for his complaining and now understands that he could have been happy in any of these jobs," I shared with Brian.

Brian breathed deeply and told me, "That is quite a leap in growth for him. He always said that work was killing him. He felt burdened by the responsibility of a family. I never asked for much. None of us did. We all felt kind of guilty for making him so miserable."

"Your Uncle Jim is now coming in. I get the impression from him that he worked in the mechanic shop, too. He was a bit of a grump, it feels like. I imagine that he was not a friendly and outgoing uncle. Did he have a heart attack, too? He is also clutching his chest."

"Yes, he also died young," Brian shared. "I still do not understand why he is here. I barely ever spoke to him. Actually, I was afraid of him."

"It occurs to me," I told Brian, "that there are marked differences between you and most of the other members of your family. They do not seem as if they were the happiest bunch when they were here in the physical world. I get the impression that you are self-aware and did not follow the family work tradition. Do you help others? Are you in the medical field? I keep seeing you working with people on improving their health."

"I am a chiropractor," Brian shared with me. "This is a second career. I started off in computer programing. I enjoy figuring things out, seeing patterns, and finding solutions. I switched from working with things to working with people."

"A spirit guide of yours has just come in," I told Brian. "He calls himself 'Dr. Lin.' I feel that he is guiding you as you work with your patients. He is showing me an image of you at work. He is standing behind you, directing and helping you in your work. He says that you are a quick learner. I get the impression from him that he was attracted to working with you because of your devotion and your intuitive aptitude."

"This is one reason I wanted a reading. I get a feeling when I am in the clinic that there is someone with me. As I am working on people, I begin to see images and I am guided to certain parts of their body. Important connections within the mind, body, and spirit that I never knew existed and that I didn't learn in school are intuitively coming to me. I am really excited by what is happening. Is there anything else that Dr. Lin wants to share with me?" Brian asked.

"He tells me to tell you not to forget the important service that you are providing for your family. He is not talking about your family here in the physical world. It is your family on the other side that he is referring to. I get the impression that this is why they are here today, your father, uncle, and grandfather. You were born into the family for a purpose. You have been healing the family patterns. I get the impression from Dr. Lin that there is a long-term history of heart disease in some form in the family. You are helping to heal not just the physical but also the mental, emotional, and spiritual health as well. He is assisting you," I told Brian.

"I think I understand. I have always felt that I wanted to help my father. He clung to his beliefs and couldn't move forward. He was always so unhappy and searching for the next best thing, never content in what was. But how am I helping them now?" Brian understandably asked me.

"Dr. Lin says that your father, uncle, and grandfather are close to you. Their guides and angels have sent them to you to learn. Through you, they are discovering how to grow and heal. I get the impression that they felt that life owed them happiness. They smoked and drank and hung out at bars, looking for a good time. Yet they were miserable. Your joy comes from giving to others and helping where you can. I get the impression that this was not something that they would have considered. Working was just a way to make money. This was their contribution to their families. They paid the bills. But in most ways, they were absent. I feel that they are learning how to open their hearts and give," I shared with Brian.

"Right before my father's death, I remember feeling that he would not be here very long," Brian continued. "Even though he was not sickly, he did not live a healthy life. He was overweight, his diet was horrible, and he liked his beer. I tried to talk to him about it, but he laughed at me. I think he thought that I was not a 'real man,' whatever that meant. He would often tease me because I exercised and ate a vegetarian diet.... Wow, the tables have turned. Now he is learning from me. I never thought that this would happen."

As Brian was talking, I felt his father's presence begin to communicate with me again. "Your father wants you to know that he respects you and he likes the person that you are. He is showing me a Buddha statue and what looks like a meditation pillow. I get the impression that you meditate. This may sound hard to believe, but your father says that he is meditating with you. His heart is opening. I feel so much love coming from him to you."

Brian laughed and told me, "You're right. The image of my tough, beer-drinking father meditating is almost too hard to believe. Please, tell him that I love him."

"Your father thanks you," I shared with Brian. "He says that he lived his life as your father with a closed heart. No wonder he had a heart attack. His spirit couldn't take it anymore. He had to learn how to feel and express love. He couldn't do it here. But he wants you to know that he can now."

7

SUICIDE IS NOT THE END: TRANSFORMING PAIN AND GRIEF

~~~~~~~~~~~~~~~~~~~~~

One of the most common reasons that people come to me for readings is to communicate with loved ones who have committed suicide. For people who have lost loved ones in this way, the journey to healing can be long and difficult. The decision to end one's life very rarely, if ever, makes rational sense to those who are left behind. They almost always feel guilty and believe that they could have done something to prevent this tragedy. Life is never the same after a loved one's suicide. Those left behind in the physical realm can experience confusion, anguish, unrelenting grief, and senseless loss. It can take a long time to fully heal and accept the heart-rending passing.

I have communicated with hundreds of spirit people on the other side who took their own lives. Their earthly family and friends come to me in part in the hope that I can shed some light on their decision to end their life. My clients sit in rapt attention in my office wanting to hear from their loved one and know that they are finally at peace. Even though they desire to understand and know why their loved one left the earth in this way, once revealed, the reasons never seem justified. The problems, stresses, depression, and suffering that led to their loved one's decision to leave the earth in this way never make sense.

Transformation

The impulse to end one's life is a confused response to the cry of a soul in crisis. From the depths of one's being, the soul sends a wake-up call to the conscious self. Serious and profound change is needed. The soul is demanding a radical departure from the old and a new vision for the future. This is not a message to end one's physical life. Instead, the deeper soul message is actually a call for transformation.

When an individual feels overwhelmed, depressed, and despondent and believes that they cannot or do not know how to deal with their present life circumstances, the soul and the personality are disconnected from one another. The soul constantly sends us direction and messages to keep us on track with our life plan. When an individual gets to the point of severe desperation and contemplates suicide, they have not been listening from within for a long time. They have missed the earlier cues and signs from their soul trying to alter their path.

Many of those in the spirit realm that I have communicated with tell me that, from their renewed, heavenly perspective, they can now see the people and help that could have changed their lives. At the time, they dismissed these opportunities and continued to willfully and even stubbornly remain on their path.

I recently worked with a woman whose son committed suicide. His first message to his mother in our session was that there was nothing anyone could have done to alter his decision. He knew that his life needed to change, but he felt that he lacked the strength and ability to know what to do and how to begin. Although there were people who could have helped him, he resisted their efforts. Now, from the spirit realm, he had gratitude for the people and positive opportunities that had been available to him. He now understood that love was always present.

On schoolhouse earth, we confront the lesson of suicide to learn how to accept a new vision of life and to engage in the process of change. It seems simple, but we humans resist and fear change of any kind. Letting go of who we believe ourselves to be and making choices and decisions to care and love ourselves can feel like an overwhelming challenge. Yet even though physical life can be demanding, painful, and difficult, it holds the raw energy of potential and all possibilities. Accepting the need for radical change in your life and putting energy into manifesting this new self is as significant and powerful as physical death.

Suicide on the Other Side

When an individual ends their physical life, they soon discover they have made a critical mistake. The soul goes into retrograde. Instead of advancing on their soul path, they must backtrack and revisit and reexperience the conditions that led to their decision.

Years ago I realized that communicating with those in spirit who left through suicide was a bit different than connecting with people who left through illness or accidents. Because the life plan for people who commit suicide has not been completed, their transition differs from others who pass from natural causes. Once in the heavenly light of the other side, they are not among the "general population." It is a bit like someone who quits school before graduating. They may no longer go to school every day, but to advance they still need to learn and complete some form of education or training. When we complete our life plan here on earth, even if we feel as if we have made "bad" decisions or made a general mess of our lives, we still graduate and celebrate on the other side. We are given an expansive freedom that allows us to create and experience the bliss and comfort that may have eluded us in the physical world.

Once on the other side, a soul that has committed suicide does not experience this kind of freedom. Instead, they enter special angelic centers where they are cared for and loved, and they participate in their healing. They become aware of what led to their decision to end their life and come to understand other actions they may have taken. Their life plan is reviewed, and they become aware of the opportunities and possibilities for change that they refused. Empathy is developed, and they feel the anguish and pain of those who were affected by their passing. Unlike the physical realm, where we can play video games, overeat and drink, watch television, and generally deny our soul needs, this is a focused environment. There is no denial and no place to hide. At the same time, it is an atmosphere of overwhelming love. Kindness and compassion are the air that we breathe. It is everywhere.

People who commit suicide need your help. Maybe more than with any other type of passing, you are essential to their healing. If you have a loved one who has passed in this way, they are most likely close and learning from you. The following session is an example of the healing effects that our actions on earth can have on a soul who left through suicide.

Accepting Self

Austin was sent to me by a psychotherapist who often refers people to me. Some people in therapy who have unresolved feelings after the loss of a loved one often benefit from a medium session. Right on time, but looking a little nervous, Austin came into my office and set up his iPhone to record the session. I said my prayer to begin the session and gave him some messages from his angel. Austin's mother and an aunt then came in. They talked about his family, shared a few funny memories, and provided some interesting information about upcoming changes in his career. Austin's mother had unexpectedly died of a brain aneurysm a few years prior. His emotional response after hearing from her was touching. Knowing that she was at peace in the spirit realm and close to her sister seemed to relax him. As my time with him came to a close, I had an uneasy feeling that there was someone present in spirit whom I could not connect with clearly.

"Is there someone else you want me to communicate with?" I asked him. "I can feel someone here, but they seem a little distant."

"Yes, there is," he said. I scanned the energy vibration where I connect with loved ones. I still felt someone's presence, but it felt fuzzy and I was unable to clearly connect. I began to suspect that this might be someone who had committed suicide. Quite often they are not in the same energy vibration as other loved ones.

I turned to Austin and explained to him, "When someone passes over through suicide, I have to tune in to a bit of a different vibration. Unless they are far along in their healing, they are not among the 'general population.'"

As I was talking to Austin, I realized that, as I suspected, the soul who was present had passed over from suicide. This awareness was enough to draw the spirit closer to me.

"Okay," I told him, "I am connecting with him now. This is a male who died young. I am not getting a family connection. Is this a friend of yours?"

"Yes," he quietly said.

"I have to tell you he seems a little reluctant to speak. He is showing me an image of buildings, quite a few of them. It looks like a school campus. I feel as if you were friends in college."

"We were roommates all four years, the best of friends." Austin confirmed the images.

"I see an image of you both. It looks like you two had fun. I see you doing the normal kinds of things that friends do, playing Frisbee and going to parties."

Despite the positive memories, Austin had a serious look on his face. "Some of my best memories are with Matt. I could not have asked for a better friend."

Even though I am aware of the drinking and drug use that goes on at college, I did not feel as if Matt had a problem in this area. I was curious, though, to know what had happened. Usually when I connect to people who passed over as a result of suicide, I feel much stronger feelings of depression and angst. I did not initially feel this with Matt. I was drawn back to him. He may have been picking up on my thoughts, as the energy began to feel more somber.

"Matt is showing me the image of a blond-haired woman. She is attractive and slim. I feel this was someone close to him, maybe a girlfriend. I feel a lot of confusion and sorrow—"

"Yes," Austin interrupted me. "This was his fiancée. They were planning on getting married a few weeks before he passed. Why did he die? No one knows what happened. Would you please ask him?"

I turned to Matt, and the images grew stronger and more intense. "I see a small terrace. Did Matt hang himself? I feel overwhelming stress and anxiety here."

"Yes, and I found him, early one morning. We had been talking about his upcoming wedding. I was his best man. We were making plans for his bachelor party. He never said anything. Why didn't he talk to me? I didn't even know he was depressed. This has plagued me for years. What could I have done differently?" Austin pleaded with me.

Despite the reluctance on Matt's part in the beginning of the session, his response was clear and strong.

"Matt was gay," I told Austin. "He didn't want anyone to know. He was ashamed."

Brian sat in silence. I knew that he was struggling with this information. He looked at me and asked, "Why didn't he just tell me?"

"He felt like he could not tell anyone. I feel as if he was involved with a few different men, but he still considered himself to be a straight man. There was, however, someone else. I get the impression that he developed feelings of love for a man. This scared him and he became very anxious." I tried my best to relay Matt's thoughts and feelings to Austin, who was clearly bewildered.

"Who?" Austin asked me. "Was it Will? They were hanging out quite a bit. I heard that after college he came out as gay."

Matt further tried to explain what he had been experiencing to Austin. "I get the impression from Matt that he grew up in a religious household. I feel as if he had a loving family. But he was afraid that they would not understand him. He knew they would reject him if he was gay. I feel like being gay would have been considered a sin in his family. Was his father involved in the church? Maybe even a minister? I keep getting an image of what feels like his father with a clerical collar around his neck."

"Yes, his father was a Baptist minister and a businessman. A no-nonsense kind of man, he wanted Matt to become a minister also," Austin explained. "I guess it would have been hard for him. He met his soon-to-be wife in the church. They had known each other since high school. They were both involved on campus with student ministries. I wish I would have known. Maybe I could have helped him. But to be honest, I know that back then I may not have been too supportive. I didn't know any gay people. On our campus it wouldn't have been accepted. This was over twenty-five years ago. How is he? Please tell him I miss him."

"I feel a strong angelic presence close to Matt," I shared with Austin. "He is being loved and helped. Matt tells me that it took a long time for him to accept the healing and love that was being offered to him. He went to a dark place after his death. Sure that he had sinned by loving a man and committing suicide, he imagined that he would go to hell. When there was no hell, Matt tells me that he created his own. Now it is better. The angels wouldn't stop trying, he says. He is feeling so much peace now .... Do you have a son?" I asked Austin. "Matt is showing me a young man who looks somewhat like you."

"I have two sons," Brian told me. "But I think he might be talking about Jeff."

"Yes, Matt feels a strong connection to him," I shared with Austin. "It's funny. I get so much love coming from Matt to you. It has something to do with your son. I get the feeling from Matt that you have helped Jeff in some way. Matt has been watching and close to you both. He tells me that he is being helped through your parenting your son. This may sound odd. I don't know. Does it make any sense to you?"

Brian nodded his head in agreement. "My son struggled, like Matt. I didn't know how much angst he was going through. His older brother is a real jock, good at sports. He was on the football and baseball teams in high school. Jeff was never very athletic. He started to fail in school and had problems with friendships. We had him go to counseling. One day his mother and I went into his session with him. Jeff told us he was gay. I will be honest. It wasn't easy at first. But I love my son. I did everything I could do to support him, even if that meant having some uncomfortable family reunions. Not everyone has been so accepting."

"I feel like in the process of helping your son, you also helped Matt. He thanks you for being a good father. The love you feel for your son helped him to know what acceptance feels like. Leaving like he did was a mistake. He knows this now." I looked over at Austin and he was slightly misty-eyed. "Matt tells me that Jeff is a funny guy. I get the impression from Matt that he is watching over him, helping him out when he can. Before we end, Matt wants me to tell you again, thank you and he loves you."

Shared Transformation

Suicide is a joint earth school lesson. When someone you love chooses to end their life, your life changes significantly as well. I have worked with people who have suffered almost unimaginable and devastating losses. The grief can be overwhelming. People are left feeling lost, confused, and often unable to continue to carry on in their day-to-day routines.

Clients often ask me, "What now? I do not know who I am or where to go from here."

When a loved one commits suicide, your life will never be the same. Grief and suffering are messengers of awakening.

The mourning period after a death can be long and arduous. When it is a death from suicide, it can take even longer. During this process, questions, self-examination, and obsessive thoughts can torment those left behind. All too often, loved ones cling to the past and to their regrets, going over and over in their mind what they could have done differently. They examine their last conversations with their loved ones looking for clues that might have saved their life. All too often, self-blame and guilt take over.

Yet, after the death of a loved one through suicide, the earth school lesson that you are being asked to learn is not one of shame and pain. Instead, it is a call into your highest purpose. When a loved one passes over, a part of you goes with them. Your life and all that you have thought to be true and real are forever altered. Just as your loved one who committed suicide is now immersed in the love of spirit, so too must you live in your most spiritual energy.

What does this mean? It is necessary for you to ask yourself why you are here. What is your purpose? What can you give? The natural inclination after the suicide of a loved one is to shut down and retreat inwardly or to immerse yourself in worldly distractions. This is the understandable human response. Yet in the higher cosmic plan, you are being called to transform and become a presence of love and peace to others.

The people whom I have seen survive and thrive after devastating losses are those who commit their lives to a greater purpose. You do not need to know what it is or how it will unfold. Just be willing to be open and to be a channel of love in the world. This does not mean that you have to quit your job, leave a relationship, move, or give up the good in your life. A way will be made.

I have a client who, after her son's suicide, was led to be a mentor in the Big Brothers Big Sisters program. Anna told me that she was sitting at her kitchen table one night thinking of her son, as she did night after night. Her mind went through the events leading to his suicide. *Was there anything more that I could have done to help him?* she wondered. But on this night, she heard a voice answer her.

"There are many that you can now help." Anna inwardly heard a voice that sounded like her son's speak to her.

Startled and surprised, she realized that there were other teenagers and other parents who might be going through what she was going through. Maybe she could not help her son, but she could help others like him.

She eventually started a local suicide prevention organization. She, along with others who had lost loved ones to suicide, began to speak in high schools, sharing their grief. The response from the students was heartwarming. Many came forward after her talks and told her how they, too, were struggling with depression and suicidal feelings. With a grant, she was able to start a crisis counseling center, which she dedicated to her son.

Anna also transformed her life in other ways. After her initial struggle with guilt and low self-esteem, she felt a gentle peace begin to unfold in her heart. Sitting on her back deck for hours watching the birds and squirrels, her sensitivity to the beauty in all of life increased. An unexpected acceptance of her son's journey in life gradually surfaced. Anna felt his presence close by and felt confident in their ability to communicate with each another. In her heart she knew that her healing and the work that she was doing to help others were having a positive effect on her son. She felt him working through her, directing her to the places and people whom she could most be of service to. In this way, her connection with her son transformed. Even though she still missed him, Anna felt that her efforts gave his life purpose.

A Past-Life Suicide

Many people believe that we live more than one life. The soul on a journey to the ultimate connection with the source of all love and life evolves and learns through many lifetimes. If this is not your belief system, you might consider the following story as a metaphor of healing and redemption.

The account of this session differs from the other stories in this book. From time to time I work with someone who can benefit from past-life hypnotherapy. Medium readings provide information, messages, and connections that are vital and important for healing and enlightenment. Participating in our healing in a more experiential and direct way through hypnotherapy can also be a powerful catalyst for growth and self-awareness. To understand our often confusing present-day challenges, past-life therapy can provide the missing piece in the puzzle.

I had had a few medium readings with Debra before we decided to have a past-life therapy session.

"My intuition," she shared with me, "is telling me that the past may hold the key to understanding my current struggles."

On the day of our appointment, she came in and seemed both excited and a bit uneasy. Despite her initial uneasiness, Debra began to easily describe what she was seeing and experiencing after the relaxation induction.

"Can you look around and tell me anything that you sense or see?" I encouraged her.

"I am alone. I feel that this is my home. It is sparse and simple," Debra continued.

I saw a few tears in Debra's eyes. She seemed to be struggling. "What is happening?" I asked.

A minute or so later, she strained to answer. "I don't know. I am very sad. Something happened. I just want to cry."

"Go back to the incident that made you sad," I directed her.

"I have a young son. It is just the two of us. I wash clothes for other people to make money."

"Are you married?" I asked her. "Do you have other family?"

Debra paused before answering. "I am not sure ... no. I think I had a husband, but he died. I don't know how I am going to support my son. I am worried. It doesn't feel like there is anyone helping me."

"Move the scene forward and tell me what happens. What do you do?" I asked Debra.

"There is another man. It feels like I marry him. Not because I love him. I don't have feelings for him. He promises to take care of me and my son," she explained.

"What happens next?"

Debra gasped, almost choked with emotion, and began to cry.

"What is happening?" I tried to direct her to put into words the intensity of her feelings.

"I don't know. Something happened to my son. I call his name and search for him in the house and outdoors. He is not here. I cannot find him. I look and look. My neighbors are also looking. He has been found. No, no … no … this cannot be."

"Take a deep breath," I advised Debra. "Breathe and let the feelings recede. Detach from them and tell me what happened."

"Someone found him. He is at the bottom of our well. He is not moving. I think he is dead."

"Breathe and relax," I told Debra. We took a few minutes to breathe, and she slowly seemed calmer.

"People seem mad. They are accusing my new husband. I am confused." She struggled to explain. "I think my husband killed him. Yes, he is confessing to throwing him down the well."

"Move the scene forward. What happens next?" I asked Debra. Despite the emotional intensity, I knew that we needed to continue. I encouraged her to detach from these difficult and painful feelings and to release them.

Debra took a deep breath and answered. "Now I am alone. I don't know why my husband did this. He is gone. I feel very guilty. I let a man into my house who killed my only child. I didn't even love him. It's my fault. I let him into our lives to make it easier. I didn't really know him …. Now I am at a cemetery. I see a headstone. This is where my son is. I visit him every day."

"Go to the end of your life," I told Debra. "How do you die?"

She quickly answered. "I see myself walking to the cemetery. I sit down close to my son's headstone. I have a bag with a container of some kind in it. This is a poison that I have put together, with berries, herbs, and other things. I drink it and lay down. Oh, I am in horrible pain. But I don't care. I deserve it." Debra began to moan.

"Are you leaving the physical body?" I asked her.

"Yes."

"Look down as you pass out of the body," I instructed her. "What do you see?"

Debra seemed much calmer now. "I see my limp body lying in the snow and mud. It's a cold winter day."

"Now what do you do?" I asked her.

"I am still alive. I see my body, but it feels very dark. I don't know where to go or what to do. I call out for my son. I want to find him," she told me. "I am lost and wandering, searching for him."

"There is an angel coming close to help you," I directed her. "Go with the angel. Feel her love and follow her. What is happening? Can you see her?" I asked Debra.

"I am going higher and higher. There is someone close to me," she told me.

"Who is it?"

"I think it's an angel. There is so much love. I just want to rest." Debra then became quiet.

A few minutes later, I continued.

"How does the life that you just experienced impact your current life? Maybe the angel will help you to understand this. Why don't you ask her?"

"I feel so much love. I don't feel as if I deserve it. I am getting the message from the angel that my constant feelings of depression and unworthiness are connected to this life. The angel is telling me that my daughter came to help me. She is like a helper spirit who agreed to incarnate with me."

Debra, I knew from past sessions, was a single parent with one daughter.

"Is there anything else that your angel wants you to know?" I asked her.

"She tells me that I am learning to make good choices in this life and to confront my feelings of unworthiness," said Debra.

I told Debra to take a few moments to allow the love of this angel to move through her body and to release the pain and stress of this past life. I asked her to fill the places in her body where there had been pain with love. She rested for several minutes, then a look of peace came over her face.

She continued. "I feel an incredible sense of love and peace. I have always felt guilty and did not know why. I feel more peace right now than I ever have."

I started to guide Debra back to normal consciousness when she abruptly began to talk.

"I think my grandmother is here. I see her in my mind's eye. It is my mother's mother. I didn't know her well. She died when I was a child. But I have seen many pictures of her. This looks like her, and I somehow know that it is."

"Can you communicate with her?" I asked.

"I don't know."

"Ask her if she has a message for you." I waited a minute or two, and then Debra began to speak.

"I sent her a thought message, asking her why she is here. I heard her say 'thank you.' Then I felt a lot of love from her to me. But I do not know why she is thanking me," Debra said.

"Send her another message and ask her," I encouraged Debra.

She quickly answered. "I got a lot of information all of a sudden. I don't know how I know these things, but it feels like she was depressed. No one ever discussed her death. She died at home. All I was told is that she died in her sleep. Wow, what a surprise. I somehow know that she took an overdose of sleeping pills. Could this be true? Do you think I am making this up?" Debra asked me.

"I doubt it," I told her. "Just listen, and you can figure that out later. What else are you hearing, or do you know?"

"My grandmother is thanking me for getting help for my depression. She knows how much I struggled in college. I even contemplated suicide. I finally went to a doctor and a therapist. They helped a lot," Debra continued.

"Is there anything else she wants to say?" I asked her.

"My grandmother is saying that it is all going to work out. The hardest part is over. I feel her love. I am so surprised this is happening," Debra told me.

"Send your grandmother love and forgiveness. I am sure she needs it."

"I will. I never heard anything but good about her. I knew that she had been depressed, but no one ever told me that she committed suicide," Debra told me and then became quiet.

I began to bring her back into normal consciousness, and she opened her eyes. We sat quietly for several minutes.

Unfortunately, it is not unusual for suicides to reoccur within families. I have worked with sons, fathers, grandfathers, mothers, daughters, and grandmothers who have endured the death of more than one family member through suicide. All too often, I have seen this tragic pattern repeat itself generation after generation.

Debra's life course could have taken a very different turn. She was depressed and had contemplated suicide more than once. Even though she did not know that her grandmother had died in this way, the genetic and past-life seed of this pattern was within her. Her ability to take positive action and seek help and healing not only saved her life, but positively affects both past and future generations of her family.

Passage to the Heavens

When a person's soul leaves the body immediately after a suicide, they usually quickly realize their mistake. Because their life plan script is not complete, they are still magnetized and pulled into the earth's force field. At the same time, the energy of their soul is ascending and being drawn into the light of divine energy. If a person passes under the influence of drugs or alcohol, there can be even more confusion.

Some of the dead that I have communicated with who passed over through suicide have told me how they have followed their physical body around searching for a way back in. After their physical death, they immediately recognize that they are still very much alive and conscious, but they do not know where to go and what to do. Still aware of those in the physical realm, they may attach to a loving and kind individual who calms their restless spirit. Searching for a connection, they might also drift in between the physical and heavenly realms.

Prayers and rituals designed to help the soul into the light of the heavens are particularly important in suicide deaths. Invoking divine help and intercession for a recently passed-over soul is like throwing a life vest to someone who is lost in open water. There are angels who patrol the astral realms searching for lost souls who are ready to accept their help. Archangel Michael in particular, when invoked, immediately guides lost and wandering souls into the light.

In the last chapter of this book, I include a meditation and exercise to help you to assist lost and wandering souls into the healing and love of the heavens.

8

ACTIVATE YOUR SIXTH SENSE:
HERE AND ON THE OTHER SIDE

Physical reality is a fickle place. We believe all kinds of things. Some of us believe that there is a God who lives in heaven, and if we do what he tells us to do then we get to go there, too. Some prefer to conceptualize a creator of all of life who is formless and impersonal. Others believe in a loving higher power, a divine presence, or a universal energy of love.

Along with our varying ideas of God, we also have differing opinions about life after death. This is debated by religious and nonreligious people alike. Some believe that death is the end and no part of us lives on. Others feel that not only do we continue to live after death, we also continue to experience happiness, learn, and evolve. Not only do we question if life continues after death, we also wonder what that life might be like on the other side. What do we look like? What do we do? Is it anything like life here on earth?

Some people, like me, believe that it is possible to communicate with those on the other side. Others feel that those who claim to connect and communicate with the dead are frauds or mentally deluded. In this same way, we have conflicting opinions and beliefs about intuitive and psychic ability, and the existence of angels, spiritual beings, ascended masters, and ghosts. For some, nothing outside of the five senses exists, while for others, physical reality is just part of a larger cosmic reality. To varying degrees, we agree and disagree on almost all aspects of the spiritual realm.

Evolution of Beliefs

During my many years as a medium, I have given more than a few readings to those who do not believe in psychic ability or the ability to communicate with the other side. They come to me usually as a last resort for a problem that they cannot find answers to or because they terribly miss a loved one who has died. Their pain, fear, and confusion motivate them to seek help through psychic sources. They may have never believed in anything supernatural, cosmic, or spiritual, but they suspend their doubts in the hope that what I have to say will benefit them. Psychic guidance and information can turn a doubter into a believer. Yet the earth school lesson that challenges us to explore the possibility of life beyond the physical realm and psychic phenomena is more about inner transformation than about simply changing a belief system.

In somewhat of a cosmic paradox, the physical realm has a bit to teach us about spiritual reality. The earth lesson of exploring life beyond the physical is not about debating who is right and who is wrong and what to believe and not to believe. Instead, it is one of awareness. When our soul recognizes an inner truth, a new world opens up. Change, evolution, and freedom come when we open our mind and heart and consider all possibilities.

Communication with those on the other side challenges the material-minded status quo. It opens us to a world that we cannot fully define and control. Some become fearful and feel threatened by this notion, while others become curious and excited. Many feel reassured and find peace in the awareness that there is more to life than what our five senses can tell us. Whatever the reaction, once we have a direct experience of contact with a loved one on the other side, the door to the spiritual realm is open. Even if we doubt the authenticity of otherworldly encounters, the heart leaps in recognition and recognizes truth.

A dream of being in the presence of a loved one, the familiar scent of a deceased family member's perfume, a glimpse of a visitor from the spirit realm, or an otherworldly message gets our attention. A tingle of energy moves through us, and we wonder, *What if?* This is the onset of the conscious evolution from a purely physical-based perspective to that of a spiritual explorer.

A Psychic Convert from the Other Side

There are some who from a young age have had a natural understanding and acceptance of psychic ability and other worldly encounters. They may have been ridiculed and teased for their beliefs and practices. Those who are intuitively attuned to the spirit realm are too often labeled as odd and strange from an early age. In the following session, the conservative father of a client of mine who had had a lifelong interest and talent in psychic phenomena came through with some surprising revelations.

"Things are really happening." Catching her breath, Elise took a seat on my couch and continued. "I am so excited to have a session today. I have been meditating every day and working with crystals, and wonderful things are happening. Yesterday during my meditation, I felt like the amethyst crystal pendant that I was wearing started to vibrate. I couldn't be sure. I took it off, and sure enough it seemed to move. I am not kidding. It was to the right of my candle, then I closed my eyes for a few minutes, and when I opened them it had moved to right in front of me. I don't think I'm crazy. Can this really happen?"

I told Elise that this was certainly possible. I suggested that we go ahead and start the session and see what comes in. As I told Elise how the reading would work, I felt the strong presence of a man in spirit trying to get my attention.

"There is a man coming through who feels like your father," I abruptly began. "He has white hair, is about average height, and looks like he was fit. I feel like he died suddenly. He touches his heart, and I get the impression from him that a heart problem ended his life."

"That is my father," Elise quickly answered. "He died several years ago of a massive heart attack. He had always been healthy, so it was a shock for all of us."

I continued listening to her father. "He is laughing and tells me that you are probably surprised that he is coming through. He didn't think that it would be like this. He says, you were right, I am still alive."

Elise started to laugh. "I would love to have seen his surprised look when he realized that there is life after death. He was so sure that there was nothing beyond the physical life. He thought my beliefs were really silly. I used to be teased and made fun of by him. I have always believed in angels and spirit guides, fairies and ghosts. My father could not have disagreed more with me. Nothing outside of the five senses existed for him."

"Your father is showing me an image of you reading a book. He is looking over your shoulder and wants you to know that he is learning alongside you. I get the impression that he is interested in the books on magic and psychic awareness that you are reading. He says that he is learning and studying such things on the other side."

It is always interesting and surprising what those on the other side are experiencing and doing. Maybe it was in part because of Elise's interest in the metaphysical that her father was involved in learning and participating in similar pursuits on the other side.

I continued trying to adequately explain what I was receiving from her father. He was enthusiastic and kept sending me colorful images. "Your father is showing me an image of himself in what appears to be some kind of school. I get the impression that he is learning how to project his thoughts and influence energy. He feels as if he is getting pretty good at it. Have you had missing objects or things falling off of shelves? I get the impression from him that he is learning how to affect physical matter."

"Do you think that it was my father who moved the crystal during my meditation?" Elise excitedly asked me.

"Your father is laughing. He has been trying to do this for a long time, he tells me. He says he is getting pretty good at it. I am not sure what this means, but I hear him tell you that he could not do this without your help."

"What does he mean? How am I helping him?" Elise wanted to know.

"That is a good question," I told Elise. "I am curious about this too. Let me ask him."

Elise's father seemed anxious to answer. "Your father is telling me that he is studying some new things. He is showing me an image of a group of people who seem to be learning more about energy, color, and motion. They seem to be practicing how to alter and affect energy through thought and intent. I don't quite understand it." When I shared this with Elise, she became more animated.

"I would love to know more. Try to find out whatever else you can about this," she appealed to me.

In response to Elise's questions, I began to see more unusual images. Her father seemed eager to share. "I see an image of a dense light, with a rainbow of colors surrounding it. It has certain auditory tones that seem to change shape and move. I get the message from your father that this is a healing tool of some kind. Now I see these people moving with it in unison, close to the earth." I tried to decipher and explain the images and the message as best I could.

"That is interesting. Even more interesting when I think of my father involved in some kind of energy healing tool for the planet. Of course, he always wanted to help others. It was very important to him," she told me.

"Your father wants you to know that you are more advanced than you realize," I told Elise. "You can affect matter and energy at will. He says that he is learning this with you. He is sending me the message that he is learning how to merge his energy field with others'. He says that it is important to know how to work in unison as one. In the earth life, everything is separate. To advance to higher states of energy, you have to be able to know how to become one with others and with divine love. He says that it is an incredible feeling. Once you do it, you want it more and more. There is nothing in the physical that can quite compare. Well, maybe loving and feeling close to another comes close."

I looked over at Elise, and she sighed when I said this. "What happened to the father that I knew?" she laughed. "He always had a desire to know the truth. But because he viewed spirituality and metaphysics as unscientific and too 'woo woo,' as he called it, he shut the door to it."

"It appears as if he has opened that door, wide open," I told her.

"Is my father working with me in any other way? Is he close?" Elise asked me with a sincere and interested look on her face.

As if this session was not already fascinating enough, Elise and I both suddenly and simultaneously saw a flash of light similar to an orb enter the room from an outside window. It happened quickly. In my second-story office, I have five windows on one wall, which looks out on trees. My client and I face these windows. Behind where we are seated there is a small desk and some office equipment. As Elise and I watched the orb of light float across the room, we jumped at the sound of my printer, which had suddenly turned on and had begun to print. Elise and I were both startled. The sound of colliding cymbals would not have been more surprising. When the printer stopped, we both got up to see what had been printed. Although the paper was full of lines, some in color and some black, both Elise and I knew that this had been her father's doing.

When we settled down to continue the session, Elise's father's energy presence was no longer as easy to connect with. Elise and I both wanted some kind of clarification as to what had just happened, so I turned to my spirit guide helpers and asked them for an explanation. I was told that Elise and her father were both learning how to affect and influence matter through will and intent. Elise had a well-developed awareness of metaphysics and a strong spirit, and because of this, her father had been able to easily connect with her. They were both practicing and learning how to influence and affect physical matter through nonphysical means, and their efforts positively were affecting each another. Although Elise was not aware of it, they often developed their abilities together. It was like two people joining forces to carry a heavy box or push a cart up a hill, my guides told me. When we work in unison with others, we are able to accomplish more than we could do on our own.

"Plus," they told me, "Elise's father was showing off a bit. Sending an orb of light into the room and turning on the computer was his way of making the session memorable."

"It worked," Elise told me as I relayed to her what my guides were explaining. "I don't think I will forget this session for a long time."

"Is it safe for Elise to be energetically connecting with her father is this way?" I asked my guides. "Nothing could be safer. This is the direction of evolution, working in harmony with others and experiencing oneness," I was told.

Our Initial Experiences on the Other Side

The idea that there is life beyond death and that we can communicate and connect with spirits on the other side may be too much for some people to accept. Yet, as physical death draws close, our spiritual senses wake us to a broader reality. Most people have a tangible experience of the spirit realm in the days and weeks leading up to their passing. They often begin to see their loved ones standing close to them or sitting on their bed. Some dream of a loved one who, from the other side, encourages and assures them of their presence and help.

Those who may have dismissed the idea of life after death as nonsense and New Age hooey soon discover when they pass over that death is not the same as dead.

When we pass over, we enter into the most sublime and loving warmth imaginable. Those in spirit describe it to their loved ones as a magnificent period of healing, forgiveness, and astonishing benevolence. We then experience our expectations of what we believe death to be. Some are met at the pearly gates of heaven by Jesus, angels, Mohammed, or another spiritual being whom they hope to be with on the other side. Others rest in a long sleep, waking slowly to an environment that they did not think existed. A few experience a cosmic oneness with all of life. They become energy merging and integrating with the pulse of the cosmos. Most are greeted by their family and friends, who joyously await their presence with a birthday party–like celebration. Unfortunately, there are some who believe that they are not "good" enough to go to a loving and peaceful environment. They expect to be met at their death with some form of hell and often create this from their expectations. Whatever our initial experience, once the veil of physicality is lifted, the energy of the divine cannot be denied for long. Eventually we come to the awareness that love, peace, joy, and all the attributes of the divine surround us.

It is always interesting to connect with loved ones in spirit who in the physical life had rigid and dogmatic views in regard to the supernatural, intuition, and psychic phenomena. Once in the spirit realm, the outer appearances that separated us from others in the physical world dissolve. We harmoniously coexist and communicate with one another through our intuition. We naturally tune in to what others are thinking, feeling, and experiencing, especially those whom we love. Intuitive development may be a hobby and a curiosity here in the physical realm, but in the spirit world it is a necessity.

Communicating with someone on the other side who has been studying and learning how to improve their intuitive ability is always a pleasure. Although it is natural and automatic to intuitively communicate with one another on the other side, spirits need further training to intuitively interact with the physical realm. One motivation for improving intuitive skills and learning more about the intricacies of energy on the other side is that it affords spirits the ability to better communicate with their loved ones still in the physical world.

Your loved ones in spirit long to reach out to you and share the love and peace that they have discovered. The way of the spirit realm is to be of love and service. It may be difficult to fully comprehend this from an earthly perspective. Here on earth, we tend to be taught the opposite. We value getting ahead and having more. Not so on the other side. The harmonious current of the spirit realm moves us in the direction of oneness and connection with all. Intuition and psychic and medium abilities offer us a way to further connect and receive the love and blessings of our loved ones on the other side.

Eternal Talent

Being a member of a family that adheres to a strict religious code of behavior can be difficult for more spiritual and freedom-loving individuals. Those who are curious to explore metaphysical concepts and delve into the supernatural have a particularly hard time. From a young age, they may have been warned of the devil, a dark and scary being that is just waiting to claim their soul. Without the support of their family, many young and talented intuitive children all too often repress their natural abilities and their desire for further spiritual exploration. If they do pursue their interests, they may hide their beliefs and activities for fear of being ostracized if exposed.

From the Stars

The following session is an example of how strong the soul's desire can be to share and help others.

When Millie came in for a session, it was evident that she was not new to intuitive and psychic phenomena. A professional astrologer for many years, she was warm, friendly, and open to whatever I had to say. The session was fairly typical. Her grandmother from spirit came in and shared a few insights and warm memories. A friend from her childhood paid her a visit, and her beloved cat who had died a couple of years prior also made an appearance. We moved on to other areas, and with a just a little time remaining, I asked her if she had any questions. Millie told me that she always wondered about her Great Aunt Adeline. Her aunt had passed long before Millie's birth, but from the first time that Millie had heard her name, she had felt a connection to her. She was often told by family members that she was a lot like her aunt, yet no one ever elaborated on what Aunt Adeline had been like. When she pushed for more information, she was told that she was "different" and "walked to the beat of her own drummer."

"I feel like I know her," Millie told me. "When I am working on someone's birth chart, I sometimes feel as if there is someone with me. I don't know why, but I feel like it might be her. Can you connect with her and find out if I am right?"

I, too, was curious and wanted to connect with Aunt Adeline. I asked Millie to speak her aunt's name. When a loved one does not spontaneously make their presence known, the vibration of speaking the loved one's name brings them close.

I immediately felt her presence, and I could tell that Aunt Adeline was quite a character. The first image that I received from her was of her wrapped in a multicolored shawl with bright red lipstick on her smiling face.

"I believe your aunt is with us," I told Millie. "This is interesting and a bit unusual. I feel like she is saying that she has been participating is some cosmic experiments of some kind and didn't mean to keep us waiting. I like her. There is the energy of liveliness and joy surrounding her. She says that she is so happy that you asked about her."

Aunt Adeline continued to send me various images. Some were easier to understand than others. "Your aunt wants to talk about her life here on earth. She shows me a big stack of papers with symbols and planets and notes strewn all over them. I see her behind a desk making more notes on what looks like an astrology chart. I think that your aunt also had an interest in astrology."

Millie said, "Really? That is a surprise. No one ever told me this. Are you sure she isn't talking about me?"

I focused on Aunt Adeline and asked her for clarification. "I know it may be surprising, but I am seeing a clear image of her working in an upstairs attic on what appear to be astrology charts. I get the impression that this was a secret. She hides the papers in a trunk."

Millie chimed in. "It would have had to have been a secret. My grandparents on that side of the family were strict Baptists, from the old South. They lived in the countryside of Georgia, outside of Atlanta. If she had an interest in astrology, they would not have been very happy about it."

"Your aunt is telling me that she gave you something, a gift of some kind. It seems like this is important. I feel love and care coming from her to you."

"Hmm." Millie stared out the window. "I don't have anything of hers. I am not sure what she is talking about."

"I get the impression that this is a different kind of gift. She keeps showing me the charts. All the work that she did, the stack of papers she worked on. I see an image of her handing them to you. I get the impression that she sent you a gift of the energy knowledge and wisdom that she acquired over the years."

"Shivers are running up my arms," Millie's said, her voice louder and more excited. "I think I know what she is talking about. Years ago after I graduated high school, I was getting ready to go to nursing school. This had been my plan for a long time. That summer I started to have doubts. I wasn't sure that I wanted to pursue nursing, but I didn't want to let my family down. They were so excited about me becoming a nurse. I just wasn't sure that I wanted to pursue this, but I didn't know what to do instead. Everyone in my family was expected to go to college and work in a traditional career. There was no room or tolerance for anything out of the ordinary. I was confused and frustrated and didn't know what to do.

"A few weeks before school started, I had a dream that changed everything. In the dream, I was sailing through the skies. It was wonderful. I'll never forget that feeling. I had complete control. I flew by the sun and moon and many other planets. I could feel them. They were talking to me, and I felt so happy. I woke up the next morning and knew that something had to change. I sat down at the kitchen table for breakfast and opened the paper to the astrology section. I am a Pisces, and my horoscope told me to *follow my dreams.* I felt as if God had spoken to me through that horoscope. My life seemed to change at that moment. I felt an electric current run through my body, and I decided then and there to become an astrologer.

"My family, of course, had a fit. But it didn't matter. I knew in my heart that this was the right choice for me. Instead of going to nursing school, I went to college and studied psychology and astronomy. I did this mostly to appease my family. I thought these areas would help me as an astrologer. I found a professional astrologer and attended his classes in the evening. I will never forget the first chart that I worked on. It was magic. In class, I was given the birth information of a person whom I did not know. Something in me opened up as I charted their planets. I had insight and awareness to information about the person that was more than just what I was learning from their chart. Do you think that she helped me choose astrology as a profession?"

"Your aunt is telling me that you have the gift. She just helped nudge you to recognize it," I told her.

Millie excitedly continued. "Sometimes when I am in a session explaining a client's chart to them, it feels as if there is someone else present. I feel like I am being given help and direction from the spirit world. I wonder if this is my aunt helping me. Would you ask her?"

"Your aunt is sending me the message that she is close to you when you do astrology. When she was here in the physical realm, she studied astrology, and now in spirit, she is learning even more. There is an energy connection between you both. She sends you information and guides you," I told her.

Millie did not seem too surprised by this. "I often feel a guiding presence when I am working. I didn't know that it was her. But it makes sense. Please tell her that I appreciate her help."

I explained to Millie that she did not need me as a go-between with her aunt. They already had an open line of communication. Millie just needed to become more aware and conscious of it. The session seemed to be winding to a close when I felt Aunt Adeline's energy begin to get stronger.

She had another message for her niece. "Your aunt is telling me that you are helping her. She wants you to know that she appreciates you very much." I shared this with Millie, and she looked surprised.

"How can I help her? I would think that in the spirit realm she has advanced teachers and access to so much knowledge," she told me.

Aunt Adeline again sent me images. "I again see your aunt when she was here in the physical. She is alone in the attic office, working on what appear to be her astrology charts. I get the feeling of loneliness and frustration. As you know, she had to hide her interests. Anything outside of the confines of organized religion would have been upsetting to the family. She was conflicted and upset. She was thought of as kooky by the family, and astrology was thought to be either connected to the devil or pure nonsense. She never had a chance to share her gifts with anyone," I explained to Millie.

"I understand," Millie shared. "It could not have been easy."

"Your aunt wanted to help others through astrology," I told Millie. "She never did. Now through you, she is getting this opportunity. There is so much gratitude that she has for you. Her heart opens with warmth and thankfulness that she can work and help others along with you."

Tears came to Millie's eyes. "I know how she feels. My family does not understand me either. I can't imagine what it was like in her time. I don't even know how she discovered astrology. She can work with me all she would like. I think we make a great team."

9

The Cure for Negativity: Doing Time in the Spirit Realm

There is an Aesop fable that tells a story about a competition between the sun and the wind. In this children's story, they challenge each another in a contest to see who can cause a man to take off his coat more quickly. The wind begins and blows as hard as it can to rip the coat off the man. But in response to the wind's force, the man pulls his coat tighter around his body. When sun's turn comes, its warm rays shine bright over the man. Within a few minutes, he sheds his coat from the heat.

This story is symbolic of the physical and spiritual realms. In the physical world, we tend to hold on to our beliefs, attitudes, and judgments. When we encounter something that opposes our views and beliefs, we usually react by holding on tight to our perspectives. We pull our beliefs closer and rarely entertain opposing views. We may judge others and form negative opinions and attitudes about them and their ideas and perspectives.

Once we pass over into the spirit realm, however, divine love is like the rays of the sun. Our hearts are warmed and comforted by a love that surpasses whatever judgments and attitudes we clung to in the physical world. We begin to shed the layers of human attitudes, emotions, and beliefs that cover our soul. Whatever keeps our soul from experiencing pure love is shed.

The Lesson of Negativity

Here on earth, we all feel negative, judgmental, and critical from time to time. This is a world of duality. We are offered the full spectrum of experiences: male and female, day and night, right and wrong, happiness and sadness, and negative and positive. Differing experiences give us the opportunity to know who we are. When we experience something that we do not like, we generally form a negative opinion about it. We may even become judgmental and critical. Yet the earth lesson of negativity is really one of discernment. When we experience something that we do not like, we begin to know more about what does work for us. Knowing who we are often begins with knowing who we are not. We miss the lesson when we dwell in negativity instead of using it as a catalyst to choose and create positive experiences.

In the physical world, negativity can become a habitual and judgmental perspective on life. It can crowd out positive thoughts and feelings and attract more of what we do not want. Immersed in a negative perception, the world becomes a threatening environment where loss, pain, and disease lurk around every corner. Happiness is elusive, loss is inevitable, and life is against us.

Negativity on the Other Side

Negativity, judgments of others, criticism, and arrogance are experienced very differently in the spiritual realms. When someone who has adopted a lifelong negative perspective passes over, they begin to realize the damage they have caused to themselves and others. On the other side, the prevailing energy of love is in sharp contrast to the negativity that we generate in the physical world. The environment of the spiritual realm is always one of calm, creativity, love, and possibilities. We cannot blame our feelings and attitudes on anything outside of ourselves. It becomes obvious that our negativity is self-generated. If we choose to live in this energy, then we do so alone. Our feelings do not affect others, and we have no power to make anyone else's life difficult. There is no payoff to our harsh and damaging feelings and attitudes. We become isolated, as there is nothing in our environment that reflects our inner discontent. We eventually realize that we have to learn, change, and grow in order to accept and embody the love that is everywhere.

In the spirit realm, we have free will and choice. There are some souls who resist the positive, loved-filled environment of spirit. If a spirit does not release their earthly destructive thoughts, attitudes, beliefs, and feelings, they are rapidly drawn back into the earth realm. Because this energy cannot exist in the love of the heavens, a soul either releases their negativity or quickly incarnates into another life. In their new incarnation, there will be negative influences that reflect their inner state of being. Inner negativity quickly manifests in what appears to be "bad luck" or "random circumstance." It is in this way that we eventually come to realize the pain that we are producing and become willing to generate and create the positive.

Chains of Love

I include the following story because it is a common one. When we make choices and decisions from a negative perspective, the impact on others is usually harmful and damaging. Many people pass over without acknowledging the harmful effects their actions have had on those they love. For those who are estranged from their loved ones at the time of their passing, it can feel like the door to reconciliation is forever shut. Death can appear to be final. But this is not the case. All that we do and do not do is reviewed once we pass over. We are made whole through confronting and healing our human frailties and missteps. Those whom we left behind with unresolved pain and heartache cannot be forgotten and denied. The spirit realm offers a new perspective and motivation for healing. If you have a loved one who passed over before hurts were healed and problems confronted, know they are with you, learning to love.

It is always a nice surprise for me when I have a client who radiates positivity. April, a professional in her mid-thirties, was this kind of client. When I opened the door for her to enter my office, I immediately felt her upbeat energy. As we sat down to begin the session, it was clear that she was nervous. Never having had a reading, she did not know what to expect and became quite talkative. I tried to settle her nerves with an attempt at humor, but I was not very successful. April told me that she was not sure why she had scheduled an appointment with me. A woman she worked with had come to see me, and she was fascinated by her experience.

"I am not sure why I am here," she said. "I almost canceled but thought I would follow through with this."

I began the session as I usually do, with a short prayer. As I looked at her energy, it was clear to me that she was a person who gave a lot to others.

"You have a beautiful heart," I told her. "Your guardian angel is showing me the deep-felt love and concern that you have for others. It is known and seen in the spiritual realms, even if you feel that it is not always noticed here in the physical."

For all of the love and care that I felt in April's energy, I also felt that she was lonely. Work occupied most of her time, and it was obvious that despite her positive attitude, she did not have many close relationships. I spent a fair amount of our session talking about love, past relationships, and what was coming her way. Still, I felt that I was not getting to the core of April's issues. I felt her wounded heart, and I knew that to fulfill her desire for intimacy, healing this pain was essential.

I asked the angels for help and immediately felt the presence of a middle-aged man from spirit. He was a boxy, broad-shouldered man who I knew was April's father who had passed over. He was quiet and reluctant to communicate with me.

"A man who feels like your father just came in," I told her. I heard a gasp from April and felt her tighten up.

"He died about five years ago," she said. "We had a difficult relationship. I did not see him for about ten years before he died. I am surprised that he is here."

April clearly was not comfortable with her father's presence. He must have felt this, too. I felt his shame and hesitation. Yet despite this, he began to communicate with me.

"Your father is sending me an image of himself with chains on his hands and feet. He is swaying back and forth in a line along with other similar spirits who are chained together. He wants me to tell you that he cannot hurt you. He is in the chain gang."

April was silent. She looked at me with a perplexed look on her face and then started to smile.

"I hate to admit it," she said, "but I am glad to hear that. He did have a sense of humor."

"Do you want me to hear what else your father wants to say, or are you too uncomfortable with him here?"

"I guess imagining him as part of a chain gang intrigues me. I would like to hear what he has to say." April now seemed to be more comfortable.

"Your father tells me that the angels have him right where he needs to be," I went on. "He says 'hard time' in spirit is not what you would think. He volunteered for it and wants to heal. He does not want to hurt others and be mean ever again. He sends me the message that until he understands how his criticism and negativity affect others, he will be chained to the angels. It's not bad, though, he tells me. He is always connected to love. This is the difference between being in shackles in the physical world and in the spiritual realms. In spirit, the chains free you."

Now that April was feeling more at ease with her father's presence, more images and emotions started to flood me.

I told April, "Your father is showing me an image of a large office building. I get the impression that this was important to him, where he worked. Oh, not just where he worked. It feels like he was important here, in charge. I see people in the building afraid of him. He seemed to know this, and he was fine with being intimidating. Being successful was important to him. He didn't feel much. Getting ahead and making money were most important."

"That is so true," April said. "I am surprised that he is aware of this. He was so sure of himself in life. Being a successful businessman, he had a lot of respect and admiration. He always thought he was right. His way was the only way."

"Your father tells me that he thought that he would be greeted by God and congratulated for his worldly successes when he passed over. It doesn't feel as if this is what happened," I told April.

I am intrigued as to what did happen. Clearly April's father underwent a dramatic change. I asked him if he could share with us what he had experienced. In response to my request, he sent me more images and thoughts.

"Your father shows me that he was not afraid to die. I feel like he had an advanced stage of cancer, but he may have actually died from a heart attack," I shared with April.

"He did have cancer. I don't know if he had a heart attack. He may have," she replied.

I continued. "Your father shows me an image of overwhelming light. This is what he saw and felt when he passed. There was so much love. I get the impression that he was uncomfortable with it. But he let go and surrendered to it. Eventually, he was led to an older man. This is a guide. The guide is telling him that it is time to feel. Your father is confused. Then he starts to feel. He is surprised. Not all of the feelings are pleasant. He understands that these feelings are what others felt as a result of his negativity and criticisms. Your father sends me the message that he also had to feel what you experienced as a result of his actions. He did not realize the pain that they caused. This made quite an impression on him."

"It made quite an impression on me, too," April shared with me. "I was always afraid of him. He could be very intimidating. I never did anything right in his eyes. I was never smart enough, pretty enough, thin enough. No matter what I did, I felt that I was lacking in some way."

"Your father is showing me an image of scales, like bathroom scales to weigh yourself on. I get a feeling of humiliation from him. He is apologizing to you."

"My father would make me weigh myself in front of him every week when I was a teenager. He thought that I was gaining too much weight. He told me that no one would be interested in a fat girl. I always thought that I was fat and unlovable," April shared. "Of course, I know better now. It has taken me a while, but I am learning to love myself just the way I am."

I looked at April, and to me she was an attractive, average-weight woman who did not need to lose weight. Her father continued.

"Your father tells me that you are beautiful and smart and talented. Maybe most important of all, people really like you. He knows that you did not get this from him," I told her.

"You know, I am glad to hear this. But I don't need it so much now. I have done a lot of healing work, and I realize that he was a sad man who was never really close to anyone. Of course, he didn't seem to notice," April sighed.

"Your father was really out of touch with his feelings. Shutting down his ability to feel at a young age, he denied his sensitive nature and vowed not to let others hurt him. It feels to me that this is part of his being in the angelic chain gang. He has to feel. He cannot get away from it. The love that he is connected to is opening his heart and healing him."

"I am glad to hear that he is changing and getting some help." April's face softened when she told me this.

I was about to finish the session, but April's father had another message.

"Your father shows me an office building again. Do you work in an office, too? He shows me you sitting at a desk. It looks like water of some kind on your desk? I am not sure what he is trying to show me."

I heard April begin to laugh.

"I have a water fountain on my desk, and yes, I work in an office," she explained.

"Now your father is showing me people coming into your office. It feels calm. I feel like your father visits you there. Being in your office with you helps him. He shows me other people leaving your office feeling better, too."

April's face brightened up as she told me, "I have always tried to make my office a sanctuary for others. I am a supervisor of a help call center for a medical software product. It is very stressful for the people I work with. I try to offer them a place to go to collect their thoughts and relax."

"It seems to work," I told her. "Even for your father. He didn't know that was important. Helping others to feel good at work is a new concept for him. You're teaching him new things. He wants you to know how much your positivity is helping him. A glow of gold and white energy surrounds you in your office. He says that you give people a little bit of heaven."

I heard April begin to sniffle. I felt her heart opening to this much-needed healing with her father. Even though she had worked hard to heal and forgive him, knowing that he was close and proud of her would help her go forward in her emotional life.

Feeling Our Choices

As loving and healing as the spiritual realm is, it is no pity party. We have to be responsible for our attitudes and actions. As part of our soul growth on the other side, we reflect upon the negative choices that we made while in the physical realm and the less-than-kind criticisms and judgments that we inflicted on others. We experience what others felt as a result of our attitudes and actions. To fully embody the love and bliss that the spirit realm offers, we must feel and discharge the pain and negativity that we produced while here on earth. Spirit guides and angels also help us to fully understand what was possible had we accepted and generated more positivity.

Loved ones on earth are essential for our growth and healing in the spiritual realm. Quite often those in spirit must visit the people in the physical realm who were affected by their actions when they were on earth. They must feel and experience the impact that their attitudes and actions had on others. Those on earth who were negatively influenced by another's actions also play an important role in this earth school lesson. There are no victims in life. Our soul has chosen its earth school lessons. If you find that you tend to habitually be in relationship with or surrounded by negative people, it is important for you to examine your choices. There is likely an important lesson that your soul is asking you to learn. When we are children, we do not have the option of leaving our families and attracting a new one. If you were born into a negative family system, you may tend to unconsciously re-create this pattern in your adult life. Remember that you now have a choice.

One way to heal the cycle of negative attraction is to heal the past. The continued healing between loved ones here and in the hereafter advances everyone. Those in spirit learn how to love and support their physical loved ones, and we in the physical also benefit. Healing a relationship with someone who has passed over is easier than you might think. Because the way of the spirit realm is love and forgiveness, your efforts are supported and strengthened.

The Artist and the Doctor

One very essential earth life lesson that we have all come here to learn is how to generate and live in positive energy. The following session is one of the many I have had with people who lived among negative and critical people but were able to stay in a positive frame of mind. This does not always happen easily. It can take a focused will and clear intent to generate positivity while in the presence of a negative individual. Yet it is an invaluable soul achievement.

Eve came to see me after the death of her husband. She had been given my name by a member of a support group. Never having been to a medium, she did not know what to expect. In her early fifties, Eve quietly sat down and we began the session. During the short prayer that I open each session with, I felt the energy of grief surrounding her.

"There are two men in spirit coming in from the spirit realm," I told her. "One feels like your father. Do you have a husband or partner in spirit?"

"Yes, they are both dead," Eve confirmed.

Eve's father came forward first even though I felt that it was her husband that she most wanted to communicate with. I spent several minutes connecting with her father. I then turned my attention to her husband.

"Your husband is holding his chest. It appears that he may have had a heart problem or died as a result of a heart issue. Is this true?" I asked Eve.

"Eric died in the bathroom while getting ready for work. He had a massive heart attack," she explained.

Eve stared out the window and I continued. "He is apologizing for leaving so much undone. I see piles of paperwork and other things, boxes of personal items. Your husband says to do with it whatever you want."

"I have had to go through all of our financial affairs. He paid all the bills and managed our money. I hope that I am doing this up to his standards." Eve looked concerned as she explained this to me.

"I get the impression that you are doing fine, maybe better than fine. Your husband is quiet. I feel a sense of regret and maybe even embarrassment with him. It has something to do with your finances. I feel as if you discovered something unexpected."

"So far the biggest surprise I have had is how much money we have, or maybe I have, now. Eric led me to believe that we were not doing well financially," Eve informed me.

"I see a busy office, actually several offices. I get the feeling from your husband that he was in the medical field. I feel that he was very successful."

"He was a surgeon in private practice, very busy," Eve explained.

When loved ones in spirit need to communicate sensitive issues, they often send me more emotional energy. I can feel their desire for forgiveness. This is what happened with Eric. I began to feel feelings of regret and sadness. I continued to share my impressions of him with Eve.

"Your husband is showing me images of beautiful places. I feel like you may have planned to visit them, but I get the feeling from him that you did not get the chance. He shows me what looks like Alaska. Did you by any chance take a cruise there or someplace similar? I see a large ship. The feelings associated with these images are sad, though."

"We had planned on going on an Alaskan cruise for our anniversary several years ago. I even reserved the tickets. But Eric said he did not want to spend the money and take the time off from work. He felt the economy was not in good shape, that we had to be frugal and cut back."

As Eve explained this to me, I felt Eric in spirit sending her apologies for denying her this trip.

"I get the impression from Eric that you were a patient and loving person. He is so sorry that you did not go on the trip," I told her. The images that I was getting from Eric quickly changed.

"Wow, all of a sudden your husband is showing me a lot of color, beautiful images. It looks and feels like paintings. I see canvases of color, like abstracts."

"I am surprised Eric is showing you these. I love painting. But he never thought I was very good. He used to tell me that my paintings looked like I just dumped a can of paint of a canvas and walked away," Eve explained. "Please ask him if he is aware of my new paintings. I got so tired of him complaining that I was wasting my time and energy that I only painted during the day when he was gone. I stopped showing him my work. But after he died, I needed something. I started painting with a vengeance. It has helped me so much to be able to express myself through art."

"Oh, I feel like he knows," I told her. "I get a very clear image of him in a room where you are painting. It has one wall covered with windows and it looks out over a garden."

Eve excitedly answered me. "Yes, that is amazing. How do you know that?"

"Your husband is showing me this." I continued to get feelings of regret from Eric. "I feel that he realizes how much his criticism affected you. He understands your artwork much better now, and he is happy you are enjoying it."

"That is almost too hard to believe." Eve looked at me in confusion. "He never had anything good to say about it."

I began to get a few images and feelings from Eric that I was struggling to understand. I decided to just tell Eve what I was experiencing and let her interpret it. "I keep seeing an image of what looks like a party or a group of people. It is very colorful and active. I am confused, though, because instead of feeling light and fun, I feel a sense of dread and even anger. Then I feel apologies from Eric. He tells me that his behavior was indefensible. Does this make any sense to you?"

Eve took a few minutes to answer me. "A few months before Eric died, we went to a party. Maybe he is talking about this. We never resolved an argument we had. We went to the opening of an exhibit of a friend of mine at a new gallery. It was a very interesting crowd, all kinds of people. I was having so much fun. My friend is gay. Eric has always had a difficult time being around gay people. He was very uncomfortable and wanted to leave early. He actually demanded we leave early. We fought on the way home. Do you think he is referring to the party?"

"I get the impression from Eric that he regrets his actions. He wants you to know that he is learning. This might be hard to hear," I told Eve. "I get the impression from your husband that he feels that his passing over is giving you a new start at life. He realizes how much his negativity affected you. You were not able to create and do what you most loved to do. He is happy for you, even joking about it. He shows me an image of you surrounded by color and energy. It helps him, he tells me. He did not know how to change, how to relax and let go. Now he has to. You are an inspiration to him."

"Eric was a good man," Eve told me. "He just always thought the worst. He worried and complained about everything. The older he got, the more suspicious he was of others. It is sad how much we missed out on. I wish that he could have felt this way when he was here, but I am glad that the heaviness is gone. Maybe now he can let himself be happy."

"He is moving in the right direction," I assured her. "Your happiness and positivity are helping him. Do all the things that you wanted to do but could not do when he was here. He is with you in spirit, enjoying them right along with you. This is his opportunity, too. Before we end, your husband wants me to be sure to tell you that he loves you. Always has and always will, he wants you to know."

"I know that he loves me." Eve looked at me with tears in her eyes. "I guess that I am running the show now. I miss him. But knowing that he is close helps."

Transform with Gratitude

I love the image of April's father surrounded by white-light chains that connect him to angelic love. I would like to think that Eric and others like him who need an extra infusion of love are also connected to the angels in this way.

We do not have to wait until we die, however, to experience the love and positivity that are always available to us. The earth challenge of transforming negativity into positivity is one that we all engage in on a daily basis. There are some basic things that you can do that will help steer you toward the positive, despite what comes your way.

Develop the attitude of gratitude. Every day before you go to bed, review the day and have gratitude for the positive that has come your way, no matter how big or small it may appear to be. Even if it is simply a smile from a stranger or an easy drive home from work, the more you notice the positive, the more it will come your way. When you have negative experiences or feel critical or judgmental, remind yourself that this is just life's way of steering you in the direction of what you truly want. Tell yourself that the negative you are experiencing is simply information that offers you a choice. Instead of indulging in what you do not like, know that it will pass. The less energy you give to it, the sooner it will transform by your positive perspective. Ask your angels and spirit guides for help. You might even want to imagine yourself attached to the angels through golden rings of love.

10

HIDDEN OPPORTUNITIES FOR SPIRITUAL GROWTH: ALZHEIMER'S, DEMENTIA, COMA, DISABILITIES

The soul never wastes an opportunity. No matter what an individual's physical appearance or condition may be, the soul is at work doing all that it can do to heal and advance the person's highest good. I have worked with many people who have loved ones who are suffering from conditions like dementia and Alzheimer's or are unresponsive and in a coma. Although it may appear that they are wasting away, confused, despondent, or unreachable, soulful activity is taking place. When I give readings to people who have loved ones suffering with these types of illnesses, the loved one's spirit is often in a suspended state in between the physical and the light of the other side. Those in these states are usually intuitively aware of me and are able to give messages to my eager clients. Less often, their consciousness is floating close and is still connected to their physical body, yet I am unable to directly communicate with them.

The Unifying Ego

The human ego unifies our consciousness. The personality self that we present to the world is just one aspect of our multidimensional self. We are our subconscious, our memories, thoughts, and feelings, our soul's entire accumulated experiences and an aspect of the collective consciousness. In the human experience, our ego bundles all these up into what appears to be one self. When people are experiencing Alzheimer's or dementia or in an unresponsive state, this veil of control is no longer present. In readings when I connect with people suffering from these conditions, I often feel as if I am communicating with more than one person. Their soul and spirit are intact. But they may be simultaneously emotionally and mentally reliving a past memory, experiencing a new activity, inhabiting a celestial realm, or even living as another person in a very different experience than their current physical situation. Even though in the human realm this will appear as mental and emotional chaos, confusion, and an out-of-touch state of turmoil, the soul is engaged in meaningful activity.

Many of the people I work with who are in these confused states are releasing past trauma, detoxing, and getting ready for their ascent into the spirit realm. We come into the earth life in part because it provides us with the opportunity for rapid soul growth and expansion. Sometimes we are given another opportunity before we pass over to accomplish what we have come to this earth to learn and experience. During the course of our lives we may have procrastinated or postponed our soul's to-do list. Behind what appears to be fragmented, fantasy, and purposeless behavior, the soul may be completing karma, releasing repressed emotional energy, and revisiting choices and decisions.

This chaotic but meaningful activity serves us in a few ways. The good that you accomplish in the physical realm is yours forever. Releasing negativity, discharging karmic debt, and loving and forgiving yourself and others before you pass into the spiritual realm assure you of a stronger, brighter afterlife. Entering into the spiritual realm as unencumbered and free as possible from unfinished business allows the soul to ascend into higher vibrations of blissful cosmic love.

Even if in human terms an individual's condition appears to be chaotic, confusing, and useless to us busy humans, the soul knows what it is doing. Trust that there is likely meaningful soulful activity going on within your loved one who is unresponsive or sitting days upon days looking out the window.

Love Beyond Appearances

The following session is a good example of the soul taking the opportunity to participate in a valuable experience before passing over into the light. Even though an individual's behavior may appear to be strange and eccentric, the soul is attracting the conditions for its evolution and healing.

When Andrew came into my office, he looked to me like a typical scientist. Living in an area of the country where medical and scientific research is a mainstay, I have bumped into quite a few scientists and academics. Andrew was a quiet, middle-aged man dressed in business casual with a pocket protector full of pens in his striped shirt. Although he had a PhD and had been a scientific researcher for many years, he was open-minded and seemed anxious to begin the session.

I said my opening prayer and soon became aware of a woman in spirit who very much wanted to talk to him.

"There is a woman coming in from spirit who has short gray hair. She wears glasses and her name may begin with an *L*. I hear her say 'mother.' She is waving her hands like she really wants to talk to you."

"Oh, yes, that is my mother. People called her LeLe, even though her real name was Pearl," Andrew confirmed.

"She is saying over and over that she is back to her old self. I get the impression that she had a good sense of humor. I hear her laughter. She tells me that the confusion has cleared. The light is back on, she says. Did she suffer from dementia before she passed?" I asked Andrew.

"For many years she had Alzheimer's," he stated. "Toward the end, she would call me by her father's name. She didn't seem to recognize me, or anyone else for that matter."

"Well, she is clear-headed now," I told him. "I see an image of a bed, like a hospital bed in a small room. I feel like this is a care facility, maybe where she spent some time."

Andrew seemed anxious to explain. "I wanted to let her stay at home, but she almost burned the house down trying to make breakfast one morning. The fire department was called when a neighbor saw smoke billowing out of a window. My mother didn't even notice. I realized I had to keep her safe. Is she upset with me for putting her in a home?"

"That is not the impression I am getting. She tells me that it was a good place to be. There is something that is funny about this. I keep hearing laughter. Did she have a male friend there? I think that this is what she is laughing about."

"That is funny," Andrew said. "Please tell me more."

I sent a message to LeLe asking her if she could communicate more about this to me. I started receiving different images, not all of which made sense.

"I feel like your mother is going back to her childhood. I see a large home in the country. I feel as if she grew up in the South, and I get the impression that this home I see was in the family for generations. Is this correct?"

Andrew explained. "That sounds like the home she grew up in. It is no longer in the family. But, yes, many generations lived in that home. I am a bit embarrassed by its history."

As Andrew said this, I got images of an old Southern estate. I saw fields with black laborers working hard. I got the impression that this had been a large farm.

"When I was young, we would visit the farm. My grandparents lived there. They loved to tell stories of the glory days when the family owned acres and acres of property and was quite wealthy," Andrew told me.

"Your mother is showing me a plaque of some kind. It is hanging in what looks like a kitchen. Actually, there is more than one. They look like framed papers. Do you know what she is trying to show me?" I looked to Andrew. His eyes were wide open and he seemed hesitant.

"I think that she may be showing you the certificates of ownership that were hanging on the wall of this farm house. Until the place sold, no one would take them down. They were slave papers. These are the people that my ancestors owned," Andrew told me in a quiet voice. "My mother, father, all of the family, were racist. They never really accepted the North winning the war. Their lives changed so much. They never got over it and accepted African Americans as equals. It was very sad."

"There is something more to this," I told Andrew. "Your mother is again showing me her hospital room. I don't know why, but she is laughing again."

Andrew did not look surprised. "I know what she is talking about. But I wonder if she recalls what happened. Do people who have Alzheimer's remember what they did once they are on the other side?" he asked me.

"Some do," I told him. "If it is important, they will recall it. Whatever happened, your mother seems to want to talk about it. It seems to have something to do with a boyfriend. I keep hearing that from your mother. I think that he may have been a black man. Does this make sense?" I asked him.

Now Andrew was laughing and shared more with me. "I went to visit my mother every Saturday morning. She could appear to be fully cognizant, but she would slip into confusion very quickly. Close to lunch time one morning, she shooed me out of the room. I didn't know why. This continued for several more weeks. She would abruptly tell me to go home around lunch time. I started to wonder what was going on. So one Saturday I told her that I wouldn't leave until she told me why. Without pausing, she told me that her boyfriend was coming to visit and she didn't want me to get in the way. I was surprised but happy to know that she had male company. This went on for a few more weeks. Finally, I asked one of the nurses about her male friend. She looked at me perplexed and told me that that she was not aware that my mother had any male visitors.

"The next week when I went to visit, I left before lunch, as usual. But I waited outside of her room. In a few minutes, a young black male nurse came and brought my mother her lunch tray. He seemed kind to my mother, but he clearly was not flirting or interested in her. On the other hand, my mother seemed beside herself with giddiness. She was smiling and flirting with him. I couldn't believe it. Here, my mother in her late eighties and a racist all of her life, believed this young black man to be her boyfriend."

"Your mother is smiling. I get the impression from her that this flirtation was a bright spot in her last months here," I shared with Andrew.

"It seemed to be," he said. "I continued to visit her once a week until she passed over. I always left before lunch so she could enjoy her 'boyfriend' visit. I never said anything to her or to anyone. It was a pleasure to see her open her heart and feel, even if the feeling was not returned or even acknowledged. For so long, her heart had been closed. She was cold and distant, especially to anyone who was not wealthy and white. This was a true blessing. I wanted to protect her and allow her to feel as much love as possible before she went over."

"Your mother wants you to know that this changed her. She thanks you for being there for her in this special way. Your nonjudgmental support has taught her a lot," I told Andrew. "I get the impression from her that you are still teaching her. She is with you more than you might think, continuing to experience how to love."

We continued with the session. Andrew's mother shared other memories and insights since passing over. Andrew's father and grandparents also came in. But no other message during our session was as delightful as the image of LeLe swooning over what she believed to be a charming male suitor. I believe that her attraction to him was more than simply the confused mental state of Alzheimer's. Her soul took the opportunity to teach her an important lesson. Despite an entire life spent in hate toward those of another race, her heart opened. In a childlike way, she experienced the innocence of love for love's sake, a lesson that furthered her soul's evolutionary agenda.

Shared Soul Lessons

Alzheimer's, dementia, unresponsive states like comas, and conditions and other mental disabilities are shared soul lessons. Those who live and care for people with these conditions are also being offered an important earth school lesson. Professional caregivers and family and friends who care for people with disabilities are practicing the lesson of selflessness, compassion, and unconditional love. Caring for a loved one who is suffering from a condition that leaves them unable to care for themselves can be demanding. It can test our patience, drain our bank accounts, strain our relationships, and even put our jobs at risk. Despite our love for another, when we have full responsibility in every area of their life, we can feel overwhelmed. Although it may be of little comfort while in the midst of this challenge, know that your soul is making great strides in experiencing the full scope of love.

Just as caring for another can test our compassion, allowing others to care for us can also be difficult. When we are mentally, emotionally, and/or physically incapacitated, we are vulnerable, dependent, and at the mercy of others. An extreme state of dependency can be the ultimate test of our trust in others and the universe, as there is little we can do to ensure that our needs will be met. Few people would willingly choose this degree of helplessness.

Our soul always seeks evolution and wholeness. Even though it is not readily apparent, when an individual experiences an extreme degree of reliance on others, their soul has voluntarily made this choice. We need one another. In the physical realm, we can become so self-sufficient that we close our hearts and attempt to control every aspect of our lives. Dependence forces us to learn how to be humble and accept the kindness and love of others. Wholehearted giving to those in need and receiving the love and care of others when we most need it move us out of our egocentric mindset and into the depths of authentic love.

Letting Go

One of the most challenging tests of love is our ability to let go. In the physical realm, we think of love as being close to one another, holding hands, talking, looking into one another's eyes, sharing activities, and cuddling. The call to experience a higher form of love often comes in the most difficult of ways.

Donna came to see me on a cold morning in February. I could tell from the look in her eyes that she was nervous and tired. As I began the session, I felt the almost overwhelming grief that surrounded her. Like a thick blanket, feelings of loss and sadness weighed heavy on her. Above Donna's head, the light of an angel suddenly appeared.

"Your guardian angel has a message for you," I began. "She opens her arms and wants you to know that you can release your sadness to her. Just ask that she take it from you. She is with you, sending love and compassion."

Donna looked straight ahead and showed no visible emotion.

"There are three people in spirit who just came in," I continued. "Two men and a woman. It feels like a grandmother and grandfather. The other man … he is tall with short curly hair. Is your husband or partner in spirit?"

Still not making eye contact with me, Donna nodded her head yes and wiped tears from her eyes.

"I feel a lot of love coming from him to you. He wants me to tell you that he finally woke up. I am seeing an image of a hospital bed. Does this make sense?"

Reluctant to speak, Donna again nodded her head yes and silently cried.

"Your husband is showing me the hospital bed again. You are sitting close to him. I get the impression that he could not speak to you. He wants you to know that he knew you were there. He shows me an image of you as a warm, bright light. He felt your pain and stress. I feel that he did not want to leave you and hung on as long as possible," I shared with Donna.

This seemed to stir up more of a reaction in her.

"Ray was in a coma for several weeks. There was an accident at his work. He was in apartment building construction, and a large beam fell on him. It left him unconscious. He never woke up."

"Ask him why," Donna pleaded with me. "Why didn't he wake up? The doctors thought he might. But he never did."

Ray was ready to respond to her question. "Your husband wants you to know that he tried. He shows me his spirit hovering over his body. He tried to reenter it. He wouldn't let go. Your husband did not have a choice," I told her. "He tried as hard as he could to stay in the physical realm. I can feel and see his struggle. He was drawn into the light. Its force kept pulling and pulling him. I see angelic spirits and others close to him, coaxing him to go over."

I knew that this was difficult for Donna to hear, yet I knew that I had to communicate as best I could what I received. I saw a tear running down her cheek. She appealed to me. "I prayed and prayed for him to heal. I asked God to open his eyes and let me talk to him, even if it was to simply say goodbye."

As Donna was sharing this, Ray was communicating with me. "Your husband is showing me an image of you sitting near his bed.

He was very close and listening to you and sending you love. He felt what you were feeling. I also feel as if your father was close. I see him sitting with you and holding your hand," I told Donna.

"I felt him, too," she excitedly shared with me. "I thought it was him. I asked him for help. He has been gone for several years. I miss him."

"Donna, at some point," I asked her, "did you accept that Ray was going to die? I ask you this because he is thanking you for letting him go. He says that it helped. Without your blessing, he may have been caught between the realms in limbo indefinitely."

With a surprised look on her face, Donna explained. "One night as I sat in his hospital room, I dozed off to sleep. I had a very real dream where I was talking to Ray. I was begging him to please come back. All of a sudden I saw a bright light come close. I felt overwhelming love and comfort. I looked around me, and I was in a field of flowers. It was warm, and I wanted to stay there for as long as possible. I felt as if I had left the sadness and grief behind, and I did not want to go back to it. Then, just as suddenly, I was back. I woke up, and I realized that this is where my husband was going. I could not deny him this. I told God that he could have Ray. Go with my love, I told him. The next morning, after a few family members had visited, he quietly died."

"Your husband knows how difficult it was for you to let go. He felt it as love," I assured her. "Your angels do, too. It was an act of selfless love."

Donna looked calmer. "Tell Ray that I miss him every day. I am glad to know that I helped him. But I still would have him back if I could."

"I am getting an image of a sliding glass door and a deck. Do you sit outside in the morning? I am also seeing a little garden with a bird-bath. Is this your home?"

"That describes my backyard," Donna shared with me.

"Ray is there with you. He is in the garden. I feel like you can feel his spirit there. I get the image of something in or about the garden. It looks like an angel. Ray is thanking you for this," I assured her.

Donna smiled for the first time and asked me, "Does he know that I planted the garden for him? I placed a small iron angel in the center of it. He loved the outdoors."

"Maybe the garden is a little piece of the field of flowers on the other side that you experienced in your dream," I told her. "You can meet him there, in that place of love."

Ray and Donna continued sharing for several more minutes, after which her father and a grandmother came in to express their love and offer comfort and guidance.

This session is a good example of a shared earth school lesson for both Donna and Ray. It tested and challenged their love for one another and illustrates the selfless love that we are asked to embody and express in this world.

The Spirit in Disabilities

Giving readings to people whose loved ones have disorders or disabilities that limit their mental functioning is similar in some ways to connecting to people on the other side. In both cases, I communicate with their spirit. Just as those on the other side have a broader and often enlightened view of their life, so do those who are living in the physical world with mental disabilities. They are, however, unable to put this awareness into words and action.

Before we are born, we choose to experience disabilities as part of our soul plan. We do this for many different reasons as there are spiritual lessons that mental, physical, and emotional challenges offer us. We may be learning how to have compassion, patience, and acceptance for ourselves and others. We may also choose to experience disabilities to help our family learn similar lessons in compassion, acceptance, and patience.

For many years I worked with people of all ages who were experiencing various disabilities. I learned a lot about myself and the power of our spirit.

In the following story, I share an unusual experience that I had while working at a treatment center for children. The depth of my interaction with the young man in this story was motivated by his father in spirit. However, this story is more about working with the spiritual energy and consciousness of someone who is in the physical realm.

Clay Communication

My first few years as an art therapist, I worked with children with severe and multiple disabilities part-time during the day. At this same time I gave psychic and medium readings in the evening and on the weekends. Although I did not initially think that there would be a connection between my intuitive interests and art therapy, they intersected, complemented, and beneficially enhanced one another. One of the classes that I went to once a week was in a residential treatment center for children with severe autism and more than one disability. The students stayed for up to six months at the center learning new skills and therapies.

Kyle, a thirteen-year-old boy who had been diagnosed with severe autism and a range of other disabilities, came to the center at about the same time I started working there. He rarely spoke and did not make eye contact or interact. He was physically present, but in most ways he was in another world entirely. If I put a crayon or paper in his hand, he would simply drop it and continue to stare at something above or beyond me.

Kyle exhibited an unusual behavior that was initially unsettling. While sitting in his chair, he would literally shoot straight up into the air a foot or so above his seat. He made an unusual whooshing sound while doing this. There was never any indication of when this would happen. He could be sitting staring at his desk and without notice launch into the air. I was young and eager to help and was intrigued by this odd phenomenon.

Through talking to his teachers, I discovered that Kyle was sent to the treatment center after the death of his father. He had three siblings at home, and his mother now needed to work full-time. The center was helping to find the mother support and help so that Kyle could return home.

After several months of working with Kyle, I felt as if I had made no progress with him. He still did not make eye contact with me and seemed to have no awareness of the art supplies that I encouraged him to hold, mold, and create with.

One night I had a dream about Kyle. Although it was fuzzy and the message unclear, I knew that his father who had passed over was trying to get my attention. I did not know why, and in a few days I no longer thought much about it. A few weeks after this dream, as I was getting ready to begin a medium session with a client, I again felt the presence of who I believed to be Kyle's father. I sent a message to him that I would connect with him after my sessions.

When I was done for the day, I closed my eyes, said a prayer, and invited Kyle's father's spirit to come close. I immediately felt the presence of the same spirit who had come to me a few hours earlier. Although I had never met him in the physical realm, when he introduced himself I knew it was Kyle's father. Through a combination of telepathy and clairvoyance, he communicated a surprising message to me.

"I want you to help Kyle," he said.

"I am trying," I tried to assure him. "I do not know what else to do." I was not sure what he wanted from me. I then listened for any more communication from him. What I received surprised me.

An intense image suddenly emerged. In it, I saw Kyle with what looked like dark-red cylinder-shaped beings spinning and surrounding him. They were all around him, erratically moving in the same way that I had seen him do many times. I understood better the source of Kyle's strange spinning. It appeared to be coming from these odd bug-like beings.

His father again addressed me. "Kyle has negative and dark energy attachments. They need to be released. Will you help him?" he asked me.

"Can you help from your side?" I sent his father the message. I assumed that the other side might be more capable of dealing with this than I was in the physical realm.

"I am doing what I can from my side. Others are helping, too. Can you help us?"

I was not sure what I could do, but I sent Kyle's father the message that I would try. In my work as a psychic and medium, from time to time I have come across people who have negative and dark attachments. Almost always these people are suffering in a variety of ways. They may be confused and disorganized, depressed, anxious, or physically ill. Negative attachments are not the cause of disabilities, and not all people who have disabilities suffer from attachments. Yet when an attachment is present, it can become a dominant force in an individual's quality of life.

I scanned Kyle's body and began to go through a process of spirit de-possession. In my mind's eye, I saw an image of Kyle. I invoked the presence of Archangel Michael and his healing angels and asked them to purge Kyle's energy field of these dark entities. While unusual images of darkness and light flashed in my inner sight, I felt surges of healing energy and activity taking place. I continued to meditate and spiritually work with him for the next several days. The day before I was to go back to the school, I still felt resistance and a struggle taking place within him. I prayed for him and sent him love, and for the first time I felt his spirit reach out to me. He was very sweet and aware of what was taking place. I could not clearly communicate with him, but I felt a connection to him that I had not felt before. I felt genuine love and gratitude coming from him.

The next day, I went into the school almost expecting Kyle to greet me. Of course, he did not. Instead, he sat in his usual seat staring out the window. When it was time for me to work with him, I sat down and handed him a lump of clay. He stuck his fingers in it and eventually scooped it up into both hands and made it into a ball. This was more than he had done in the past, and I was happy that we had gotten this far. I left him with the clay and made my rounds to check on the other children. I returned several minutes later. Lying on his desk was a clay figure. It looked surprisingly similar to the cylinder-shaped attachments that I had clairvoyantly seen in Kyle's energy field. I had been working for a week to detach these bug-like beings, and I was startled to see a clay replica of one sitting on his desk.

I looked at Kyle hoping that he would make eye contact with me. Instead, he looked above me, below me, and to the side, but not directly in my eyes. But he did speak. Over and over he said the word "demon."

I could hardly believe what I was hearing. Despite his severe disabilities, his spirit was awake and present. He did know what was happening, and I felt that he wanted me to know this. When our class time was over, I carefully put his clay demon in my bag. I later placed it on an altar in my home, where it stayed for many years.

Kyle's behavior did not radically change after this. He never made eye contact with me, and he still rocked back and forth and seemed distant. But I never saw him abruptly shoot up in the air suspended above his seat again, and he was visibly more relaxed. His hands no longer curled into tight fists, and his neck and back no longer seemed to be muscularly strained and tight.

I do not know why Kyle's soul chose a life of disabilities and limitations. But during the time that I worked with him, I learned and grew in many ways. I understood better the special energy nature of those who similarly struggle and the love and that we can mutually exchange.

Invoking Archangel Michael

Archangel Michael is a protective spiritual presence who is fearless and assertive. He is the angel to call upon if you feel a negative or dark presence or spirit present. All you need to do is send him a message, and he will immediately draw close. Ask for his help in detaching and removing any influence that is attached to you or your home, animals, or possessions. Allow his angels to surround you with their healing light. Michael encases negative beings and transports them into the light of the heavens, where they can heal and transform. You will feel a sense of ease and calmness when this happens. As the divine patrol of the spiritual realms, Michael can also help loved ones who get lost on the way to the heavens after their passing.

11

WANDERING SPIRITS: HELPING LOST SPIRITS

~~~~~~~~~~~~~~~~~~~~~~~~~~~~~~

My mother passed over to the other side on August 27, 2001. She had been diagnosed with colon cancer a year earlier. I woke up the morning that she died knowing that she would leave the physical world that day. I could feel it. Even though I had been working with the spirit realm for many years, never before had spiritual energy moved me in this way. I sat down to meditate to better understand and tune in to the strange sensations that I was experiencing. As soon as I closed my eyes, I felt what I can best describe as an unrelenting, powerful energy vacuum. I knew that my mother had no choice but to leave the physical body. She was being pulled into the spirit realm. I realized that it would be impossible to resist this intense force. When it is our time, we must go over. There is no negotiating. I was humbled by the magnitude of this power. My mother died several hours later. As another unexpected gift, I felt it when she was in the light.

In New Age and metaphysical circles, the term "the light" is used to describe our spirit realm home. Also referred to as heaven, the divine realm, paradise, the source of all life or bliss, and many other names, the light is the source of all love and wisdom and is our eternal residence. When my mother passed over, I became more aware of why it is called the light. In an unexpected synergetic energy connection with her, I felt the love that she was surrounded by. I knew that she was not alone and that her suffering and pain were over. I clairvoyantly saw radiating and pulsating light. Her spirit was lifted into another dimension, and she was floating in a sea of translucent energy. Love and deep peace surrounded her. It was a wonderful gift to feel and know what she experienced during her transition.

The force of energy that I felt when my mother passed over was transformative. Just as we depend on air, food, and water to maintain our physical body, the light is a vibrant source of energy beyond anything that we can fully comprehend. When it is our time to make our transition, the physical body drops away and only the energy body remains. The spirit realm has a natural cycle of change similar to that in nature. We cannot stop the sun from shining or the leaves from dropping away in the fall, and we cannot forestall our entrance into the spirit realm.

When we shed the body, we still have consciousness, free will, and we are very much ourselves. We can still make choices and decisions.

Wandering Spirits

Unfortunately, not everyone who passes over goes directly into the light. Instead, some souls after physical death wander confused in the lower vibrations of the astral realm. The astral realm is a vibration of energy that lies in between the physical realm and the higher vibrations of pure love and spiritual energy. When an individual passes over and stays in the astral realm, it is like being stuck between floors in an elevator. You can sense the heavier and denser physical vibration below, and you may be aware of what is above, but you are not fully on either level.

There are some people who, when they pass out of the physical body, simply refuse to believe that they are "dead." Often they believe that there is no such thing as life after death. After their physical body has died, they discover to their surprise that they are still very much alive. Many in this state erroneously reason that they cannot be dead. Other spirits remain close to the earthly realm because their consciousness was impaired at the time of their physical death. This can happen if someone passes over in an accident, has a cognitive illness, or is under the influence of drugs and alcohol. Their conscious awareness is clouded over or altogether detached from what is happening to the physical body. They have missed the process of their physical passing. Not aware of what is happening, they search for something familiar in the physical world to connect to.

Spirit Attachments

Spirits who have died in accidents or who have illnesses like dementia or Alzheimer's often wander in the astral realms trying to find their way to back to something familiar. They live in a kind of fog, not sure where they are. Because their consciousness is still attuned to the physical world, they can usually see people, their homes, and recognizable objects. Yet because they no longer have a physical body, their attempts to connect and live in the world as they used to are illusive and frustrating.

Those in the astral realm also need a source of energy. They no longer need food, water, and air to survive. Instead, they need the life force energy that is found in the light and in people who are still physical. To receive energy and feel connected to the physical realm, they often attach to a loving and dynamic person from whom they can absorb energy. They do not do this because they are negative or mean harm, but simply because they do not know what else to do. Being connected in this way is calming and helps them to feel comforted.

Lost and wandering souls in the astral realm may also attach to a particular location that people frequent or one that has a buildup of psychic energy. I have encountered spirit wanderers in churches, spiritual retreat centers, historic battlefields, and energy centers like Machu Picchu, the Mayan ruins, and Sedona, Arizona. Wandering souls can also attach to physical objects, especially mirrors, electrical appliances, and jewelry.

I once had a woman contact me after she and her family had experienced alarming phenomena. Her quiet suburban home had been turned upside down by sudden and strange occurrences. One morning she awoke to find all of the clothes in her closet off the hangers and lying on the floor. Her children started to wake up in the middle of the night, crying and insisting that there was a little boy in their room going through their toys. The fire alarm in her home started to spontaneously go off at random times, and the sound of running footsteps could be heard in all parts of the house. She sent me several photographs of flashes and streaks of color that everyone had begun to see in the home.

When I clairvoyantly tuned in to the energy in her home, I immediately saw two young children running and playing. I also got the impression that they had come into her home through an old television. When I asked her about this, she told me that a friend had given her an old black and white television that she had found at a home auction. A collector of memorabilia, she was thrilled to have it. I helped the children find their way into the light, and the house settled back down to normal.

Ghosts

Ghosts are a little different than spirit wanderers. They are usually aware that they no longer have a physical body, but they just do not want to leave the earth. There are many reasons for their clinging to the physical world. Sometimes ghosts do not feel as if they are "good" enough to go to heaven. Often they were religious individuals who believed in a hell. Out of fear of spending eternity burning or in the company of a devil, they hold fast to the material world.

There are some ghosts who do not want to give up their earthly possessions or allow others to live in what they consider to be their homes. Usually stubborn spirits, they like to scare those in the physical world and create all kinds of commotion. Because of their refusal to evolve and leave the earth, they can become very good at slamming doors, making creepy noises, creating cold and warm spots or breezes of air, touching people, and causing all kinds of bizarre, frightening, and weird phenomena. Over centuries, some have had a lot of time to practice interrupting and creating mayhem in the physical realm. Yet however scary they may appear to be, people in the physical body have dominion over the physical world. Ghosts gain power and energy by provoking fear. Once you become aware that ghosts have no real power, their ability to create havoc usually disappears.

When a soul does not go over to the other side, their consciousness does not evolve. They remain in the mental and emotional state that they were in when they "died." This is why many ghosts seem to be reliving their lives over and over, as if they were still in the same situation and conditions. They may be suffering through a battle that ended decades ago, still lost and looking for their mother or father, or drifting in a shadowy fog between realms. Because their consciousness is still attuned to and focused on the physical realm, they desperately need our help.

The following session illustrates how helpful we can be to those trapped in this in-between state.

Please Enter

I had given a few readings to Anna. A nurse supervisor at the Veterans Hospital for many years, she sounded distressed when she contacted me for another session.

"I just feel as if something is off. I cannot describe it," she told me. "Can we do a short session to find out what is going on?"

Because I knew Anna to be a down-to-earth and practical, intuitive woman, I gave her my first opening. When she came into my office, she did not look like her usual spunky self. Her skin was a little ashen and she told me that she was tired all the time.

"I had a full checkup," she told me. "Blood work, tests, the whole thing. Except for high cholesterol, everything checked out fine. I wasn't surprised, though. Whatever is going on with me isn't a health problem. I just don't know what it is."

I began the session with a short prayer. Not knowing what to expect, I remained open-minded and adopted a receptive attitude. As I did this, a middle-aged man suddenly appeared.

"A man with slightly graying hair, about average height, just came in," I told Anna. "He looks a little confused. I hear the name 'Robert.' Does this mean anything to you?"

"Not that I can recall. I know a Robert, but he is a tall man with very little hair," Anna told me, looking a little confused.

"He is showing me what I believe to be your office. I see just one small window. It's not very big, and there is what looks like a poster of puppies on the wall. I see him sitting in a chair next to you," I told her.

"Yes, that sounds like my office. But I still cannot place a Robert. These days, people are in and out of my office all day. He could have been there and I just do not remember. Why is he here now? I don't understand," Anna said.

"He is telling me that he is waiting for you to tell him what to do and where to go. He thinks that you are in charge. He passed over, but I don't think he knows this."

I sent Robert a message asking him if he knew that he was no longer physically alive. He looked at me with an authoritative grin and told me that he would know if he was dead and that he was not.

"He doesn't realize that he has passed over," I told Anna. "My impression is that he thinks that he is in the hospital and that you are in charge. He is waiting for you to direct him as to where to go next. This is most likely why you are tired. He is following you around. Not knowing what else to do, he has attached himself to you."

"Can you do anything to help him?" Anna was understandably alarmed. "I know he needs direction, but I do not know how to help him."

I have encountered lost souls many times. Even though we tend to think of them as threatening and scary, they need help and direction. So I sent a message to my angels asking them to send someone from the light who Robert knew and trusted to help him cross over. In a moment, I felt the presence of what appeared to be his mother. Then Robert was gone.

"Robert's mother came for him. He has gone into the light," I told Anna.

"Thank you so much. I already feel better," she said with a sigh of relief.

I continued the session with Anna, discussing some other topics of interest. We talked to her mother on the other side, and she had some questions about her son. Anna left feeling much lighter and relieved to not have Robert connected to her.

I did not expect to hear from Anna and so was surprised when she contacted me less than a month later.

"I think he is back. I was feeling like my old self for a couple of weeks. Then out of nowhere, I started to feel tired and drained again. I woke up last night, and I felt that there was someone at the foot of the bed. I had the odd sense of a man staring at me. It scared me. I didn't know what to do. With as much confidence as I could muster, I told him to go away. But the next day, I felt that same feeling of being drained. Why is he back?" Anna asked.

I scheduled another session with Anna as soon as I could. When she came in to see me, the ashen, tired look was back. This time she was also frustrated and unsettled. This, too, proved to be a surprising session.

"I don't feel as if Robert is back. There is someone with you, but it is not him. This man is older, and it does not appear as if he knows where he is," I shared with Anna.

"Who is he? Why does this keep happening?" she frustratingly asked me.

"I get the impression that he, too, died in the hospital but did not go into the light."

I went through the same process of helping this older gentleman over.

"A sweet woman who feels like his wife is helping him," I told her. "He seems very happy and relieved to see her."

"Why are these lost souls coming to me?" Anna was still confused. "How can I stop this from happening? I want to be helpful, but enough is enough. I feel like I am the Holiday Inn of the spirit world."

"Quite often, people who pass over who are confused or afraid of the afterlife are attracted to loving and strong people like you. They feel safe and comforted being in your presence. I feel that these two souls died in the hospital where you work. I keep seeing them in your office with you," I explained to Anna.

"A thought just came to me. Do you think that this has anything to do with the location of my new office? I was recently transferred downstairs. My office sits directly above the hospital morgue, which is in the basement. When I think about it, all of this started after I changed offices." Anna sounded nervous as she explained this to me.

"That would make sense," I told her. "When people pass over and do not go immediately into the light, they may try to stay with their body. Once in the morgue, they sense you above them and perceive you as a source of love and positivity."

"So now what do I do? I need my job and I can't change offices."

"You can do the same process that I did with them," I explained to Anna. "You already are aware of their presence. When you feel heavier energy connecting to you, ask your angels to send someone from the light who knows this person and whom they would trust to come and get them. Also, every morning before you go to work, imagine white light completely surrounding you. Ask your angels to protect you, and set the intent that only what is in your highest good can come close."

Anna did not look convinced. "I will give it a try," she said.

After this session, I expected to hear a progress report from Anna. Instead, I was surprised when I did not receive a call or e-mail from her. Then several months later, I bumped into her at a bookstore event.

"How are you?" I asked. "Are all things clear?"

"I have been meaning to call you," she told me. "When I went back to work after our last session, I got another visitor. I did what you told me to do. I saw myself surrounded by white light and asked for protection, and it seemed to work. I guess I got lazy, though, and forgot to keep it up. A few weeks later, I woke up in the middle of the night with the eerie feeling that I was not alone. I realized that someone had followed me home from the hospital again. I did what you suggested and asked an angel to help this soul go into the light. It was very quick. I felt that whoever was with me went over right away.

"As I lay there in bed half-asleep, an idea came to me. Of course, it may have been my angel's idea. I saw a big white door suspended in the air with a sign on it that said 'Please Enter.' I looked inside the door, and it was filled with white light. I knew that this doorway would lead these lost souls to the other side. When I went to work the next day, I visualized this door in my office. Whenever I feel even a hint of a soul drifting up from the basement, I direct them to the door. It seems to be working. I guess there really can be a doorway to heaven."

Earth Lesson: Recognizing Home

When I first traveled through Mexico many years ago, my bus pulled into a busy and hectic station in Mexico City. After it dropped me off, I watched it drive away with no passengers aboard. I had no idea where to find my next bus. It took over an hour, but I went to every bus terminal in the station and looked for the route that would take me to my destination. I could not find it. With my limited Spanish, I asked a few people where I could catch my bus to Oaxaca. Although I could figure out how to ask my question, I could not understand the answer. With a fair amount of pointing, gesturing, and deciphering a few words, I finally understood that I was at the wrong bus station. In the midst of my confusion, a man came forward and explained to me in English how to get to where I needed to be. I was quite grateful, as without his help, I would have likely continued to walk aimlessly around the station for hours wondering what to do next.

When people pass over and do not go directly into the light, their experience may be somewhat like this. Without clear direction and the ability to communicate with anyone who can tell them the way to go, they can wander around feeling disconnected and lost. When we encounter a soul who has lost their way, we are participating in a shared earth lesson.

Those of us in the physical world are learning that we have the ability to assist and help others in the spirit realm. When you accept this lesson, you realize your spiritual power.

People often ask me why angels do not simply reach out and gather up all the lost and wandering spirits and bring them into the light. I have to admit that I have wondered this myself. After working with many lost spirits who have not gone into the light after their physical death, I have come to the realization that they are still focused on a physical perception. They cling to the physical world because this is the only reality that they are aware of.

Mediums traverse the physical and spiritual and travel between the realms as messengers. We speak both languages. Just as I listened to the Spanish-speaking man who explained to me in English where to go to catch my bus, the dead listen to us.

We all share the same space. It is our perception that determines what we experience. A spirit who chooses to stay here clinging to their home or possessions can only accept the help of an angel if they recognize the angel. Because they still have a physical perspective, we are still a part of their reality. They see us, hear us, and often try to interact with us, even if it is just to scare us away.

If you have an interest in ghosts and other spiritual beings, then an aspect of your life plan is to learn the earth lesson that you, too, are a spirit.

Spirit Responsibility

With the awareness that before and after your physical life you are a spirit being comes responsibility. Instead of viewing ghosts and spiritual phenomena as terrifying and strange, it is important to own your power to assist and help where needed. One of my pet peeves is the further alienation of lost souls by ghost hunters, who seek only the thrill of encountering the dead. When we are only interested in capturing proof of the existence of ghosts, we miss a valuable opportunity to be of service. It is an act of love and spiritual maturity to help and assist lost and wandering spirits into the place of love and peace where they can join with their loved ones, heal, and evolve. It is a hell to be trapped between realms. Spirit soldiers wandering in battlefields, children waiting for decades for their parents to come home, lost spirits at sea, and lonely ghosts living in attics and basements need our help.

There are some ghosts and negative entities that refuse to go into the light, and they are best left alone. But for the most part, these lost souls need to go home. I rarely encounter a wandering spirit who stays here once a loved one from the light comes for them. I consider it almost child abuse to not help a lost child spirit into the light. I know that it is not always easy to sense the presence of spirits and to know who they are and if they are willing to go over. However, when in doubt, always try to cross them over. If you suspect that you are in the presence of a spirit, know that you can be of service. In the last chapter of this book, I include an exercise to show you how to help wandering and lost spirits.

Your Eternal Home

We are fortunate that we have such a beautiful, peaceful, and loving home to return to one day. The physical realm is a lovely place with unspeakable joys, laughter, and triumphs. Yet it pales in comparison to the spiritual realm of bliss and love. There is no evidence that you will find in the physical world to prove the existence of the celestial heavenly home. It is only in your heart that you know this truth.

Those who persistently deny the existence of life beyond the physical take the risk of having to learn one of the earth school's most difficult lessons. When we cling to the idea that the physical expression of life is all that there is, we might confront a bit of a dilemma when we pass out of the body. If our expectation after physical death is that there is no life and that we cease to exist, then we can go into a sleep-like state of unconsciousness. If we resist the spirit's impulse to ascend into the light, we might aimlessly wander or lose our way in the astral realms.

Eventually all lost and wandering spirits make their way into the light. Unfortunately, it may take some time. However, angels and loved ones on the other side never give up trying to assist the lost ones. Once we become aware that we are spirit and that the physical body is just a convincing disguise that will one day fall away, we can never be lost. When you embrace the unseen spiritual realm as part of the totality of life, you can move through existence as a free spirit.

The following session shows the simple, loving way that we can naturally guide our loved ones after their transition into the spirit realm.

Feeding the Dogs

A successful businesswoman and CEO of a technology recruiting service, Karla was a no-nonsense kind of person. At our first session, she came into my office, sat down, and started to question me about my credentials. Karla scheduled a session with me to gain insight into her business and map a strategy for the future. Most of our time together was devoted to her career. As we were coming to a close, an older woman in spirit gently made herself known.

"There is woman coming in from the other side. She feels like a grandmother. I hear the name 'Marge.'"

"That is my mother's mother," Karla explained. "Her name is Marge."

"She wants to thank you. She is sending you love and gratitude," I told her.

"I cannot imagine what she is thanking me for," Karla said with a surprised look on her face.

Marge responded and I began to see images and receive more information. I told Karla, "Your grandmother is showing me an image of a car. I feel as if there may have been an accident. I am feeling a lot of confusion with your grandmother. She is telling me that you helped her. I get the impression that this is what she is thanking you for. Does this make any sense to you?"

For the first time since our session began, Karla showed some emotion. She looked down, cleared her throat, and told me, "My grandmother died in a car accident. She was driving down a country road near her home and lost control of the car. No one quite knows what happened. Her car was found down an embankment up against a big boulder. It was very sad. She was such an independent woman. I am not sure how I helped her. I was miles away. I didn't hear of the accident until later in the day."

Marge was persistent. I told Karla, "I keep seeing an image of the car. I get the impression that your grandmother did not know that she had died. Did she have dogs? I feel that she wanted to get to her dogs. I see her trying to walk home," I explained.

A moment of recognition seemed to come over Karla. She anxiously shared with me, "Oh, you're kidding. I thought that was a dream. A few nights after my grandmother died, I had what I thought was a dream about her. I saw her pacing back and forth. I heard her talking about her dogs. She wanted to feed them, but she couldn't find them. I told her that the dogs were fine and that my cousin was taking care of them. Her dogs meant everything to her. She had two little poodles. My grandmother looked at me relieved when I told her this. I told her that I was happy to see her and that she looked very much alive. With a surprised look on her face, she asked me if she was dead. I told her she died in a car accident. I asked her if she had seen Grandpa yet. He died about ten years ago. Then I felt him close, too. That was the end of the dream."

"I am not sure that was a dream," I tried to explain to Karla. "Your grandmother was lost. I feel like she didn't know that she had died. She wanted to make sure her dogs were all right. Instead of going to the light, she wandered around looking for them. You helped her more than you know."

Karla still looked confused. "Did she really come to me? Did I really help her?" she asked me.

"Your grandmother is thanking you for reuniting her with your grandfather. It might have seemed like a dream, but she really came to you looking for help."

With a bit more confidence, Karla said, "I am so glad that I helped her. She was always so caring and good to me. It would be just like her to want to make sure her dogs were being taken care of. Are you certain that she is on the other side and with my grandfather?"

"She is in the light," I assured Karla. "She says that you were the one that she knew could help her. Have you thought of getting a dog yourself? Your grandmother seems to be encouraging this."

"I never wanted any pets," Karla told me. "I am so busy with work, it doesn't seem fair. Recently a friend of mine adopted a rescue dog. For a moment I thought about it. Even called up the rescue group and asked them what dogs they had available. I almost did it. Then I came to my senses and realized that a cat may be more my style. That was probably my grandmother influencing me. She loved her dogs. Tell her maybe one of these days I will get one for myself."

"Your grandmother just wants you to always feel loved," I told her.

There Are Two

The following session moved me beyond my preconceived ideas of what is possible. It also made me more aware of the challenges that are taking place in our midst without our ever knowing it.

An attractive woman in her early forties, Rachel came to see me on the recommendation of a friend. I started the session and quickly realized that she had a concern about her son.

"Do you have a son?" I asked her.

She quickly responded, "I have three sons and a daughter."

"This son is about six years old and has dark hair," I explained.

"That is Jack," Rebecca anxiously answered. "He is the reason that I am here."

"I get the impression that he has emotional mood swings that he cannot control. I see him not sleeping well. He is anxious and excited at night and then tired during the day. He has some food allergies. Yet there is something else going on with him that I have not seen before. His energy is very confused," I explained.

"He has had a physical and seen a psychologist, and I have done everything I can think of to help him. Something is off. I don't know what. He is distracted and having trouble in school. I was told that you could help us. Do you think that he needs medication? I don't know what else to do." Rachel looked concerned as she told me this.

I refocused my attention and was surprised by what I intuitively received. "There are two," I told her. "There are two spirits inside of Jack." As I shared this, more information came forward. "I feel that another soul went into Jack's body soon after he was born or maybe right before he was born. I see you in a hospital. There was a woman giving birth at about the same time that you were. Something unexpected happened. I feel that there was a problem with the delivery. The baby didn't make it. The soul of that baby girl passed into Jack. She was lost. I feel as if that soul believed that this was her body. Both of the souls are still inside of his one body."

Despite this startling information, Rebecca did not look as taken aback as I thought she might. She told me, "I heard rumors of a stillborn at the hospital when I was there. It's odd, but it makes sense. Something seemed off at his birth. I was only in labor for three hours. I had no problems, but I felt very uneasy. Like there was something happening that I could not control."

I explained to her, "I am going to help the soul that came in at birth go into the light. It will not take long."

I asked for an angel and Mother Mary to carry this trapped soul to the light. There was no resistance. I felt readiness and a sense of relief from the trapped soul. In a moment, I felt that she was gone.

I told Rebecca, "The other soul is in the light. It was not difficult. You should see immediate changes in Jack. He still needs to go through a process of integration and fully spread out into his body, as he has never had this opportunity. But he will be more grounded, and his true personality will begin to surface."

"I am not as surprised as you might think," she told me. "Jack has had such odd behavior. Call it mother's intuition, but I have felt that something was odd for a long time."

This was a lot for Rebecca to take in. However, I seemed to be a little more surprised than she was. We talked some more about Jack and what to expect. She thanked me and we ended the session.

The following day I received an e-mail from Rebecca. In it, she said: "The evening after our session, I asked Jack how he was feeling and if he felt any different that evening than he had that morning. Jack has had a lot of health issues, so this is not an unusual question for me to ask him. He said that he had been feeling *weird* and further that he felt that something important was missing and it made him feel different. To me, this was confirmation that this extra soul had gone to the light. I found myself happy and relieved as well as strangely a little bit sad."

I thanked Rebecca for letting me know how Jack was doing and asked her to let me know if anything else came up.

A couple of days later while I was doing my morning meditation, I received a message about Jack. I felt as if he was trying to convince this other spirit to come back into his body. An hour or so later, I received another e-mail from Rebecca.

"Today, Jack slept until 10:00 a.m. He has never slept that late in his life and normally wakes at 7:30. I asked him how he was feeling, and he told me that he was feeling good. I am a bit worried, though, because he told me that he figured out what was wrong. He said that there was a spirit missing, a good one. But then he told me that it was back, so now everything was okay. I am really concerned. What do I do? Do you think the spirit came back?" she asked.

I immediately contacted Rebecca and told her that during my meditation I, too, felt that Jack was trying to convince this soul to come back into his body.

I advised her to sit Jack down and explain to him that the spirit that was close was his friend but that she was meant to be a spirit and not live inside of his body anymore.

I told her, "Tell him that he will feel her presence close to him from time to time, but she needs to be free. She is in the spirit world, and he is in the physical world. She loves him and wants him to be happy as a boy in the world, because she is happy as a spirit. Jack might get sad and upset, but be firm but gentle in reminding him that this is how it has to be."

A day later I heard back from Rebecca. She told me, "I did speak with Jack, and he was initially very resistant and said that he did not want to do as I was asking. In the end, he said that he understood and would let the spirit be free."

I hope you have been inspired by these client sessions and see a bit of yourself in them. You are important to your friends, family, and community both here in the physical realm and on the other side. In the next section, you can explore and develop your natural medium abilities. I have included a quiz to help you better explore your medium type, as well as instructional exercises, visualizations, and meditations. In the last chapter, there are meditations and practices to empower you to directly help those on the other side.

Section 3

DEVELOP YOUR NATURAL
MEDIUM ABILITIES

12

DISCOVER YOUR MEDIUM TYPE

The ability to communicate with the other side may seem like a mysterious gift that just a few people possess. During medium sessions, clients will sometimes ask me if they, too, might have this ability. They may have experienced instances of direct contact with the other side or moments of fleeting connection, and they wish to harness their medium potential.

You may wish to explore your medium ability for a few different reasons. You may be curious and want to learn more about the spiritual realm, you may wish to feel closer to your loved ones who have passed over, or you may desire to become a professional medium and help others to connect with their loved ones.

There are people like myself who from an early age have been aware of and able to communicate with those on the other side. Yet everyone shares this innate gift. With a bit of dedication, understanding, and practice, it is possible to develop your latent abilities and become a more skilled medium.

How Your Loved Ones Get Your Attention

Developing your innate medium abilities begins with becoming aware of the often subtle and elusive interactions that you are most likely already experiencing with those on the other side. Sometimes we have surprising encounters with the spirit realm that are unmistakable and easily recognizable. You may visually see a deceased loved one, smell their favorite perfume, or hear their voice speaking to you. I had a client tell me that while on the phone with her daughter, the reception went blank for a moment and she heard what sounded like her husband who had passed over say, "I love you."

These kinds of encounters are exciting but not as common as those times when you suspect that a loved one is close but are just not sure. A loved one's presence may be experienced as a feeling of comfort or warmth in your heart, a penny you find on your doorstep, or a light in your home that flickers. Have you ever had a dream of a loved one that seemed to be more real than a dream? You felt their presence and their love and awoke feeling as if you had been with them. That spontaneous insight about someone on the other side that helped you to understand them better may be a loved one sending you a thought message. While reading a self-help book or practicing meditation, have you ever had the feeling that there was someone beside you, learning along with you?

It is easy to discount these types of interactions, yet your loved ones reach out to you in these and other subtle ways. Even when you are not aware that you are doing so, you are intuitively receiving the thoughts, love, warmth, and comfort of those who have passed over. Intuition is an innate sense that we all possess which bypasses conscious reasoning and empowers us to connect with our loved ones in spirit.

The Four Medium Types

Intuition is a fascinating and enriching aspect of our true and authentic nature. It is the key to understanding ourselves, our world, and the world of spirit. When we die, we shed the heavier and denser shell of the physical body. What is left is the energy body, or spirit, an intricate system of consciousness, love, and wisdom. The energy body is not confined by the material laws of matter. It allows us to connect and communicate with others in the physical and nonphysical realms through energetic intuitive impulses. Even though we tend to think of ourselves as physical beings, we are also energy beings. The physical part of you is just a temporary earth suit. It will one day be shed and what will be left is the pure energy and spiritual vibration of who you really are. You are able to intuitively connect with your loved ones in spirit because you, too, are an energy being. The physical body is simply a convincing decoy. Those in spirit communicate to you through their intuition, and you receive their messages through your intuition.

Just as we all have a particular learning modality, we also have a specific way that we absorb intuitive energy vibrations. Some people learn best when material is presented visually. Others are more auditory and like to listen to lectures or taped information. Many people are kinesthetic and do best with a hands-on approach to learning.

Similarly, there are four basic ways that we intuit. We may absorb energy vibration through our thoughts, our emotions, the physical body, and our energy field. An emotional intuitive is attuned to emotional energy. A mental intuitive intuits thoughts and mental energy. A spiritual intuitive intuits through the energy field, or spirit, while a physical intuitive absorbs energy into the body.

Although you likely intuit through all four of these modalities, there will be one or two that are stronger and that you are more naturally attuned to. You connect and communicate with those who have passed over into the spiritual realm through these same intuitive modalities. I call these different ways of naturally connecting with the other side your *medium type.*

To gain confidence and trust your ability to communicate with the other side takes practice and an open attitude. Do not expect to immediately get the kind of verifiable evidence that your logical brain may desire. It is best to become sensitive to the shifting vibrations and energy sensations that you may experience and quiet the thinking and analyzing mind. You may want to see, hear, and talk to those in the spirit realm like you do with the people in your day-to-day life on earth. This may or may not happen, and most likely it will take some practice and further development to fully trust what you receive. To begin, let go of your expectations of how you want to communicate and discover how you already are communicating.

Medium Type Quiz

This quiz will help you to determine if you are primarily an emotional, mental, physical, or spiritual medium. There is no right or wrong answer. Just go with the answer that feels most right. Record your scores in the answer grid at the end of the quiz.

Scoring:
3 points = most of the time
2 points = sometimes
1 point = rarely

1. Just thinking of my loved ones on the other side provokes an emotional reaction in me.
2. I usually know what my loved ones on the other side would think about my decisions.
3. Loved ones in spirit try to get my attention by blinking the electrical appliances or lights in my home.
4. I see those in the spirit realm as streaks of light or orbs.
5. I easily forgive the wrongs done to me by those who have passed over.

6. Since my family and friends have died, I find myself wanting to learn more about them.

7. I feel closer to my loved ones on the other side when I hold one of their possessions.

8. I have memories of living on other nonphysical planes of existence.

9. I feel the love and care of my family and friends who are on the other side.

10. I carry on conversations with loved ones who have passed over.

11. I sometimes can smell the perfume, cigar aroma, or another scent of a loved one who has passed over.

12. My loved ones often visit me in my dreams.

13. I feel the love of the heavens and long to share it with others.

14. My loved ones send me signs through synchronicity or meaningful coincidence.

15. I often sense the presence of spirits.

16. I often catch a glimpse of my loved ones in spirit.

17. My heart fills with love in unexpected moments and I know that a loved one is with me.

18. I want to learn more about what happens to us after we die.

19. When I go to my loved one's favorite places, I feel their presence there.

20. From a young age, I have known when angels are present.

21. I want to help heal the grief and loss that people feel when a loved one transitions.

22. I want to understand the mysteries of the universe.

23. Nature spirits communicate with me.

24. I visit the spiritual realms in my dreams and daydreams.

25. I desire to feel the love of my loved ones on the other side.

26. I want to know what my loved ones on the other side think about the current conditions in my life.

27. I want to feel the presence of my loved ones who are in the spirit realm close to me.

28. I want to see my loved ones who have passed over.

29. I intuitively feel the love of those on the other side.

30. I have an intuitive connection to the one mind and consciousness.

31. I feel the presence of the divine within nature.

32. I have always felt that I am a visitor here. My true home is in the spirit realm.

Scoring:
3 points = most of the time
2 points = sometimes
1 point = rarely

	A		B		C		D
1		*2*		*3*		*4*	
5		*6*		*7*		*8*	
9		*10*		*11*		*12*	
13		*14*		*15*		*16*	
17		*18*		*19*		*20*	
21		*22*		*23*		*24*	
25		*26*		*27*		*28*	
29		*30*		*31*		*32*	
Total							

Add your totals for columns A, B, C, and D.

If your highest sum is

A: You are an emotional medium

B: You are a mental medium

C: You are a physical medium

D: You are a spiritual medium

In the next chapter, the characteristics and unique abilities and challenges of each medium type are explored and explained.

13

YOUR MEDIUM POTENTIAL

W e all intuit information. Most of the time we are not aware that we are absorbing energy information and connecting with those in the spirit realm. Knowing the natural way that you intuit will help you to recognize when and how you are already acting as medium. With this awareness, you can begin to further develop and refine your abilities.

You are likely to have one or two medium types that are stronger than the others. It is best to be comfortable with each mode of intuiting, and the ideal is to be balanced in all four types. This will empower you to be able to consciously communicate with the other side when and how you choose. Keep in mind that those in spirit communicate through similar types of modalities. Some on the other side transmit messages through visual images and others through mental thought, and some are more attuned to emotional energy.

Each medium type has specific intuitive abilities and potential obstacles for development. Read the following descriptions for each of the four types. Although you are likely to see a bit of yourself in each one, you will also be better able to clarify your primary way of communicating with the other side.

The Healers

Emotional Intuitives

An emotional intuitive is an emotional sponge. These people soak in the feelings and emotions of those close and far away. It does not matter if a loved one is in the next room or thousands of miles away; their ability to intuit others' emotions is remarkable. Without knowing that they are doing so, they often absorb the emotional energy of a situation, a group of people, or even past and future events. They tend to be sensitive and responsive to others' needs regardless of time and space. If you get a call from a friend who says that she has been thinking of you and wonders if everything is all right, she is most likely an emotional intuitive.

Emotional Mediums

Emotional mediums feel and absorb the emotional energy of those who have passed over. Have you ever felt an unexpected and sudden surge of love flow through your heart? Have you ever woken up in the morning and seemingly out of nowhere you were able to let go of ongoing anger and forgive someone on the other side who had caused you pain? When you think of loved ones who are no longer in the physical realm, do you ever feel flooded with emotions? These kinds of confusing experiences might very well be real encounters with loved ones on the other side. Because emotional mediums are intuitively wired to communicate and connect with the spirit realm through emotional energy, they feel more and more deeply than the other types. Emotional mediums tend to be compassionate, empathetic, and attuned to the higher states of divine love.

Emotional mediums can feel the present-time emotions of those in spirit, although this may seem like simply the recollection of good feelings or random memories. Without knowing the source of their emotions, emotional mediums may feel spontaneous feelings of joy and bliss and the assurance that they are loved. A good example of this is my mother, who felt the love of my grandfather in spirit. Even though she was still angry and resentful after many years, divine love crept into her heart. Although she did not consciously know that she was intuitively connecting with him, the love that she felt coming from his spirit helped her to heal.

Our loved ones send waves of positive emotional energy to us when we are scared, confused, or in pain, or when we need to undertake a difficult task. When we feel overwhelmed and alone, they surround us with feelings of peace and calm reassurance. An emotional medium is the most likely type to receive and feel these emotional gifts from the other side.

Understanding Emotion

If you are an emotional medium, it is important to learn how to balance the deluge of emotions that you often intuit. The challenge is to both feel the emotional energy that you are receiving and detach and understand it at the same time. Otherwise you are likely to feel overwhelmed with emotion and not be able to differentiate your personal feelings from the emotional energy that you are absorbing from the spiritual realm. I know that it seems like a paradox to be able to both feel and detach at the same time. But once you become more aware of the innate way that you connect with those on the other side, the better able you will be to sense the difference between your emotions and those that you are receiving from the spirit realm. Even if you are not sure where the emotions that you are feeling are coming from, this is the beginning step to further medium communication. Once you become aware that what you are feeling is coming to you from an outer source, you can begin to dialogue and elicit other information. Your ability to intuit the emotions of those in spirit is the doorway through which other medium abilities can be developed.

Conduits of Divine Love

Emotional mediums tend to be sensitive to the needs of others and may seek to become a professional medium in order to help heal those here and in the hereafter. With a soulful desire to be of service, emotional mediums often use their intuition to promote reconciliation and forgiveness between those in the physical realm and their family members on the other side. They know that it is never too late to heal wounds and resolve disagreements and misunderstandings.

A session with an emotional medium can be transformative. To varying degrees, most mediums are aware of the emotions of those in spirit. This is often referred to as *clairsentience*. An emotional medium, however, is an expert in adeptly handling the wide range of emotions that are often generated when people are reunited with their departed loved ones. Their sessions often provide a sense of healing and peace to everyone involved.

If you are an emotional medium, you may disregard your intuitive gifts as less genuine or authentic than the other kinds of medium skills. Because you do not see those on the other side sitting beside you or you do not catch the scent of their cologne or hear them speaking, it may not feel real to you. Yet intuitively tuning in to the vibrations of emotional energy is a powerful way to connect. Emotional mediums can heal the long-lasting pain and hurt between individuals regardless of time and space and bring closure to people who are deeply mourning their loved ones who have passed over. It is not just the words they speak. Emotional mediums exude love and forgiveness. In their presence, pain is released and healing and forgiveness emerge. Emotional energy is likely the most powerful energy that we experience and generate in both the physical and spiritual realms. An emotional medium is adept at harmonizing, balancing, understanding, and putting into words the complexities of emotionally charged energy. In this way, they mend, restore, and nurture those in the deepest states of grief and overwhelming loss.

Angels often use emotional mediums as conduits of divine love. These people are connected to the purest vibrations of love. It is their sustaining grace. Without it, they become depressed and ungrounded. Often overwhelmed by the depth of emotions that they unknowingly absorb, emotional mediums need to remember to open their heart, release the pain and wounds of others, and receive cosmic love.

The Knowers

Mental Intuitives

Mental intuitives intuit energy information through their thoughts. They are natural telepaths who knowingly and unknowingly send and receive thought messages. With the ability to simply know information and facts without knowing how they know, they are natural problem solvers. They are driven to understand and increase their knowledge and awareness in all areas. Attuned to the higher states of consciousness, mental intuitives can see the big picture and bring cohesive understanding to complex issues and situations.

Mental Mediums

Mental mediums are able to intuit the thoughts of and receive energy information from those in the spirit realm. However, they are not always aware that they are doing so. Have you ever been riding in a car or doing a mundane task while carrying on an inner conversation? New ideas, the solution to a pressing problem, or an aha moment suddenly emerges, bringing with it fresh insight. These moments of illumination might be coming to you from your Uncle Ed, your grandmother, your mom or dad, or even a spirit guide. A mental medium often unknowingly engages in an inner dialogue with those on the other side throughout the day. Because receiving the thoughts of others comes so easily to mental intuitives, they often do not believe that they are actually communicating with the other side. Mental mediums often doubt their intuitive ability. After receiving intuitive information, they will often tell me it was "all in their head." To which I say, "Exactly! You're a mental medium."

Mental mediums receive the thoughts of those in the spirit realm in a few different ways. Sometimes auditory intuitive messages can be heard as an inner voice. Other times it may seem as if intuitive messages are heard externally. Have you ever heard your name called, but you are alone? Many people hear messages from the spirit realm in this way. This is known as *clairaudience*. Mental mediums also receive spirit messages *telepathically*. Telepathic communication is the ability to send and receive thoughts back and forth from one mind to another or to know the thoughts of another or of a group. Mental mediums also have the ability to simply know and become aware of energy information, which is known as *claircognizance*. This can feel like a large bulk of knowledge has suddenly been dropped in your lap. Mental mediums tend to more easily receive facts and information like names and dates from those in the spirit realm than the other types.

Thought Messages from Spirit

Loved ones in spirit send us thought messages all the time. They love us and do all they can to help us. This is so common that we rarely realize the supernatural source of our thoughts and ideas. From their vantage point, they can often see what is coming our way, both the hurdles and the opportunities. Our loved ones try to alert, warn, and signal us of approaching positive, negative, and unexpected events. It can take a bit of training in the spirit realm for them to learn how to effectively do this. Unlike an emotional intuitive, who might feel fear or stress when they feel a warning coming to them from the spirit realm, a mental medium can often intuit information in a calm and decisive manner.

Because mental mediums are comfortable with processing thoughts and complicated information, spirit guides often work through them to bring useful guidance and enlightenment to others. Because of their innate connection with the mind and consciousness, mental mediums can also be interested in receiving wisdom and inspiration from otherworldly and extraterrestrial life forms. If you have the ability and passion to contribute and use what you intuitively receive in positive ways, your spirit guides may utilize you for a higher purpose.

Resistance and Other Obstacles

Like all of the medium types, the mental medium has a couple of obstacles to be mindful of. Because energy information tends to pour into their consciousness, mental mediums can become distracted and unfocused by the sheer volume of thoughts. At times they absorb so much thought energy that they become overwhelmed and are unable to make a decision or take action. In order to effectively understand the constant mind chatter that they might be experiencing, mental mediums have to learn to slow down, breathe, and clear their mind. Meditation can be very helpful.

Mental mediums tend to enjoy logic and rational thinking. They like patterns, systems, and thinking that make sense to them. To be a medium, you must, however, be comfortable with the abstract and not knowing. Intuiting information without attempting to prematurely understand and pin down what you receive is another challenge for the mental medium. Because of their inclination toward rational thinking, not all mental mediums believe that they have the ability to communicate with the other side. Without scientific proof that life after death exists, they may not believe that there is consciousness outside of the physical body.

Mental mediums may be skeptics who view psychic and medium ability as farfetched and delusional thinking. Their world is logical and rational, with no room for this kind of silliness. Acceptance of their innate medium ability does not always come easy. They will often deny and dismiss their own intuitive experiences as unreliable coincidences. Their doubts, however, do not always prevent the persistent flow and influx of other worldly thoughts, ideas, and insights from the other side. Mental mediums can live in a vigilant paradox of denial. While they readily receive information from the other side in the form of insights, ideas, and helpful information, they discredit the source. They may choose instead to attribute their flashes of intuitive brilliance to their individual thoughts. However, once they accept the possibility that they are intuiting information from nonphysical sources, mental mediums are quick studies who often rapidly develop their natural medium abilities.

Mental mediums are often motivated to become professional mediums by their thirst for knowledge and wisdom and to further explore the vast, unknown, and unseen world. They can be exceptional mediums who provide exacting information, unique ideas, and a cohesive understanding of the spirit realm.

The Manifesters

Physical Intuitives

Physical intuitives absorb and receive information energy primarily through their body and the physical world. They often describe their intuition as a gut feeling. Physical intuitives tend to unknowingly absorb the energy of others and their environment directly into their physical bodies. If they are surrounded by positive people, this will feel uplifting and energizing. In a negative or stressful environment they are likely to experience unexplained headaches or stomach problems or become tired. Physical intuitives also have a special connection to nature. Through the natural world—the stars, seas, animals, and plants—they receive cosmic energy and inspiration.

Physical Mediums

Have you ever wondered if something in nature like a bird, snake, cloud, or butterfly was sending you a message? Do you sometimes find coins, certain stones, or feathers on your path and wonder if someone on the other side sent them to you? Do the lights in your house sometimes blink or the chimes of a clock suddenly ring and you are certain someone in spirit is trying to get your attention? A physical medium often experiences more demonstrable psychic phenomena than the other types of mediums. Their loved ones in spirit are likely to try to contact them through blinking the lights in their home, creating static on the phone or television, and other unusual interruptions of electrical, Internet, and audio wavelengths. Physical mediums are also likely to naturally connect with those on the other side through synchronistic encounters with nature and material objects. Because their intuition is connected to the more dense vibration of the physical, their loved ones in spirit often use electric currents, animals (especially birds), coins, phone lines, and more physical phenomena to get their attention.

Psychometry

A physical medium communicates with those on the other side in a more somatic way than the other types. Their physical body is a finely tuned sensor that absorbs energy vibrations. Because of this, they are especially adept at connecting to the other side through psychometry. Psychometry is the ability to hold or touch an object or look at a photograph and receive intuitive energy vibrations from it. Many mediums connect to the spirit of their loved ones on the other side by holding a personal object or looking at a photograph. A ring, car keys, a piece of clothing, or a hairbrush are also good conductors.

Physical mediums tend to have pictures of their loved ones in their home or office. This is not just a sentimental gesture. They create and feel an energetic connection with their loved ones on the other side by simply looking at and holding their photo. Physical mediums are also more likely to want to have their departed loved ones' objects, furniture, and knickknacks throughout their home. A client of mine with physical medium tendencies had her garage and basement stuffed with her beloved mother's furniture. These items were so important to her that when she moved across the country, she hired an extra moving van to move these things rather than sell them. I also had a client whose daughter died after a lengthy illness. Her daughter had driven a compact car that she adored. My client sold her new hybrid car to drive her daughter's older-model car. It not only helped my client to feel closer to her, she felt her daughter's spirit as a visceral presence when she drove it.

All of us are likely to have pictures of our loved ones and possess a few of their personal items. But for a physical medium, these things are their lifeline to the other side. They experience an energetic connection with their loved ones through them. An emotional medium absorbs their loved ones' presence through their emotions and feelings. A mental medium carries on internal conversations with their loved ones and receives their thoughts and ideas, and a spiritual medium intuits their loved ones' presence or connects with them through visions, dreams, or apparitions. A physical medium experiences a tangible connection to their loved ones on the other side through their photographs or items. For a physical medium, a personal object or photograph is like a cell phone to the other side. These objects transmit cosmic vibrations.

Putting Energy into Words

With a little effort, a physical medium can become aware of the energy vibrations that they are receiving from the other side through certain objects, photographs, or occurrences in the natural world. Their challenge is to go a step further. Once this phenomenon is accepted, they must then discern the message. For the other medium types this is easier, as their innate intuitive functioning is wired to understand the thoughts, feelings, and visions that they are receiving. Physical mediums may need to develop the capacity to put into words the energy messages that they receive. They might be aware of signs from the other side, but to develop their medium abilities they need to extend their skills into translating and discerning the meaning behind the vibrations.

Some physical mediums are not comfortable or willing to dialogue with nonphysical energy. It can feel too abstract and unreliable. The challenge for these mediums is to accept that there is life after death and that we have the inherent ability to connect and communicate with our loved ones who have passed on. Accepting nonphysical life forms as viable and meaningful sources of love and wisdom accelerates a physical medium's development. Once a physical medium perceives spirit within physical form and puts words to their impressions, their intuitive gifts come into full bloom.

In Service to Others

Physical mediums often pursue a professional medium career to be of service to others. Once they refine their ability to assign words and meaning to energy vibration, they can hone in on practical and down-to-earth guidance from the spirit realm. Their bodies become a reliable instrument for receiving love, help, and care from the other side.

Well-developed physical mediums can excel at more practical matters and are able to receive from loved ones on the other side advice in areas such as finances, the buying and selling of property, locating lost items, and even needed car repairs. They also tend to more easily receive information about the health conditions and illnesses of those in spirit while they were still in the physical world. In medium sessions, I usually tune in to the health problem or illness that led to a loved one's passing. This is a common way for me to identify for my client the loved one whom I am speaking to.

Physical mediums can be natural channels. A channel is an individual who becomes a receptive and accessible vessel for a spirit to communicate through. The difference between a channel and a medium is that a medium communicates with a spirit. A channel allows a spirit to enter their body and communicate through them. There are conscious and unconscious channels. Putting their conscious awareness aside, an individual becomes an unconscious channel when they do not know what a spirit says or does when they are within their physical body. With a conscious channel, the individual is aware of what the spirit may be saying and doing.

The first time I witnessed an unconscious channel was when I was in my early twenties and attending a Spiritualist church. It was one of my first visits to the church, a small window front on a busy street in San Francisco. The speaker took his place behind the podium. He said a few opening words, then put his head down for a moment. He then began to speak to us in a women's voice. His mannerisms completely changed. He held his body more fluidly and laughed and carried on with the audience. About twenty minutes later, he put his head down again and in a man's voice asked what the talk had been about.

The Seers

Spiritual Intuitives

Spiritual intuitives receive energy information through the energy field. This might be a little harder for some people to understand. All living things emit an electromagnetic energy that is for the most part invisible to the eye. This is commonly referred to as the *aura*. Many intuitives and mediums are able to see or sense the aura or energy field that surrounds the body. This can look like a multicolored glow from a light bulb or rays of the sun. A spiritual intuitive will often comment that they pull information out of the air or that they sense things and have no idea how or why they do.

Spiritual Mediums

Do you ever see flashes of light or color or the image of a loved one who is on the other side? Do you ever feel, in your home or car, the presence of a loved one who has passed over? Have you ever woken up and felt that you were busy and active all night while in the dream state? Do you sometimes feel that you are in the company of an angel? These are common experiences for a spiritual medium.

A spiritual medium receives intuitive impulses in a more elusive way than the other medium types, so their connections may tend to feel imaginary and dreamy. A spiritual medium is likely to have encounters with ghosts, spirit guides, and divine beings. Having a depth of spiritual wisdom, they can also often intuit the lessons and higher purpose within their own lives and the lives of others.

Spiritual mediums are connected to the other side in ways that can be hard to fully appreciate. For most spiritual mediums, the other side is not far away and abstract. Because this type of medium intuits through their energy field or spirit, they have a natural and comfortable affinity with spiritual and lofty vibrations. Spiritual mediums tend to be aware of the soul purpose and lessons that others are meant to be learning here and in the beyond. Because of this, they can provide a wide range of useful guidance and information.

The Sensitive Aura

A spiritual medium's aura, or the electromagnetic energy field that surrounds their physical body, is usually expansive and flowing and can reach out across time and space. It absorbs and receives spiritual energy and connects them to those on the other side. Not all spiritual mediums are aware of their highly sensitized aura, so they may be confused by the images, flashes of light, and random apparitions that they randomly perceive. Without intent and thought, they can have one foot in the physical world and the other in the spiritual realm.

The spiritual medium's highly sensitive energy field is intertwined with their nervous system. Spiritual energy can affect them in baffling and unpredictable ways. They may be attracted to meditation and altered states of consciousness and find transcendent spiritual states soothing, nurturing, and comfortable. Intuiting too much energy can also cause a spiritual medium to become spacy, forgetful, and lazy. A physical medium picks up the denser physical vibrations and communication with the other side as *real*. A mental medium whose energy is focused in thought can talk themselves out of believing in otherworldly communication, and an emotional medium can be overwhelmed by the emotions they receive. A spiritual medium does not have these concerns. For most, communication with the other side is an accepted reality. Their issue instead is their tendency to allow their consciousness to freely drift in spiritual currents and lose touch with the practical reasons for further developing their skills.

Clairvoyance

Many mediums can visually see spiritual beings. However, this ability comes most naturally to spiritual mediums. The ability to visually see energy information is called *clairvoyance*. Clairvoyant images vary in intensity and depth. They may fade or drift, be a partial image, or be more third-dimensional looking. Quite often these visions and images are more inward and dreamlike. However, a clairvoyant vision can appear in the external world as solid and physical. In medium readings, spirits commonly communicate information to me in this way. Quite often a loved one on the other side will describe such specific details as the flowers in my client's garden, the color of their bedroom walls, a specific picture, or the pattern on their china. I initially become aware of loved ones in spirit through clairvoyance. I am usually able to see those on the other side in surprising detail. Their clothing, the expression on their face, the way they stand or sit, and their jewelry all can stand out. I can assure you that we still have style in spirit.

Natural Mediums

Unlike the other medium types, a spiritual medium is usually aware that they are connecting and communicating with the other side. They are innately wired to be aware of nonphysical reality. For an experienced spiritual medium, the spiritual realm is so familiar it can feel like a second home. They visit it through their dreams, daydreams, and visions and like to escape there as often as possible.

As children, many spiritual mediums were able to sense and communicate with deceased family members, angels, and spirits. They may have memories of seeing their grandpa who passed over years earlier sitting in the rocker and their Aunt Anne helping in the kitchen. Spiritual mediums are also more likely than the other types to encounter ghosts and other spiritual entities. Because they naturally bond with spiritual energy, they can become stressed and anxious in the presence of ghosts and wandering and lost souls. Although they are aware of these spirits, they do not always know how to detach and disengage from them. It can be confusing to encounter random spirit strangers and dream of loved ones and other celestial visitors. At a young age, many spiritual mediums began to repress and hide their intuitive ability. Not wanting to be thought of as kooky and different, they do their best to silence their natural intuitive talents. For the spiritual mediums who grew up feeling misunderstood and not accepted, developing their medium abilities later in life can be an emotionally healing experience.

Engaging with the World

Although spiritual mediums are naturally attuned to the spiritual realm, some avoid sharing and developing their gifts. They may like floating in the lofty extrasensory experience of spiritual energy so much that they become ineffective in the physical world. Instead of fulfilling their earth lessons, they can live in an alternate reality of daydreams and fleeting spiritual sensations. Satisfied with their stimulating inner world, they become unmotivated and dissipate their potential. For this type of spiritual medium, energy is a transcendent seduction that need serve no purpose in the world. In the everyday earthly realm, they may feel as if they are strangers from another place. The challenge for these kinds of spiritual mediums is to discover meaning and purpose in the here and now.

However, many spiritual mediums go in the opposite direction. At ease and usually adept at communicating and connecting with those on the other side, they desire to become professional mediums. They retain a distant memory of life in the ethereal cosmos and love to visit its special magic and love-centered warmth as often as possible. With devotion and drive, they develop their abilities in order to bring those in the physical and spiritual realms together. They see the interplay between the two realms and seek to understand the bigger purpose and meaning in life. For them, the physical world is a temporary assignment in their overall soul plan. Like a magnet, they feel as if they have been pulled to the earth to be of service for a greater purpose. Just taking the leap to acknowledge their medium abilities and practice and share them with others is all that they may need to do to further develop as a medium.

14

Mastering Medium Abilities: Exercises and Meditations

∾∾∾∾∾∾∾∾∾∾∾∾∾∾∾∾∾∾∾

The natural impulse to develop the ability to communicate with those on the other side is a call from your soul, awakening you to your true identity. Although from the human point of view it may seem that spirit communication is simply an interesting pastime, when you are motivated to develop medium abilities your soul has a bigger agenda in mind. A new you comes to light when you engage the power of your spirit. As you expand your circumference of awareness, you begin to participate in the full continuum of life. The physical realm is just one aspect of the vast multidimensional spectrum that we are all a part of. The spirit realm is all around us. It is where you are right now. As you develop your ability to communicate with the nonphysical, you wake up to a larger vision of reality. Your innate medium abilities are the doorway through which your most powerful self emerges.

In this chapter, I provide exercises and meditations that enable you to develop and refine your innate intuitive connections with the other side into useful medium abilities. However, learning how to effectively communicate with your loved ones, angels, and guides involves more than just acquiring and practicing skills. In the process, your spirit awakens and emerges and the eternal you is activated.

When you communicate with the spirit realm, you begin to better understand your own spiritual nature. You begin to interpret and perceive reality through a much broader lens.

It is important to approach the spirit realm with respect and with an open mind and heart. This is more than a parlor trick and a way to impress your friends and family. When you open yourself to the other side, you invite transformative energy into your consciousness. You will change, grow, and evolve.

Guidelines

To achieve the best possible results in your efforts to further develop your intuitive medium type, I recommend the following practices.

Become Aware of Your Intent

Why do you want to communicate with the other side? Your reasons for wanting to develop your medium abilities are just as important as your level of intuitive proficiency. The spirit realm cannot support your desire to connect if you are only interested in becoming more powerful or special or if you wish to separate yourself from others. You will still be able to develop your intuitive abilities, as this is a normal and natural function that we all have, but you will not attract the highest degree of help and guidance from the spirit realm.

This is not because your angels and guides are ignoring or punishing you. Instead, it is because self-centered ego thoughts and feelings are a dense vibration. They weigh you down and prevent you from accessing the higher levels of wisdom and love. What you perceive and connect with will be nonphysical energies that are in the denser astral levels of spirit. Because these energies are usually fear-based thoughtforms and negative entities, you may become confused and frustrated instead of enlightened and filled with love. Your loved ones, your angels and spirit guides, can only work with you if your intent is based on greater principles. Open-hearted loving, giving, sharing, supporting others, and service is the way of spirit. When your intent is pure, you align yourself with love and wisdom.

Be Humble and Receptive and Have a Good Sense of Humor

Approach the spirit realm and your loved ones with a simple and receptive openness. There is no room for ego when you make contact with those in spirit. I have been working professionally as a medium and psychic for over twenty-five years, and I am continually humbled by my experiences with the other side. Almost every day I realize how little I really know. Our human understanding is very limited. We do not know why things happen and the true significance of the small acts that we perform each day. The physical world is a dim reflection of the beauty, love, and magnificence of our eternal nonphysical reality. Let go of your expectations, preconceived ideas, and biases, and be curious and open. Receive, pause, and do not jump to conclusions. This perspective will accelerate your growth by leaps and bounds.

Although it is important to be reverent and respectful of the other side, develop a sense of humor. Don't take the spirit realm too seriously. The other side certainly doesn't. They laugh, tell jokes, drop things in our path, and even at times try to scare us, just for fun. Laughter is expansive energy. It loosens the energy field and lifts the consciousness to higher levels of clarity and truth.

When doing the following exercises, do not take yourself too seriously. This limits and restricts your ability to receive. Sometimes in between especially intense medium sessions, I try to take a few minutes to watch a short online comedy video or go to my favorite humor sites. I search for a laugh. It lightens up the energy and allows me to become more receptive. Stress and tension act like sand bags that keep an air balloon tethered to the ground.

I have a friend who was getting ready to begin a new career venture. The night before she was to launch herself into her new work, she had a humorous dream. She knew that it was significant, but she was not sure exactly what it meant. In the dream she was the lead singer in a band with four musicians who called themselves the "Call on Us Gang." The band was getting ready to perform in front of a large group of people, and although she had never sung or played an instrument before, she was excited and ready. When she asked me about the dream, I immediately saw her band mates surrounding her. They were her spirit guides who wanted her to know that they were her back-up band.

"Tell her to call on us. We are always here to help her," they told me.

Remind yourself that even though you are not always aware of it, your spirit guides and loved ones on the other side are your band, singing and playing along with you.

Pay Attention to Your Earth School Lessons

When you engage with the spirit realm, your earth school lessons intensify. Developing your medium abilities is not an escape from your everyday mundane responsibilities and challenges. It does not excuse you from participating in the ups and downs of life. As much as you might like it to be, it is not a magic formula that makes your problems and issues immediately disappear. Although you must still meet your challenges, medium development enhances your insight and ability to learn and participate in your earth lessons. You still engage in everyday issues, such as relationship, career, financial, and health concerns, but with a renewed understanding of the significant role that they play in your soul plan. As you do this, your life begins to transform.

When you develop your ability to communicate with the other side, you begin to receive the higher vibrations of divine love and wisdom. This is the energy that your loved ones on the other side reside in. When you open yourself to their energy, the divine flows in. You are refining yourself from the inside out. The conditions and circumstances that do not support your highest self fall away. This might at times feel like loss and the opposite of what you desire. Yet like a snake shedding its skin, this is only temporary. Eventually you integrate the compassionate cosmic flow of spirit energy within the circumstances of your life. Effortlessly, you create new conditions and positive experiences. What you need spontaneously comes to you before you even ask. You naturally attract people who can support, love, and respect you. Your physical body is rejuvenated and made healthy by the inflow of vibrant spiritual energy. Love fills your heart and mind, and you are never alone. Despite the ups and downs of physical reality, you bathe in an inner knowing that you are safe and loved. Fear evaporates, and you become a light of strength and guidance to others.

Know That You Are Worthy of Love

Love yourself. If you have low self-esteem, habitually engage in negative self-talk, and lack confidence, you unconsciously sabotage your attempts at developing your medium abilities. Do all that you can to heal past wounds and love and take care of yourself. Close your eyes, breathe, and ask your angels for help and healing. Do this every day.

Developing your medium abilities requires patience, practice, and trusting yourself and the spirit realm. If you lack confidence in yourself, you will have a hard time trusting the intuitive impressions, thoughts, and feelings that you receive. Even if you receive clear and accurate information and guidance, you may doubt and disregard your abilities.

The source of your intuition and your ability to communicate with the other side is your spirit. Your loved ones on the other side, your spirit guides and angels, want to connect with you and they will do all that they can to reach out to you, love you, and facilitate communication.

Meditation

There is no getting around it: to develop your medium abilities, you must have a regular meditation practice. If you have read even one book or taken a class on developing intuitive or medium abilities, you most likely have heard of the benefits of meditation. I, too, believe in its importance. Think of meditation as opening the door and welcoming into your home friendly and loving company. Your loved ones, angels, and spirit guides respond when invited. Meditation allows your mind and heart to open and receive their energy vibration.

Despite the value of meditation in inducing an inner state of calm and intuitive receptivity, many people are frustrated in their attempts and give up. Like others, you may have a difficult time settling your mind and releasing constant inner talk and tumultuous emotions. In this busy, multitasking world that we live in, it can at times be difficult to go from full speed ahead to relaxed. I have found that before settling down to meditate, engaging in a transition activity can be beneficial to inducing a more ready state. Before attempting to meditate, you might want to read a passage from an uplifting book, light a candle, listen to relaxing music or nature sounds, or write in a journal. These activities prepare your mind and emotions to wind down and receive. Sometimes it can be helpful to engage in a physical activity, like running, yoga, swimming, or walking your dog. To get the most from a meditative state, it is best to gradually slow down, shift gears, and relax.

When you are ready to meditate, find a place in your home where you can be undisturbed for a period of time. Sit on the same comfortable cushion or in the same chair and try to meditate at the same time every day. This has a couple of benefits. You train your mind, emotions, and body to relax each time you sit in this spot, and you increase its psychic energy. Then each time you meditate, you can tap into this energy and add to its potency.

When I teach classes in my office, a student often sits in the chair that I use when I do readings. I have been using this same chair in the same spot in the room for many years. For the student, it is like sitting in a psychic vortex. In no time they are the class star, amazing others with their psychic ability.

I suggest that you meditate without the thought of communicating with the other side until you are comfortable with achieving a relaxed and quiet state of mind.

Meditation to Prepare for Communicating with the Other Side

- Begin by closing your eyes. Slowly inhale and notice your thoughts, then release them through the out breath. Continue to breathe in this relaxing breath. Move the breath through the body, and exhale any stress or tension through the out breath. You might want to set a timer for five or ten minutes to begin and then slowly increase the time that you spend in meditation.

- As you become comfortable with this relaxing process, you will begin to look forward to this quiet inner space. In meditation, you enter an interior world. In this inner realm, your intuitive senses awaken and you can tune in to subtle sensations and the soft presence of spirit.

- Once you are comfortable with simply breathing and relaxing, strengthen your meditative state by imagining that you are breathing white light down through the top of your head. Move this breath through your body. White-light energy originates in the higher vibrations of love and peace. It is the divine breath. When you visualize white light, you invite unconditional love and blessings into your body, mind, and spirit.

- As you breathe white-light energy down through the top of your head, move it through your body and exhale it through your heart. Continue breathing in white light. Allow it to circulate throughout your body, loosening and relaxing any stress and tension. Then exhale through your heart.

- Feel your heart begin to open. Release any negativity, old wounds, and hurts through the out breath. Bathe your heart in the divine breath.

- As you continue to breathe in white light, imagine your mind and heart opening. Feel your consciousness expand as your mind merges with the divine mind. Feel the presence of love as soft energy filling your heart. Continue to breathe in this energy. Rest, open, and allow love to fill you.

- When you are ready, send warm thoughts of love and gratitude to the spirit realm. Open your eyes.

It is helpful to have a journal or tape recorder close by when you do this meditation. Quite often you will spontaneously receive impressions and images, hear voices, or feel sensations. Even though at the time these kinds of inner occurrences may seem insignificant, I suggest documenting whatever you receive. Many times we disregard what we intuitively obtain as unimportant. Then days or weeks later we begin to observe a pattern or understand the significance of what we are experiencing.

Preparation for Connecting to the Other Side

Having a loved one pass over to the other side can be one of life's most painful experiences. The grief can be overwhelming and last for weeks and months. Your world can feel like it has been turned upside down. When someone we love leaves the physical world, we can feel like we are torn in half. In energetic reality, we are, as loving another creates an energy bond. When the energy field that love creates shifts due to the passing over of one person to the spirit realm, we can feel raw and vulnerable. Even when we have the assurance that our loved ones are alive and well on the other side, we still miss their company and physical presence.

Most people want to communicate with those on the other side whom they most love and miss. Yet for the beginner it is these beloved spirits who may be the most difficult to initially connect with. Strong emotion, grief, sadness, and mourning create an emotional barrier that can diffuse and create static in your attempts to feel a connection. For this reason, I recommend that in the following exercises you pick a relative or loved one to communicate with who has been in the spirit realm for several years and one whom you no longer are actively grieving. It can also be helpful to have a friend or more than one person to develop your abilities with. You can tune in to one of their relatives, and they in turn can tune in to one of yours. Once you are feeling more confident in your intuitive receptivity, you can invite other loved ones into your practice. As your medium abilities develop, it will be easier to clearly communicate with and tune in to those with whom you share a deep emotional connection.

Loved ones on the other side like to communicate with us. Sometimes people ask me if they might be interfering with the activities of those on the other side or disturbing their rest. I have found that those in the spirit realm are eager to connect with us. Remember, they have free will and choice to refuse our invitation. We can never force or make someone become available to us. At the same time, be open to the possibility that whoever comes forward in these exercises may not be the person you are expecting. There may be someone present on the other side who shares similar strengths in intuiting and is better able to communicate and help you to develop.

Exercises to Develop Each Medium Type

The following exercises are designed for each of the four intuitive medium types. To be able to connect and communicate with the other side, a little experience and practice with all four of the intuitive types is helpful. Your medium type is the doorway through which you naturally access energy information. It is the path of least resistance. Begin with your innate medium type, as it will then be easier to develop the other types.

There are exercises to develop three levels of expertise for each type:

Level One: Discern Energy Vibrations

Level Two: Convert Energy into a Usable Form

Level Three: Communicate and Dialogue with the Other Side

I suggest that you begin with the exercise of your primary medium type. Practice this until you are satisfied that you have experienced the objective. Then practice each of the other three types one at a time. When you have completed all four exercises, you can then move to the next level of expertise. Once you have mastered all the exercises on all three levels, you will be ready to hold a medium session.

I suggest that you have a journal to write in or a tape recorder to document the sessions. Whatever information you intuitively receive may seem insignificant and minimally important at the time. However, days, weeks, or even months later you will discover patterns and be able to gain new insights into your experiences. Later review of your practice sessions will also help you to track your progress.

I suggest that you practice these exercises in the same place every time that you do them. As the psychic energy in this location intensifies, it supports your efforts and helps you to slip into and maintain a receptive state. If you have a regular meditation area, this is a good place to begin.

Choose the person whom you would like to connect with. Again, it is best to begin with someone who has been in the spirit realm for several years and whose passing you are no longer mourning. You might want to choose someone different each time you do the same exercise. This will help you to experience the subtle and at times dramatic differences in energy from spirit to spirit.

I find it helpful to have a short ritual with which to open myself to spirit's influence. You might what to say a short prayer to call forth divine protection. In these meditations I ask you to imagine white light. Seers, psychics, and healers can often see the divine vibration as white light. When you visualize white light, you invoke this divine presence.

My prayer goes something like this:

Divine Spirit,
As I draw close to the spirit realm
I ask for the white light of your love and protection.
I also ask for my angels, guides, and (speak the name of the person
from spirit whom you want to connect with) to be present.
Surround us with love and
open my heart and mind for the highest good.

It is not necessary to use this prayer. Any ritual that prepares you to open to those on the other side and relaxes you will work.

Level One: Discern Energy Vibrations

Emotional Mediums

Level One Objective: Differentiate your emotions from the emotional energy that you are intuitively receiving from the other side.

The biggest challenge for emotional mediums is to learn how to differentiate their emotional energy from the emotional energy that they are intuitively receiving from someone on the other side. This exercise will help you to tune in to the emotional energy of a loved one in spirit. It also highlights the subtle and unique emotional differences that you will experience from one spirit to another.

Write down or tape-record a list of your current feelings. Write down whatever feelings surface. Don't analyze or drift into overthinking. This list might include feelings you have had during the day or the past week and feelings about doing this exercise. You do not have to understand what you feel; just write it all down.

This exercise involves developing the psychic skill of *clairsentience*, which is the ability to connect with energy information through feeling.

- Close your eyes and begin to breathe long, deep breaths. Notice your breath and send it through the body, loosening and relaxing any stress and tension. Imagine that you are breathing white-light energy down through the top of your head and releasing it through the exhale. Keep breathing and relaxing in this manner a few more times.

- Breathe and imagine white-light breath coming down through the top of your head and surrounding your heart. Breathe this white light of love into your heart. Imagine that your heart opens like the petals of a flower. Keep breathing white light down through the top of your head and into your heart. Feel your heart expand and open.

- Draw into your awareness a loved one who has passed over. Repeat their name a few times. Send the person the message that you would like to communicate with them. Ask your loved one to send you an emotion or feeling. Gently repeat this request a few times. Keep breathing and relaxing. Feel your heart opening.

- Imagine that you are receiving into your heart the emotional energy of your loved one. You might want to repeat their name a few times.

- Keep inviting and receiving your loved one's emotional energy. As you do this, name the emotions and feelings that surface. You might want to say them aloud if you have a tape recorder. It may take some time and practice to fully discern and name what you are receiving.

- When you feel as if you have completed all that you can at this time, open your eyes and thank your loved one for their presence. Ask them to continue to work with you at another time.

Physical Mediums

Level One Objective: Become aware of the subtle vibrations that emanate from a photograph or personal object of someone on the other side.

The challenge for the beginner physical medium is to become aware of nonphysical energy. Because physical mediums tend to be grounded individuals who disregard what is outside of the confines of material reality, they can at times have difficulty becoming consciously aware of energy vibrations.

In this exercise, you will need a picture or object of the loved one with whom you would like to connect. If you do not have such an item, you can write the person's name and birthday on a piece of paper. Receiving a loved one's vibration from a personal object or photograph is called *psychometry*. It is a common technique used by mediums to connect with those on the other side. This exercise will help you to develop this ability.

Write down or tape-record your expectations for this exercise. Be honest about what you think may or may not happen. Write down any reservations that you may have. Don't analyze or judge as right or wrong whatever thoughts or feelings surface. When you have written down as much as is possible at this time, become aware that you can put aside your beliefs and expectations. Begin this exercise open to whatever occurs.

- Close your eyes and begin to breathe long, deep breaths. Notice your breath and send it through your body, loosening and relaxing any stress and tension. Imagine that you are breathing white-light energy down through the top of your head and releasing it through the exhale. Keep breathing and relaxing in this manner a few more times.

- Hold in your hand the picture, object, or written name of the person whom you wish to connect with. Continue to breathe and imagine white light coming down through the top of your head and moving through your body. Keep breathing white light down through the top of your head and through your body, and exhale any stress and tension.

- Draw into your awareness the loved one whose object you hold in your hand. Repeat their name a few times.

- Imagine that you are receiving energy from the item. Check the sensations in your body, most notably in your hands, head, heart, stomach, and solar plexus.

- Keep receiving your loved one's energy in this way. Try to put words to the vibrations that you are receiving from whatever you are holding in your hands. You may experience a sensation of increased energy, a part of your body might feel heavier or lighter, you may feel an ache or pain, or your hands or head may tingle. Say the words aloud if you have a tape recorder. It may take some time and practice to fully discern and name what you are receiving.

- When you feel as if you have completed all that you can at this time, open your eyes and thank your loved one for their presence. Ask them to continue to work with you at another time.

Mental Mediums

Level One Objective: Differentiate personal thoughts from the thoughts and impressions that you are intuitively receiving from the other side.

The challenge for mental mediums is to become aware of the difference between their personal thoughts and those thoughts and impressions that they are intuiting from those on the other side. Mental mediums are open receptacles for the thoughts and ideas of others, including those who have passed over. Constant mind chatter is an issue for many mental mediums. In this exercise, you will learn how to differentiate your thoughts from the impressions and thoughts that you are receiving from those on the other side. This exercise will help you to develop *telepathy*, the ability to intuit the thoughts of others both here and in the beyond.

Write down or tape-record your thoughts. Observe and listen. Do not judge or regulate what you are thinking. Just let the thoughts surface one after another. It does not matter if you think about this exercise, your loved ones in spirit, your day, or what is for dinner. Just write down whatever comes to mind. Don't analyze or judge as right or wrong. After several minutes of writing, begin the exercise.

- Close your eyes and begin to breathe long, deep breaths. Notice your breath and send it through your body, loosening and relaxing any stress and tension. Imagine that you are breathing white-light energy down through the top of your head and releasing any tension or stress through the exhale. Keep breathing and relaxing in this manner.

- Continue to breathe and imagine white light coming down through the top of your head, and imagine that as you exhale, your mind becomes clear. Any thoughts or stress evaporate as your mind fills with white light. Keep breathing white light and clearing your mind in this way. Breathe down through the top of your head and through your body, and exhale any stress and tension.

- Speak the name of the loved one on the other side whom you would like to connect with. As you say the person's name, breathe and allow your mind to clear. Become aware of any thoughts and impressions that you receive as you repeat your loved one's name. Do not analyze or think about what you receive. Just observe, accept, and say aloud whatever you become aware of. You can speak this into the tape recorder.

- When you feel that the process is complete, thank your loved one for sharing their thoughts with you. Open your eyes and write down whatever you have received.

Spiritual Mediums

Level One Objective: Focus on the energy that you intuitively receive from a loved one on the other side.

A spiritual medium's awareness of energy is opposite that of the physical medium. Physical mediums tend to be attuned to the denser physical vibrations. They usually need to increase their sensitivity to the subtle vibrations of the unseen. Spiritual mediums are all too aware of the energy of the cosmos. They can feel overwhelmed and be preoccupied with trying to understand and discern the energy that flows into their porous energy field. They are celestial energy sponges.

Become aware of what you would like to experience in this exercise. Whom do you want to contact and why? Write down or tape-record what comes to you. During the exercise, stay focused on communicating with a loved one on the other side. Although interesting sensations and compelling visions may surface, remind yourself to tune in to a loved one on the other side.

- Close your eyes and begin to breathe long, deep breaths. Notice your breath and send it through your body, loosening and relaxing any stress and tension. Imagine that you are breathing white-light energy down through the top of your head and releasing any tension or stress through the exhale. Keep breathing and relaxing in this manner.

- Continue to breathe and imagine white light coming down through the top of your head. As you exhale, visualize a clear and open space above your head. Thoughts and stress evaporate as you continue to breathe in white light. Imagine that this open space above your head takes the shape of an energy funnel and enters the top of your head. Keep breathing white light and clearing your mind as this funnel creates an open space within you.

- Repeat the name of the loved one on the other side whom you would like to connect with. As you say the person's name, breathe and imagine their energy entering the funnel-shaped space. Become aware of any impressions and sensations or feelings as you repeat your loved one's name. You may feel an increase in energy, especially in your head, spine, or hands. This might be like a buzzing or a buildup of pressure. You might feel more spacy or like you are floating, and you may see flashes of color or light and images of your loved one. Do not analyze or think about what you receive. Just observe, receive, and say aloud whatever you become aware of. You can speak this into the tape recorder.

• When you feel that the process is complete, thank your loved one for working with you. Open your eyes and write down whatever you have received.

Level Two: Convert Energy into a Usable Form

The next step in developing your ability to communicate with the other side is learning how to discern, understand, and put into words the energy information that you receive. We all receive intuitive information and we all unknowingly connect with our loved ones in the spirit realm. We just do not always know that we are doing this. Even if we are aware that we are receiving energy from the other side, we do not always know how to decipher its meaning. This next level of development will help you to transfer the energy that you receive from the other side into a form that you will be able to communicate with and better understand.

Imagination

Learning how to employ your imagination to work in unison with your intuition helps you to put words and meaning to energy information. There is, of course, a difference between connecting with those on the other side and simply imagining that you are doing so. Yet, when used correctly, aligning your imagination with your intuitive ability can be invaluable. When they work hand in hand, your imagination can provide you with additional information and an avenue for deeper communication. The key is to first tune in to the energy vibrations of your primary medium type and allow this to guide you.

Clairvoyance

In these exercises you will be developing the psychic skill of *clairvoyance*, which is the ability to perceive energy information in the form of an image. The image that you observe may be a symbol, a figurative or a realistic representation of energy. In this exercise, I ask you to "allow an image to emerge." If an image does not automatically surface, consciously use your imagination to create one. You may feel as if you are making this up. That is perfectly fine. Go with this and remember that your imagination is the facility through which you give meaning and form to energy. You may "see" the image through your inner vision or you may instead know, think, or feel it. This may seem unusual, but as you practice these exercises, it will make more sense. If an image does not feel "right" or if it fades and feels as if it does not have energy, ask for another image to emerge that better represents the energy that you are intuiting. This might not make logical sense to you, but do it anyway. In time, you will begin to get an inner intuitive feel for what is actual energy information and what is simply your imagination.

You will also be asking the person in spirit whom you are inviting into this exercise to send you a message through an image. It is highly likely that you will not understand the image that you receive. Keep in mind that your loved ones in spirit are also practicing communicating with you. They may, like you, be learning and improving their intuitive ability to communicate. Accept whatever you receive. In time, you will understand the meaning behind it.

I have learned to not overthink the images and information I receive in readings. Recently I gave a reading to a client who came to see me to communicate with his sister who had passed over. During the session she kept showing me the image of a cartoonish-looking elephant. It seemed odd, and for a minute or two I said nothing. Finally I described the elephant to her brother, and he started to cry. A week or so before her passing in an automobile accident, she had given him a T-shirt with a cartoon elephant dancing on the front of it.

The meaning or significance of the images that you receive is not important. This exercise is designed to help you transfer energy from your innate medium modality into different forms.

Emotional Mediums

Level Two Objective: Imagine an image that represents the emotional energy that you are receiving from the other side.

Physical Mediums

Level Two Objective: Imagine an image that represents the energy that you are receiving from a personal object or picture of your loved one on the other side.

Mental Mediums

Level Two Objective: Imagine an image that represents the thought energy that you are receiving from the other side.

Spiritual Mediums

Level Two Objective: Imagine an image that represents the energy vibrations that you are receiving from the other side.

Beginning Meditation for All Medium Types

- Close your eyes and breathe in long and deep, relaxing breaths. Move the energy through your body, and exhale any stress and tension. Continue this cleansing and relaxing breath. When you feel relaxed, imagine that you are breathing white light down through the top of your head. Move this breath through your body, and exhale any stress and tension.

- As you breathe in white-light energy down through the top of your head, move it through your body and exhale it through your heart. Continue breathing in white light. Allow it to circulate throughout your body, loosening and relaxing any stress and tension. Then exhale through your heart.

- As you continue to breathe in white light, imagine your mind opening. Feel the white-light breath fill your mind with white light. Exhale any stress and tension. Continue to breathe in white-light energy, and feel your heart and mind open.

- Breathe in white-light breath and move it through your body. Imagine your body filling with white light, open and relaxed. Continue to breathe in this way. Breathe in white light and imagine it expanding beyond the physical body and surrounding you. Imagine that your energy field opens and glows with this white light. Continue to breathe white light into your mind, heart, body, and spirit. Feel yourself invigorated and at one with the spirit realm.

- Now proceed to one of the four meditations to complete the exercise.

Emotional Mediums

- Breathe white-light energy down through the top of your head and exhale through your heart. Draw into your awareness a loved one who has passed over. Repeat their name a few times. Send them the message that you would like to communicate. Ask your loved one to send you a message. Gently repeat this request a few times. Keep breathing and relax. Feel your heart opening.

- Imagine your heart opening and receiving the emotional message of your loved one. You might want to repeat their name a few times. If you do not feel much, ask your loved one to intensify the energy.

- Allow an image to emerge that represents the emotional energy that you are receiving. Continue to breathe and relax. Ask yourself, "If the emotional energy that I am receiving was an image, what would it look like?"

- Continue this process until you have a sense of an image. Accept whatever you receive without needing to figure out its significance and meaning. The image that you receive may elicit an emotional response or feeling from you. This may seem perplexing, yet it is a sign of its genuineness.

- When you are ready, send warm thoughts of love and gratitude to your loved one. Open your eyes. Write down or speak into the tape recorder a description of the image that you received.

Physical Mediums

- Hold an object or a picture of your loved one or a piece of paper with your loved one's name on it. Breathe white-light energy down through the top of your head and exhale through your heart. Draw your awareness to the picture, object, or piece of paper in your hand. Repeat the name of your loved one a few times. Send them the message that you would like to communicate. Ask your loved one to send you a message. Gently repeat this request a few times. Keep breathing and relax.

- Imagine that you are receiving an energy message from your loved one through whatever you are holding in your hand. You might want to repeat the name of your loved one a few times. If you do not feel much, ask your loved one to intensify the energy.

- Allow an image to emerge that represents the energy that you are receiving. Continue to breathe and relax. Ask yourself, "If this energy that I am receiving was an image, what would it look like?"

- Continue this process until you have a sense of an image. You may not see but rather know what this image is, or you may experience the image as a gut feeling. Accept whatever you receive without needing to figure out its significance and meaning.

- When you are ready, send warm thoughts of love and gratitude to your loved one. Open your eyes. Write down or speak into the tape recorder a description of the image that you received.

Mental Mediums

- Breathe white-light energy down through the top of your head and exhale through your heart. Draw into your awareness a loved one who has passed over. Repeat their name a few times. Send them the message that you would like to communicate. Ask your loved one to send you a message. Gently repeat this request a few times. Keep breathing and relax.

- Breathe down through the top of your head, filling your mind with white-light energy. Imagine a clear and open space in your mind. Imagine that you are receiving energy from your loved one. You might want to repeat the name of your loved one a few times. If you do not feel much, ask your loved one to intensify the energy.

- Allow an image to emerge that represents the energy that you are receiving. Continue to breathe and relax. Ask yourself, "If this energy that I am receiving was an image, what would it look like?"

- Continue this process until you have a sense of an image. Most likely you will experience a sense of knowing or your mind will fill with thoughts. If this knowing or your thoughts were an image, what would it look like? Accept whatever you receive without needing to figure out its significance and meaning. Try not to overthink what you are receiving. Just breathe and observe without trying to make sense of what you receive.

- When you are ready, send warm thoughts of love and gratitude to your loved one. Open your eyes. Write down or speak into the tape recorder a description of the image that you received.

Spiritual Mediums

- Breathe white-light energy down through the top of your head and exhale through your heart. Draw into your awareness a loved one who has passed over. Repeat their name a few times. Send them the message that you would like to communicate. Ask your loved one to send you a message. Gently repeat this request a few times. Keep breathing and relax.

- Breathe down through the top of your head, filling your mind, body, and spirit with white-light energy. Imagine a clear and open space within you. Feel energy move through you.

- Focus on the energy of the loved one that you are inviting into this exercise. Imagine that you are receiving their energy. You might want to repeat their name a few times. If you do not feel much, ask your loved one to intensify the energy.

- Allow an image to emerge that represents the energy that you are receiving. Continue to breathe and relax. Ask yourself, "If this energy that I am receiving was an image, what would it look like?"

- Continue this process until you have a sense of an image. You may see many images, flashes of color, light, or fragments of fleeting visions. Ask for one image and focus on this. Accept whatever you receive without needing to figure out its significance and meaning. Try not to overthink what you are receiving. Just breathe and observe without trying to make sense of what you receive.

- When you are ready, send warm thoughts of love and gratitude to your loved one. Open your eyes. Write down or speak into the tape recorder a description of the image that you received.

Level Three: Communicate and Dialogue with the Other Side

In this exercise, you will begin to communicate and dialogue with the other side. Do not do this exercise until you have practiced all four medium type exercises for levels one and two. It is necessary to have some practice with all four of the medium types, as those on the other side may send you messages through any of these four channels.

Emotional Mediums

Level Three Objective: Imagine an image that represents the emotional energy that you are receiving from the other side, and let it communicate to you.

Physical Mediums

Level Three Objective: Allow the object or picture of your loved one in spirit to communicate to you. You can also use a piece of paper with your loved one's name on it.

Mental Mediums

Level Three Objective: Imagine an image that represents the thought energy that you are receiving from the other side, and allow it to communicate.

Spiritual Mediums

Level Three Objective: Imagine an image that represents the energy vibrations that you are receiving, and allow it to communicate.

Medium Opening Meditation

- Close your eyes and breathe in long and deep, relaxing breaths. Move the energy through your body, and exhale any stress and tension. Continue this cleansing and relaxing breath. When you feel relaxed, imagine that you are breathing white light down through the top of your head. Move this breath through your body, and exhale any stress and tension.

- As you breathe in white-light energy down through the top of your head, move it through your body and exhale it through your heart. Continue breathing in white light. Allow it to circulate throughout your body, loosening and relaxing any stress and tension. Then exhale through your heart.

- As you continue to breathe in white light, imagine your mind opening. Feel the white-light breath fill your mind with white light. Exhale any stress and tension. Continue to breathe in white-light energy, and feel your heart and mind open.

- Breathe in white-light breath and move it through the body. Feel your body filling with white light, open and relaxed. Continue to breathe in this way. Breathe in white light and imagine it expanding beyond the physical body. Imagine that you are surrounded by an orb of white light. Feel your energy field open and relaxed. Continue to breathe white light into your mind, heart, body, and spirit. Feel yourself invigorated and at one with the spirit realm.

- Now proceed to one of the four meditations to complete the exercise.

Emotional Mediums

- Breathe white-light energy down through the top of your head and exhale through your heart. Draw into your awareness a loved one who has passed over. Repeat their name a few times. Send them a message that you would like to communicate. Keep breathing and relax. Feel your heart opening.

- Create an inner image of your loved one. You can imagine them from a photograph or just use your imagination and create an image. Perceive this in as much detail as possible. What are they wearing? What is the expression on their face? You might want to repeat the name of your loved one a few times.

- Keep in mind that you may not actually "see" an image. You may instead feel or simply sense it. When you feel as if you have a sense of an image, ask yourself, "What emotion or feeling am I receiving from my loved one?" Continue this process until you feel an emotional connection.

- Send feelings of love to your loved one. Listen and ask them if they have a message for you. Be patient and listen. You may begin to experience a wide range of emotions or a deep sense of peace and feelings of being loved. You may feel a warm embrace of healing energy. They may also answer you with another image or symbol, a thought, or the spontaneous recall of a memory.

- Keep breathing and relax. Continue in this way until you feel the energy begin to fade. Do not try to analyze and figure out what you receive. If you do, you may lose the energy connection.

- When you are ready, send warm thoughts of love and gratitude to your loved one. Open your eyes. Write down or speak into the tape recorder a description of the image that you received.

Physical Mediums

- Hold in your hand a photograph or an object of your loved one or a piece of paper with your loved one's name on it. Breathe white-light energy down through the top of your head and exhale through your heart. Draw into your awareness the loved one who has passed over whom you wish to connect with. Repeat their name a few times. Send them the message that you would like to communicate. Keep breathing and relax.

- Create an inner image of your loved one. You can imagine them from the photograph you are holding or just use your imagination and create an image. Perceive this in as much detail as possible. What are they wearing? What is the expression on their face? You might want to repeat the name of your loved one a few times.

- Keep in mind that you may not actually "see" an image. You may instead know it or simply sense it. When you feel as if you have a sense of them, scan your body and check for any changes or shifts in how you feel. Do you feel lighter or heavier? Are you experiencing any aches and pains, or do you feel energized? Pay attention to your stomach and solar plexus. Continue this process until you feel a shift of energy in your body.

- Send feelings of love to your loved one. Listen and ask them if they have a message for you. Be patient and listen. You may feel your loved one's presence as a touch on your hand or shoulder or a warmth close by, or a light in your room may flicker. They may also answer you with a feeling, another image or symbol, a thought, or the spontaneous recall of a memory.

- Keep breathing and relax. Continue in this way until you feel the energy begin to fade. Do not try to analyze and figure out what you receive. If you do, you may lose the energy connection.

- When you are ready, send warm thoughts of love and gratitude to your loved one. Open your eyes. Write down or speak into the tape recorder a description of any images that you received.

Mental Mediums

- Breathe white-light energy down through the top of your head and exhale through your heart. Imagine white light quieting your mind. Notice your thoughts, and release them one at a time. Breathe and relax. Draw into your awareness the loved one who has passed over whom you wish to connect with. Repeat their name a few times. Send them the message that you would like to communicate. Keep breathing and relax.

- Create an inner image of your loved one. You can imagine them from a photograph, or just use your imagination and create an image. Perceive this in as much detail as possible. What are they wearing? What is the expression on their face? You might want to repeat the name of your loved one a few times.

- Keep in mind that you may not actually "see" an image. You may instead know it or simply sense it. When you feel as if you have a sense of them, breathe and quiet your mind. If you begin to have an influx of thoughts and become distracted, draw your awareness back to the breath and the image that you have created.

- Send feelings of love to your loved one. Listen and ask them if they have a message for you. Be patient and listen. You may hear, spontaneously know, or receive information through thoughts. They might also answer you with a feeling, another image or symbol, or the spontaneous recall of a memory. Do not overthink this process. You may begin to have thought after thought. Keep breathing and focus on the image of your loved one. Thought messages from the other side are likely to surprise you with their simplicity.

- Keep breathing and relax. Continue in this way until you feel the energy begin to fade. Do not try to analyze and figure out what you receive. If you do, you may lose the energy connection.

- When you are ready, send warm thoughts of love and gratitude to your loved one. Open your eyes. Write down or speak into the tape recorder a description of the image that you received.

Spiritual Mediums

- Breathe white-light energy down through the top of your head and exhale through your heart. Imagine sending white-light breath down through your entire body. Breathe and relax. Feel energy move through you. Draw into your awareness the loved one who has passed over whom you wish to connect with. Repeat their name a few times. Send them the message that you would like to communicate. Keep breathing and relax.

- Create an inner image of your loved one. You can imagine them from a photograph, or just use your imagination and create an image. Perceive this in as much detail as possible. What are they wearing? What is the expression on their face? You might want to repeat the name of your loved one a few times.

- Keep in mind that you may not actually "see" an image. You may instead know it or simply sense it. If you begin to see flashes of light or color, especially purple, this is an indication that you are receiving higher vibrations of energy. You may also see many images and become overwhelmed by your perceptions. If this happens, repeat your loved one's name and focus on an image of them.

- Send feelings of love to your loved one. Listen and ask them if they have a message for you. Be patient and listen. You may feel their tangible presence close to you. Their image may begin to communicate with you. They might also answer you with a feeling, another image or symbol, a thought, or the spontaneous recall of a memory. Again, focus on the energy that is coming from your loved one. If you begin to have image after image emerge, focus on the images that feel the most intense.

- Keep breathing and relax. Continue in this way until you feel the energy begin to fade. Do not try to analyze and figure out what you receive. If you do, you may lose the energy connection.

- When you are ready, send warm thoughts of love and gratitude to your loved one. Open your eyes. Write down or speak into the tape recorder a description of the image that you received.

Level Four: Hold a Medium Session

Congratulations! You are ready for a medium session. The following exercise will help you to make use of the many skills that you have been practicing. Be ready and willing to receive energy information through all four medium types. Unlike in the other exercises, you will not ask for a particular loved one from the other side to draw close. Instead, allow whatever spirit is present to communicate to you. Before you begin, I recommend that you say the prayer of protection from earlier in this chapter or a similar one. Intend to invite only a loving presence from the light into your practice.

- Close your eyes and breathe in long and deep, relaxing breaths. Move the energy through your body, and exhale any stress and tension. Continue this cleansing and relaxing breath. When you feel relaxed, imagine that you are breathing white light down through the top of your head. Move this breath through your body, and exhale any stress and tension.

- As you breathe in white-light energy down through the top of your head, move it through your body and exhale it through your heart. Continue breathing in white light. Allow it to circulate throughout your body, loosening and relaxing any stress and tension. Then exhale through your heart.

- As you continue to breathe in white light, imagine your mind opening. Feel the white-light breath relaxing and quieting your mind. Exhale any stress and tension. Continue to breathe in white-light energy and allow it to expand your heart and open your mind.

- Breathe in white light and imagine it expanding beyond the physical body. Imagine that you are surrounded by white light. Breathe white light into your mind, heart, body, and spirit. Imagine that you are at one with the spirit realm.

- Send a thought or feeling message to those in the spirit realm. Ask for a loved one to come close and communicate with you. Keep breathing and relaxing. Be patient and calm.

- Pay attention to any sensations, emotions, thoughts, and images that you receive. Do not try to figure them out or overthink. Simply stay in a receptive mode. Breathe, relax, and receive.

- When you sense a loved one, receive a visual image, see streaks of light or color, or you simply know that a presence is close, ask for a message. Continue breathing and relaxing, listening and receiving.

- Allow images, thoughts, feelings, and sensations to surface. Do not rush this process or expect too much. If you are confused or overwhelmed or feel very little, ask the spirit to increase the energy and strengthen the quality of an image.

- Keep breathing and relax. Continue in this way until you feel the energy begin to fade. Do not try to analyze what you receive. If you do, you may lose the energy connection.

- When you are ready, send warm thoughts of love and gratitude to your loved one. Open your eyes. Write down or speak into the tape recorder all that you received. Include descriptions of any thoughts, feelings, body sensations, and images.

Interpreting What You Receive in a Session

The following is a list of guidelines for interpreting the images, thoughts, feelings, and impression that you receive in the exercises.

- Assume the beginner's mind. Do not try to immediately understand and figure out what you receive.

- Energy is alive. What you receive may change and evolve. Let it.

- Trust your initial impressions.

- Expect to be surprised.

- Use your intuition to interpret what you have received. Accurate intuitive interpretation involves both the left and right brains. Allow your left (thinking) mind to suggest an interpretation. Use your right (intuitive) brain to confirm and get a sense of what feels correct.

- If you intuitively receive numbers, letters, words, or names, use free association to discern the meaning. For instance, the number four may indicate four days, weeks, or months. Get an intuitive sense of what feels right to you. Some words and names have literal meaning. For example, if the name John comes to you in some way, it is likely that John is present. Names of towns and places, like Chicago or the gym, might signify these actual places.

- Use your intuitive type to guide you in interpreting what you intuitively receive. An emotional medium can use their feelings as a barometer for what feels correct or inaccurate while interpreting a message. A mental medium can trust their inner sense of knowing as an interpreting guide. A spiritual medium can tune in to their angels and guides for further help, and a physical medium can confirm accurate interpretations through their gut feelings.

- Know that even if what you receive seems confusing at first, you will, probably at a later time, receive a flash of understanding.

- Take your time and don't push. Relax and try to enjoy the process. You may spontaneously and unexpectedly receive the interpretation days or weeks later.

15

MEDIUM HELP 911

Death is the great awakener. When someone you love passes over to the other side, a bit of you goes with them. Even when you know in your heart that they are safe in the heavens among family and friends, you still miss them. Grieving is a process that, like death, can shake us to our core. Compassion, understanding, and supportive friends and family can help us through the difficult and lonely days and nights. But still it is not easy. When someone passes over, we can experience an emptiness that nothing seems to be able to fill. However, when death makes its way into your life, you are forever changed.

Although you may be grieving the passing of a loved one, it is important to be aware that you can still be a source of help to them. When death arrives, our loved ones seem gone forever. But they are not. You still miss their phone calls, warm presence, a touch on the hand, and their laughter. Yet learning how to communicate and connect with them not only helps you, it also supports them in a variety of ways.

The following exercises, meditations, and suggestions provide a way for you to be of further help and be of service to a loved one. In the process, your relationship with them will evolve in unexpected ways. Although they are now living in another dimension, it is still possible to feel an unexpected comfort and a tangible sense of their presence.

Talking About Death

Helping our loved ones during their transition to the other side can have a significant positive impact on their journey into the spirit realm and on our continued relationship with them. In our culture, we are embarrassingly afraid of talking about death. While we can lovingly tend to a loved one's physical needs, we are less comfortable discussing and talking about the dying process. I know that it is not easy to broach the topic. You may not feel as if it is your place to discuss death with someone who is dying. Yet I have found that most people who are in the process of making the transition find it a relief to share their thoughts and feelings. They are usually thankful when someone brings up the topic. Many people who are aware of their imminent passing fear that if they approach this topic with their friends and family, it will only upset them and cause them undue pain. If you would like to broach the subject of dying and the other side with a loved one, open the door to conversation in a gentle way. If your loved one is ready and willing to take the discussion any further, they will recognize and seize the opportunity.

It can be helpful to begin by talking about your personal feelings and beliefs about life after death and communication with the other side. However, do not expect others to necessarily readily agree with you. My mother was a Methodist minister and was not at all interested in metaphysics, New Age beliefs, psychics, or mediums. Yet when she was dying of cancer, she wanted me to talk about what I knew of the other side. This might not necessarily seem noteworthy, unless you knew my mother. A Bible-believing woman with a graduate degree in religion from Duke University, she was not a fan of my work as a psychic and medium. That all changed when she was dying. The closer she got to passing over, the more she wanted me to tell her what I knew of the other side. Even though in her work as a minister she had cared for many who were in the process of dying, when physical death came close she did not know what to expect and needed reassurance. In response to her questions, I told her what I knew of the other side. Our discussion helped to calm her anxiety, and an inner peace settled in. Assure your loved ones that the other side is a realm of love, acceptance, compassion, and forgiveness. Let them know that they will not feel any more pain or discomfort and that their family members and loved ones are waiting to welcome them home.

If your loved one does not share the same beliefs as you, do not argue or try to convince them that you are right. Listen and let them share their thoughts. Whatever their perception of the afterlife may be, assure them that they will experience unconditional love and peace.

The Hand of Spirit

When physical death is imminent, almost everyone begins to see and sense their loved ones on the other side. Sometimes they connect and communicate with their loved ones through dreams. Often their family and friends in spirit can be seen sitting on their bed or watching over them. At times, people deny their loved ones' presence and believe that they have an overactive imagination or that they are experiencing a hallucination. Loved ones on the other side come close to us during our transition to comfort and guide us. Asking a loved one if they are aware of a family member on the other side can help them to accept their presence and accept their help.

Close to the time of passing over, many people become fearful as to where they are going and what to expect. It is difficult for some to let go and leave the physical body. It can be helpful to tell your loved one that a family member or loved one will come and help them over. If they have a beloved pet on the other side, it may also come forward to comfort and help them.

When your loved one feels that their time has come to make the journey to their spirit home, tell them to go toward the light. This might seem like an overused and trite comfort, but to a loved one who is passing over, it can be a much-needed support and guide. You might also let them know that an angel or loved one will take their hand and guide them.

Passing Alone

Do not be surprised if your loved one passes when they are alone. One of the most common regrets that I hear from clients in medium sessions is their guilt at not having been present when their loved one passed over. If this happens to you, it is no accident.

I had a client who quit her job and moved across the country to care for her father after he was diagnosed with cancer. For over a year she lived in his home and took care of all of his needs. He spent the last week of physical life in the hospital with his daughter by his side day and night. She stepped out of the room to get breakfast one morning, and when she returned, she discovered that her father had passed over. She was racked with guilt for not having been with him during his last moments. When she came in for a reading, her father immediately came forward from spirit to thank her for her love and care. He also explained to her that he could not leave in her presence. It was too difficult. He felt the other side pulling him into spirit, but his daughter's love was keeping him in the physical realm. He apologized and told her that when she left the room that morning, a light in space opened and filled him with love, and he could not resist. She assured him that she understood and she was glad that he had passed over in love. This was her concern. She was at peace knowing that it was not her bad timing, but rather fate, at work.

Timing

The time of passing is not random. It is as meaningful as our time of birth into the physical world. It is a joyous event when a soul unites with the source of all of creation. Family members who are caring for ill loved ones sometimes ask me if I can tell them when their loved one will pass. Watching a loved one go through the process of dying can be difficult and even overwhelming. Yet the time of death is a personal and intimate exchange between an individual and the heavens. It is not always for us to know.

When the light of the other side draws close, blessings and unexpected wonders often take place. Many people tell me of the deep and profound look of peace on their loved one's face when they passed over. Honor physical death as a path to pure love, even if a loved one passes over unexpectedly in an accident, through drugs or alcohol, in war, or in a widespread tragedy. Know that once they are in the light, unfathomable love, peace, and forgiveness greet them.

Meditations and Medium Type

Your innate intuitive awareness provides you with an often ignored avenue of loving service to your loved ones during the time of transition. You do not have to be an expert intuitive or medium to tune in to and facilitate healing and provide assistance to the dying. The time immediately before, after, and during someone's passing is a time of increased energetic potency. As a loved one shifts their energy into the spirit body, they are aided by powerful angelic and divine forces. Positive energy is heightened during the time of transition. Tuning in and connecting with your loved one through visualizations and meditations can have a profound effect on both you and your loved one.

The meditations that follow are for all of the four medium types. Each type experiences the same process in different ways. Tune in to energy information through the modality that works best for you. Emotional mediums experience the energy of the other side through their emotions. Mental mediums receive communication through thought messages, while spiritual mediums may see their loved ones as flashes of light or color and have a tangible sense of their presence. During the exercises, physical mediums might want to hold in their hands an object or photo of their loved ones and feel an intuitive connection to them through their body.

In these meditations, I ask you to use your imagination to create images. Keep in mind that you may not actually visually see the image. Instead, you might have a sense of knowing or feeling it. The same is true of feeling and invoking love. You may sense or simply know that love is present and yet not feel it the way an emotional medium might. Go with the strengths of your medium type.

Letting Go Meditation

This meditation can be done before and after someone's passing. It can be very difficult at times to let go of our loved ones. You may feel helpless in your ability to take care of them and nervous as to where they are going and what may be happening to them. You may also feel alone and not want to let them go. It is important to remember that your relationship with your loved one will continue after physical death. Although your connection with them will be very different than what it was in the physical world, love transcends all boundaries. As you let go of the physicality of your relationship and embrace the spiritual, you will find that your loved one is always within reach.

- Light a white candle and get into a comfortable position. You may want to lie down for this exercise. Close your eyes and take a long, deep breath, then exhale any stress and tension. Continue to breathe in white light, sending the warm energy of the breath to any part of your body that is sore or tense or tight. Then breathe out the tension or stress. Continue with this cleansing breath. Each time you breathe, draw in warm, relaxing white light and exhale any tension from the body.

- Imagine an image of your loved one standing and facing you. You can visualize an image from a photograph or just create one within your imagination. Notice as much detail as possible, such as what they are wearing and the expression on your loved one's face. Imagine that you are standing about an arm's length away, facing your loved one.

- Imagine a beam of white light extending from your heart to your loved one's heart.

- This beam of light radiates love. Breathe in the love that is moving between you and your loved one. Send love to them. Keep breathing in white-light energy and sending and receiving this love to your loved one.

- Continue to experience and strengthen the love connection between you and your loved one. Imagine that the white-light energy expands and surrounds you both within a glowing, light-filled orb.

- Invite your angels to enter within this orb. Ask that any negativity, misunderstandings, wounds, and hurts between you and your loved one, past or present, be released and dissolved. Request forgiveness and healing. As you do this, imagine that any dark energy that may exist within you or your loved one falls away. In its place, imagine that love and light fills you and your loved one. Forgive yourself and your loved one for any intentional or unintentional pain that you may have caused each another.

- Imagine that the orb of light that you and your loved one are within begins to separate. Now there are two orbs of light; you are in one and your loved one is in another. Send a message to your loved one encouraging them to allow their orb of light to take them into the divine source of all light.

- Feel a white-light beam of energy from your heart to your loved one's heart. It is strong and eternal. You can feel the love and peace that surrounds your loved one. You know that they are being cared for and loved by divine forces.

- Send a message to your loved one asking them to send you a sign when they are in the light. Breathe and let go. Feel the presence of your loved one in your heart.

- When you are ready, open your eyes and write down any thoughts, feelings, or impressions that you may have received.

Help for a Traumatic or Unexpected Passing

If you have a loved one or know of someone whose passing was unexpected or traumatic in some way, the following meditation can be helpful. Those who pass over through suicide, accidents, war, mental or emotional disorders, widespread tragedies, or while under the influence of drugs or alcohol need special help with their passing. Sometimes people who experience these kinds of deaths are not aware of what is happening. It is easy for them to lose their way to the heavens or cling to the physical realm.

To ensure that your loved one who is transitioning goes quickly into the light, I recommend that you ask for divine intervention. When you invoke help from the celestial realm, it is always available. Joining forces with higher energies ensures that your loved one will make their way into the heavens.

There are many divine beings willing to come to your aid. Some people feel comfortable invoking Jesus, some prefer to ask for angelic or archangel support, and others may ask for help from the light or any number of divine gods, goddesses, and deities.

I ask for help from Mary, the divine mother. She is the intermediary between the physical and spiritual realms and guardian of the grace and miracles of the divine feminine. Prayers of intervention through her many names are invoked throughout the world. She is love and healing, and most people, regardless of their religious and spiritual beliefs, are comfortable with her. She guides and comforts your loved ones as they pass over. She is particularly close to children and those who suffer. Many people invoke the presence of Archangel Michael. Like Mary, he is an intermediary between the realms and he will safely guide your loved ones to the light. Whatever your beliefs may be, invoke divine goodness and love to help those whose passing is difficult.

Divine Intervention

Janet, a long-term client of mine, recently experienced the traumatic passing over of her high school–aged daughter when a car that she was riding in was hit by a drunk driver. Janet was told by the paramedics that her daughter, Jessica, died instantly. The grief that she felt over the sudden loss of her daughter was almost unbearable. Janet called me soon after her passing to ask me to make sure that Jessica had gone into the light.

She told me, "I feel that Jessica's spirit is still here. This should give me peace. But I feel that she is unsettled and restless. Can you make sure that she went into the light?"

I took a moment, closed my eyes, and felt Jessica's spirit in this same state. She seemed to be searching and restless. It felt, to me, that she did not know that she had died.

I asked for Mary and her angels to surround Jessica and take her to the light. I immediately felt Mary's presence and a swift flow of love energy. Then Jessica was gone. I knew that she was being taken care of. A few hours later, I felt Jessica thanking me. She was at peace in the presence of her grandparents and being comforted by the angels.

To the Light Meditation

This meditation will empower you to help those who have passed over make their way into the healing light of the divine presence. It can be especially helpful if you sense or intuitively feel that someone who has passed over is confused or has lost their way to the light.

- Light a candle for your loved one. Get into a comfortable position. You may want to lie down for this exercise. Close your eyes and take a long, deep breath, then exhale. Continue to breathe, sending the warm energy of the breath to any part of your body that is sore or tense or tight. Then breathe out all of the tension or stress. Continue with this cleansing breath. Each time you breathe, draw in warm and relaxing white light and exhale any tension from the body.

- Breathe in white-light energy down through the top of your head. Exhale it through your heart. Keep breathing in white light and exhaling it through your heart. As you do this, imagine that a white-light bubble begins to surround you. You are completely protected within the energy of this bubble. Only what is in your highest good can enter. Keep inhaling white-light energy and exhaling it through your heart into this bubble.

- Repeat the name of the person who has passed over. Breathe and keep repeating their name. Send them warm, calming white-light energy. Send love and imagine that white light completely surrounds the person.

- Send a prayer to the divine. This can be to Mary, Archangel Michael, the Goddess, divine energy, or whatever or whomever you feel a connection to. Ask for this divine being or energy to draw close to your loved one and guide them to the light.

- Send a thought message to the person you are assisting encouraging them to trust and allow the love that is close to guide and help them. Repeat their name and this message a few times. Send them the thought message that they are no longer in their physical body. They belong in the warmth and love of light. Encourage them to go fully and completely into the light.

- Ask for a loved one on the other side who may know the person whom you are helping to draw close. Ask the person you are helping to go with their loved ones into the light. Breathe, send love, and repeat these messages a few times.

- When you feel the energy connection began to fade or if you have the intuitive awareness that the person you are helping is in the light, let go and shift your attention to your energy. Ask your angels or your divine helper to clear you and release anything that is not in your highest good. Fill yourself with love.

- Send gratitude to your divine helpers. Open your eyes. Write down or record any intuitive impressions that you may have received.

What to Expect

These meditations combined with your love, concern, prayers, and other acts of care have a positive effect on your loved ones during their transition. Even if you do not experience a tangible connection with the person, as you do these meditations and other activities, they will be able to sense your efforts and greatly benefit.

There are countless ways that your loved ones may attempt to make their presence known to you. Remember that those on the other side are also learning how to better communicate with you. Their efforts may at times be clumsy and confusing. Encourage them by paying attention and sending gratitude when you sense their presence or receive a feeling, thought, or other type of intuitive message.

Those on the other side who had an interest while in the physical world in intuitive, psychic, and medium development will have an easier time communicating with you. Intuitive skills and abilities transfer with you when you pass. If you have a loved one who was engaged in intuitive awareness development during their physical life, they will be better able to send you signs and messages.

The Answer

Your loved ones on the other side want to assure you that they are alive and well. There are several ways that they may attempt to communicate with you. We often doubt the thoughts, feelings, sensations, and communication that they send us. You can ask your loved ones to confirm their presence through a sign. They will do their best to respond. Not only will they try to reply to requests, but it is likely they will continue to surprise and connect with you in a variety of ways.

Dreams

Many people who pass over visit their loved ones in the physical realm through their dreams. These dreams are often memorable and leave the dreamer feeling comforted and at peace. Many people who have encountered their loved ones in dreams tell me that it felt more like a direct visitation with their loved one than a dream.

Scents

Have you ever smelled your grandmother's favorite perfume or caught the unmistakable scent of your father's aftershave? Transference of a familiar scent is a common way that those in spirit let you know they are present. They might also send you the scent of flowers or their favorite foods.

Lights

The spirit world has a special connection to electricity. Because those in spirit live in a much stronger energy vibration than that of the physical world, they are able to affect and manipulate electrical wavelengths. Lights in your home that blink, burn out quickly, or seem to dim or get brighter may be under the influence of your loved ones. The spirit realm can also manipulate street lights and the lights in office and commercial buildings.

Appliances

Those on the other side may be responsible for coffee makers that spontaneously turn off and on, kitchen gadgets that burn out, microwave buzzers that sound without being turned on, and refrigerator lights that blink or go out.

Clocks

Another favorite sign from the beyond is stopping clocks or changing time. Spirits can also ring the chimes on grandfather clocks, stop or interfere with the time on your wristwatch, or play with your car or cell phone clock.

Television

I have a friend whose television turned on every night around midnight. This started soon after her father died. When it woke her, she would get out of bed, sit and watch it for a few minutes, say good night to her father, and go back to bed. Those on the other side may also change the channel or give you an intuitive message to turn on the television or change the channel. If you listen to this inner prompting, you will likely discover that one of your or their favorite shows or sports teams is playing.

Phones

Those on the other side love phones. Landline or cell phones, it doesn't matter. Using a phone as a means to get our attention is the perfect metaphor for illustrating their desire to communicate with us. They can actually call us, speak through the phone, and send us messages. Although this often appears to simply be a random technology glitch or a garbled and incoherent message, many of the mysterious phone activities that you experience may be coming from the beyond.

Alarms

At the exact time of my mother's passing over, the speaker phone in my bedroom turned on at 4:04 a.m. The dial tone was so startling, it sounded like it was amplified. Spirits can also ring the doorbell, sound the car alarm, and ring the bell of a timer.

Birds and Feathers

One the most common ways that the spirit realm likes to get my attention is by dropping blue jay feathers on my path. I become more aware and alert if I find one on my doorstep or one crosses my path. A client of mine recently commented that there seemed to be an abundance of blue jays in my back yard. Your loved ones may try to get your attention through birds and feathers. Pay attention to the winged creatures around your home. Birds are often the go-between mediators between the spirit and physical realms.

Stray Animals

Have you ever discovered a stray cat or dog outside your door? Or has one ever wandered up to you and you knew that there was something special about it? The spirit realm works through animals and nature. Take in and love those lost animals that make their way to you. They bring with them a special message of love. Even if you cannot keep them, open your heart and accept their love. Then find them a good home.

Coins

Finding coins and money is another common way that loved ones like to get our attention. If you repeatedly find the same denomination of coin, a loved one is likely sending them to you. Everyone loves to find money, and the spirit realm loves to send it to us. I recently found a ten dollar bill on my morning walk. It was a cosmic assurance of abundance just when I needed it.

Clouds

Have you ever looked up into the sky and noticed clouds in the shape of a heart or some other meaningful formation? Angels and loved ones in the light want you to know that they are with you, in the light of the sky. Listen when your intuition tells you to look up. There might be a confirming sign looking down on you.

Butterflies

The spirit realm loves butterflies. With their vibrant and delicate wings, they are almost spirit. I had a friend who was going through some difficulties. She so much missed and wanted the advice and support of her father, who had passed over a few years prior. One day while driving in her convertible, she felt her father's presence beside her. A moment later, a butterfly landed on the side of her forehead. It stayed seated there for the entire drive of over twenty miles. She took several pictures of it with her cell phone, sure that no one would believe her.

Missing Jewelry

Have you ever lost a ring, an earring, or a necklace, yet you remember exactly where you put it? Then several days later it is back where you thought you had placed it. Has a crystal, key ring, or small object disappeared or appeared out of nowhere? Not all of those on the other side are capable of moving, materializing, and dematerializing objects, but some are. Your loved ones on the other side are learning, often right along with you, how to better communicate and connect with the physical realm. In advanced stages, many are capable of affecting solid matter in astounding ways.

Music

Those on the other side experience music differently that we do. While we hear it with our external senses, they feel it as vibration. Music can be soothing, exciting, stimulating, and enjoyable in both realms. Have you ever heard a favorite song of your loved one at a time when you had been thinking of them? Have you been intuitively prompted to turn on the radio and one of your favorite songs was playing? This is another way that our loved ones communicate and connect with us.

Rituals

Since the beginning of time, traditions throughout the world have honored the rites of passing through various rituals and ceremonies. Depending on your beliefs and spiritual practices, you may have a particular way of commemorating a loved one's passing. Whatever your tradition, there are a few actions that you can take that will help the spirit of your loved one to release negativity and ascend quickly into the heavenly realm.

Creating a shrine for your loved one can serve as a vessel for continued blessings for the person. You have most likely seen shrines erected along highways or streets where people have passed over through accidents. These shrines help those in both the physical and spiritual realms. They purify the energy of a place of passing and help the loved one's spirit to leave the earth in love and peace. They also provide loved ones with a focus for their grief.

In your home or yard, an altar can serve as a potent location where you and your loved one on the other side can meet and be in each another's presence. Those in spirit are uplifted and helped by these gestures. They experience and feel shrines as love and an honoring of their most positive qualities. You can place on the altar photos of your loved ones, flowers, crystals, some of their favorite personal objects, and even their favorite foods. You can also place any items that you consider holy or pictures of spiritual masters and teachers.

I find that writing a short note to a loved one and placing it on an altar is a good way to send them a message. You might also want to light a candle and place it on an altar at the same time every day for seven consecutive days after a loved one's passing. This small act sends them positive energy for their journey into the light. In readings, loved ones on the other side often describe the altars, shrines, small gardens, or bird feeders erected in their honor. Their spirit is close and at peace.

In Service to the Spirit Realm

The physical realm is just one aspect of a vast, multidimensional, living, evolving reality. You are part of this unseen celestial masterpiece. It is within you, surrounding you, and it is you. We tend to operate from just a sliver of what is possible. As you harness the power of your spirit, your world expands and new realities become evident.

One of the most important contributions that mediums provide is a glimpse of the other side that is so different from what our fears may generate and have us believe. Popular media has magnified our uncertainties and suspicions of what may lie beyond the known. Vengeful ghosts, extraterrestrials who want to destroy our world, and dark creatures from the pits of evil that prey on the innocent are just some of the images that films, books, and video games have planted in our consciousness. Although these kinds of negative and evil beings can be entertaining, a part of us may wonder if they are more than just fantasy. Some people fear that the unseen realm might be a reflection of the human world, a threatening and scary place.

In the physical world, we may sometimes live in fear of being hurt, robbed, or destroyed by an unexpected catastrophe or deranged person, but there is nothing to lose in the spirit realm. The spirit body never dies. When love is the strongest force and power, false threats fall away. While there are negative thoughtforms and confused and dark entities in the lower vibrations of the spirit realm, they only have power if you allow them to. Once in the spirit realm, fears dissolve like mosquitoes against a flame. It is that simple. This is the great awakening that awaits you in the change called death. Our loved ones on the other side want us to know this truth. The light is a realm of love, service, and support. This is the way of the beyond.

I encourage you to experience the power of your spirit in the here and now. As you engage in medium work, you are in service to the divine realm of love. Leagues of angels and guides travel with you and guide your step. You become an important link in the connection between the worlds.

Invitation to Your Gatekeeper

As you become more comfortable with your natural connection to the other side, I encourage you to further explore and communicate with your spirit guides. You can request the assistance of an angel or guide who can serve as a gatekeeper between the physical and spiritual realms. A *gatekeeper* is a spirit guide or angel who guides and protects you during your interaction with the spirit world. They ensure that no spirit entity or influence that is not in your highest good enters or attaches to your energy field or your physical body. They also help your loved ones on the other side to better communicate with you by untangling energy information so that it is understandable. They can amplify your communication with your loved ones by providing an increase in psychic energy. The fact that you are reading this book is an indication that you likely already have a guide who is helping you as a gatekeeper.

The following meditation will allow you to become more familiar with your guides and angels and better communicate with your gatekeeper. If you do not receive the kind of clear connection and communication that you would like, this does not mean that you do not have a spiritual being guiding and protecting you. Practice this meditation often, and ask your guide or angel to send you a sign or signal of their presence. Remember to tune in to your strongest medium type during the meditation.

Meditation for Connecting to Your Gatekeeper

- Settle into a comfortable position. You may want to lie down for this exercise. Close your eyes and take a long, deep breath, then exhale. Continue to breathe and send the warm energy of the breath to any part of your body that is sore or tense or tight. Then breathe out all of the tension or stress. Continue with this cleansing breathing. Each time you breathe, draw in warm, relaxing white light and exhale any tension from the body.

- Continue to breathe and imagine a place in nature that is tranquil and inviting. The sun is shining down on you, helping you to feel warm and relaxed. The warm sunshine stands for all that is positive in life, like love, kindness, and compassion. You feel and sense trees, flowers, and vegetation gently swaying in a slight breeze. You may hear water from a stream, river, or waterfall flowing in the distance. Perhaps you can also hear the sound of birds chirping overhead.

- Everything in this environment is an expression of love and goodness. The flowers, the gentle breeze, and the soft sounds of water in the background are all vibrating in the essence of love.

- Imagine the white light of protection completely surrounding you. Send a thought message to your angels and spirit guides and ask for the presence of your gatekeeper. Breathe and relax. Continue to open your heart and feel love move through you.

- You may sense the presence of your gatekeeper as warmth and love. You may hear a message or receive instantaneous images, feelings, thoughts, or bodily sensations. Keep breathing and relaxing.

- Stay in this energy for as long as possible. Listen, feel, see, and accept whatever comes to you. Do not become concerned or stressed if you do not immediately experience anything.

- When you feel the energy begin to recede, thank your gatekeeper for his or her help. Open your eyes and write down any thoughts, feelings, images, or messages that you experienced. Keep in mind that your gatekeeper may send you a message or sign of his or her presence days later or when you least expect it.

The Light Is Where You Are

The light is not so much a location as it is a vibration of all love, strength, and peace. It is the source of energy where angels, guides, archangels, and spiritual beings reside. When we pass over, this is our home. We think of reality as a place within time and space. However, in the unseen realm, reality is made up of energy vibration. It is within you and surrounding you.

Whenever you engage in medium work or other spiritual activity, it is important to invoke the energy of the light to protect and guide you. When you do this, you surround yourself with an impenetrable coat of love and safety. This will repel any lost or confused entities or negative thoughtforms and keep them from intruding or interfering in your practice.

Here is a simple prayer of protection:

Invocation of Light
Divine source of all of life, surround me with the
white light of love and protection.
I invoke the highest love of all of
creation to be above me,
within me, by my side, within my heart,
mind, body, and soul, protecting and guiding me.

Helping an Earthbound Spirit into the Light

It is likely that at some point you will encounter a lost or wandering spirit or ghost. These earthbound spirits are still focused on the physical realm. Even though they can ascend into the higher vibrations of light and love at any time, they often feel confusingly bound here. They do not always recognize that they have passed over, they may not feel good enough to go into the light, or they may be stubbornly holding on to their home or property. Whatever their reason for clinging to the physical world, they need our help to find their way to the freedom of the light.

One of the most common ways to recognize the presence of an earthbound spirit is through unusual feelings or a strange phenomenon that often accompanies their presence. You may hear them walking through a house, shutting doors or tapping on walls, see them as fleeting images or streaks of color, feel their presence as cold spots of air, or hear them speak as strange noises and sounds. You might also intuit their presence as an uncomfortable sense of heaviness or dread, smell them as a distasteful odor, or wake up at night with the sense that you are not alone. They may try to get your attention in an attempt to feel less lonely, or they may try to contact you to ask for your help. More stubborn spirits may try to scare you, hoping that you will leave what they consider to be their home or property.

If you sense that there is an earthbound spirit present, I encourage you to go through the process of helping it into the light. Your efforts are never wasted. Even if there is not a spirit present, you may unknowingly help an undetected spirit miles away.

There is a difference between helping a loved one into the light and helping an unfamiliar spirit. When you have a personal connection to a loved one, they accept your influence and trust your guidance. But you will not have this kind of personal connection to a ghost, wanderer, or lost spirit. In the case of an earthbound spirit, it is not necessary or even advised that you personally connect with whomever you are helping over. Because earthbound spirits are already focused on the physical realm, a personal connection with them only further confuses them and keeps them bound here.

Your job in helping a ghost or lost spirit over to the light is to act as a medium between the realms. It is important that you do not get personally involved with the spirit. Instead, focus your efforts on invoking the presence of an angel, guide, or spirit in the light who knows and can influence the earthbound spirit. Even though these divine helpers are always present, an earthbound spirit is usually not able to recognize them.

If you are new to working with the spiritual realms, I recommend that you only work with earthbound spirits who reside in a physical location that you can visit. As you become more confident and adept with crossing spirits over, you can do this in a meditative state from your own home.

- Go to the location where the earthbound spirit has been felt to reside. Do not ask for signs or phenomena to confirm their presence. This only creates vibrational disharmony and makes crossing over more difficult. It is enough confirmation that you or another has felt or sensed a presence. There is never any harm with this process. Any earthbound spirit who is present (and even those who are not) will benefit.

- Inwardly repeat your prayer of protection several times. As you do this, imagine that you are surrounded by white light. Ask that your gatekeeper angel or guide be present to assist you and the earthbound spirit.

- Ask for the assistance of a divine being. I ask for Mother Mary or Archangel Michael and their angels. However, ask for the presence of whatever divine being you feel most connected to. Ask for their presence, and imagine the earthbound spirit surrounded by their love.

- Send a thought message to the earthbound spirit telling them that you are here to help. You can do this by projecting a thought either aloud or silently. Tell the earthbound spirit that there is a place to which they can go where they will feel loved and better than they have in a long time. Tell them that there is a loving spirit close by. Ask that they become aware of the presence of this divine being. Ask them to let this being touch them or send them love. Repeat these suggestions.

- Send the earthbound spirit the thought message that the physical realm is no longer their home and that they cannot stay here any longer. Be firm but loving. Assure them that there is a place of love and peace waiting for them.

- Ask for a loved one in the light who knows the earthbound spirit to be present. Spirit loved ones can be very clever and can convince even the most confused souls to go with them. Ask the divine being who is present to guide the earthbound spirit and their loved one on the other side who is helping them into the light. Imagine in your mind's eye the earthbound spirit going into the light with their loved one.

- When you feel the energy begin to fade or if you receive an intuitive confirming sign, begin to withdraw your energy. Imagine yourself surrounded by light. Ask your angels and guides to clear your energy field of anything that is not in your highest good. Send love and gratitude to your spirit helpers for all of the guidance and help that you have received.

Some people like to burn sage, sprinkle sea salt, or place crystals in a location that has held earthbound spirits. This ensures that any negative thoughtforms or residual energy will be cleared and transmuted.

You can do this process whenever and wherever you sense an unsettled and earthbound spirit. You will be liberating and freeing unfortunate lost spirits into perfect love and peace and contributing to the ascension of the planet.

Conclusion

The Enlightened Medium

~~~~~~~~~~~~~~~~~~~~~~~~~~~~

As you come to the end of this book, my hope is that I leave you inspired to further explore and develop your relationship with those on the other side. Experiencing a tangible connection with the spirit realm can be healing, comforting, reassuring, and enlightening. It shifts your perspective and heralds the beginning of a new understanding of yourself and the universe. If you have been grieving the loss of a loved one, establishing a new means of communication and connection with them will ease the pain. Whatever your motivation may be in developing your natural medium abilities, you now know that you play a meaningful role in helping those on the other side.

While reading through the client stories in this book, you may have identified with some of their challenges and unexpected life lessons. Even when you struggle through life's ups and downs, your efforts create a positive flow of energy here and in the hereafter. The small acts that no one seems to notice influence and benefit your highest purpose and your loved ones on the other side. My wish is that you now more fully understand the importance of your daily choices, decisions, and actions. You are never alone. Your loved ones on the other side, your spirit guides and angels, are with you. There is an underlying soul plan at work in all that you experience.

Medium Types

As you continue to develop your medium abilities, there are a few things to be aware of. One of the most frequently asked questions that I receive from people who have read my book *Discover Your Psychic Type* has to do with the scores they receive after taking the intuitive type quiz. Once you take the medium type quiz, you may have similar questions. Your scores for each type may be close to one another, or there might be a significant gap between your strongest medium type and the other types. Whatever your scores are, the optimum is to be balanced in all four types. To fully cultivate medium abilities, it is necessary to be familiar with and develop intuitive ability with all four types. The exercises and meditations in chapter 14 were created to help you do this.

While it is important to develop all four medium types, your strongest type will be your most reliable compass and guide. Take time on a daily basis to listen within. Become aware of what you may be intuitively receiving through your thoughts, feelings, body sensations, and energy field. Allow the messages that those in spirit are sending your way to unfold and guide you.

Trust Your Process

As you practice the exercises and meditations, do not become discouraged if you do not immediately receive the kind of tangible interaction and communication with your loved ones on the other side that you expect. It often takes time to align your inner intuitive receptors with your conscious awareness. At other times you may hear, see, feel, and receive messages from the other side, only to suddenly feel distant and unable to connect. If you have been experiencing positive medium communication, you might also go through a period of doubt. Your logical mind may interfere, and you may begin to distrust your intuitive capability and even, at times, your sanity. It is also possible that you may suddenly become fearful of working with the spirit realm.

Even though it seems that the opposite is true, these are actually signs that you are making progress. These kinds of experiences are a normal part of integrating the flow of spiritual energy into the more ego-based aspect of your consciousness. I encourage you to continue to practice and refine your medium abilities. When your determination and devotion feel tested, remember that it is often darkest before the dawn. Quite often, a breakthrough into a higher level of medium receptivity and self-trust will follow a period of distrust and uncertainty.

Reading this book is just the beginning. Continually putting what you have learned into practice is the next step. Those in the spirit realm will respond. As you continue to devote yourself to communicating and connecting with your loved ones, spirit guides, and angels, it will become second nature to receive their direction and guidance.

Whatever your interest may be in exploring the other side, your innate medium abilities should no longer be in question. You may decide to further refine your skills in order to help and give messages to others, or your interest might instead be to feel closer and better able to communicate with your loved ones in spirit. However you desire to use your medium abilities, the spirit realm supports you in your efforts.

Cosmic Revolution

We need the love of the heavens. Your loved ones, spirit guides, and angels send comfort, wisdom, compassion, and healing your way. Accept this and share it. Assist those in the physical world who are suffering, and continue to evolve, grow, and move into new territory with your loved ones on the other side. Remember that you are a powerful being who can positively affect those in the physical and spiritual realms. With power comes responsibility. The ability to communicate with the other side is not simply an entertaining trick. It is an accelerated path of soulful evolution and growth that affects you on a personal level and has an impact on the collective whole.

In many ways, the other side operates in reverse of the laws of the material world. What is small and obscure here often has a remarkable force in the beyond. Even a slight amount of effort to reach out beyond the veil to those on the other side will yield positive results. As you develop and refine your medium skills, you evolve and transform. You become a citizen of the universe, a change maker, and the bringer of a new way. Do not underestimate your influence.

We are on the cusp of a transformation of a magnitude that the world has never experienced. As we move closer to environmental, economic, and humanitarian disaster, our ability to support ourselves on Mother Earth is questionable. In response to this crisis, there is an influx of spiritual energy flowing into the planet. As you interact and continue to connect with the other side, you naturally integrate these higher spiritual vibrations into your soul and the soul of the planet. It is a wonderful achievement to be a part of this evolution. As I wrote this book, I felt the stirring of hope growing and expanding in my heart. Individually and collectively, we are moving beyond the boundaries of physical limitations. Be the empowered and enlightened intermediary between the physical and spiritual realms that you are meant to be. You are an essential part of the creation of heaven on earth.

READING LIST

Baldwin, William J. *Spirit Releasement Therapy: A Technique Manual.* London: Headline Books, 1995.

Dillard, Sherrie. *Discover Your Psychic Type: Developing and Using Your Natural Intuition.* Woodbury, MN: Llewellyn Publications, 2008.

———. *Love and Intuition: A Psychic's Guide to Creating Lasting Love.* Woodbury, MN: Llewellyn Publications, 2010.

———. *The Miracle Workers Handbook: Seven Levels of Power and Manifestation of the Virgin Mary.* United Kingdom: John Hunt Publishing, 2012.

Fiore, Edith. *The Unquiet Dead: A Psychologist Treats Spirit Possession.* New York: Ballantine Books, 1995.

Newton, Michael. *Destiny of Souls: New Case Studies of Life Between Lives.* St. Paul, MN: Llewellyn Publications, 2000.

Schwartz, Robert. *Your Soul's Plan: Discovering the Real Meaning of the Life You Planned Before You Were Born.* Berkeley, CA: Frog Books, 2009.

To Write to the Author

It has been a joy to share my psychic and medium adventures with you. You inspire, motivate, and teach me. I would love for you to share your insights and experiences with me.

You can e-mail me at sgd7777@yahoo.com or go to my website, www.sherriedillard.com, and sign up for my newsletter for updates. I also invite you to follow me on Facebook, www.facebook.com /sherrie.dillard.

—Sherrie Dillard